PENGUIN BOOKS

STUPID WHITE MEN

Michael Moore is the award-winning director of the ground-breaking documentary *Roger & Me*, which became the largest-grossing non-fiction film of all time, and the creator and host of the Emmy-winning series *TV Nation* and *The Awful Truth*. His latest film is *Bowling for Columbine*. He lives in Michigan.

STUPID WHITE MEN

... and Other
Sorry Excuses
for the State
of the Nation!

MICHAEL MOORE

PENGUIN BOOKS

PENGUIN BOOKS

Published by the Penguin Group
Penguin Books Ltd, 80 Strand, London WC2R 0RL, England
Penguin Putnam Inc., 375 Hudson Street, New York, New York 10014, USA
Penguin Books Australia Ltd, 250 Camberwell Road, Camberwell, Victoria 3124, Australia
Penguin Books Canada Ltd, 10 Alcorn Avenue, Toronto, Ontario, Canada M4V 3B2
Penguin Books India (P) Ltd, 11 Community Centre, Panchsheel Park, New Delhi – 110 017, India
Penguin Books (NZ) Ltd, Cnr Rosedale and Airborne Roads, Albany, Auckland, New Zealand
Penguin Books (South Africa) (Pty) Ltd, 24 Sturdee Avenue, Rosebank 2196, South Africa

Penguin Books Ltd, Registered Offices: 80 Strand, London WC2R 0RL, England

www.penguin.com

First published in the USA by ReganBooks,
an imprint of HarperCollins Publishers Inc. 2001
First published in Great Britain with new Introduction, Epilogue and
minor text changes by Penguin Books 2002

73

Printed in England by Clays Ltd, St Ives plc

FOR AL HIRVELA

It's amazing I won. I was running against peace, prosperity, and incumbency.

—GEORGE W. BUSH, JUNE 14, 2001,
speaking to Swedish Prime Minister Goran Perrson,
unaware that a live television camera was still rolling

CONTENTS

INTRODUCTION

THIS EDITION OF *Stupid White Men* is being published for the English-speaking world outside of North America, the continent where the vast majority of the pathetically stupid, embarrassingly white, and disgustingly rich men live.

This book was initially written for Americans and Canadians (well, really, just Americans; Canadians are pretty smart and hip to the evils of America—they just bought this book to be nice to me because they know I like them).

I wrote *Stupid White Men* in the months preceding September 11, 2001. The first 50,000 copies of it came off the presses on the evening of September 10. Needless to say, those books were not shipped out to bookstores across the nation on the following day as had been scheduled.

I asked the publisher, ReganBooks (a division of Harper-Collins), if we could delay the release for a few weeks. As a resident of Manhattan, I did not feel like going on a book tour at that time. The editor at HarperCollins agreed—just as a bomb siren went off at their corporate headquarters. "I gotta go," he said, "they're evacuating the building." His last words were: "We'll get back to you in a few weeks."

Well, there were no further bombs and the few weeks went by. I hadn't heard anything, so I called up the people at Regan-Books/HarperCollins and asked them when the 50,000 copies of my book (which were now sitting in a warehouse in Scranton, Pennsylvania) were going to be put on sale. What I heard next was not what I expected to hear anywhere inside a free country:

"We can't release the book as it is written. The political climate of the country has changed. We would like you to consider rewriting up to 50 percent of the book . . . removing the harsh references to Bush and toning down your dissent. And we'd like you to give us $100,000 to reprint the books we've printed." They suggested that I remove the chapter entitled "Dear George" and change the chapter title of "Kill Whitey" ("Mike, 'Whitey' is not the problem right now." "Whitey," I responded, "is ALWAYS the problem"). They said they would like me not to refer to the 2000 Presidential election as a "coup," and that it would be "intellectually dishonest" not to admit in the book that, at least since September 11, Mr. Bush had done "a good job." They closed by saying that "At ReganBooks, we're now known as the '9-11 publishers'—we've got a couple of quickie books on the Twin Towers heroes in the works, we're publishing the autobiography of the police chief, and we're doing a photo book of the tragedy. Your book no longer fits with our new image."

I asked if these orders were coming from "on top"—meaning the owner of the News Corp., which owns HarperCollins—Mr. Rupert Murdoch. No one would respond.

So I decided to respond to them: "I am not going to change 50 percent of even one word of this book. I can't believe what you are telling me. You already accepted this book and printed it! Now you are afraid—or worse, you are trying to censor me to conform to the corporation's political philosophy. At a time when we are supposed to be fighting for our freedom, this is how we do it—by reducing our freedoms here at home? Shouldn't this be the time when we are expanding our freedoms, to show that, no matter how much we are attacked, the last thing we are going to do is to be like those nations which suppress freedom of expression and dissent?"

Yeah, tough talk—but the truth is I was very scared. Many people told me I had better cool it, that I should find a way to compromise or I will never see this book on a single shelf. So I wrote to the publisher and tried to find a happy medium, offering to write some new stuff, and promising to go through the book and make sure there was nothing in it that would be insensitive to those who lost loved ones on September 11. I tried to appeal to their sense of what *real* patriotism should be about—standing up so that all points of view are heard—and I told them how confident I was that they were the ones to publish this book because they weren't afraid to take those risks.

The response I got was the publishing world's equivalent of "fuck off." They wanted a significant rewrite, they were not going to budge on their insistence that I censor large portions of the book, and, yes, they wanted that $100,000 check made out from me to Mr. Murdoch's enterprise.

This went on for nearly two months. I tried to speak to the president of ReganBooks, Judith Regan, but she would not return my calls. I was told by more than one person at News Corp. that Regan was, since September 11, spending many of her days over at the Fox News Channel where she also has a late-night weekend cable show, perhaps the worst talk show on American television (having landed her very own imprint in his publishing fiefdom Murdoch had topped that with her own show on his news channel).

I have been told by sources inside the News Corp. a number of things relating to the near-banning of my book, but British law does not allow me to publish these things in this British edition of my book. (Hey, former owners of America and much of the World—that's right, you Brits! Get a friggin' Constitution with a Bill of Rights and a First Amendment (Freedom of Speech and the Press), will ya? You started out great with the Magna Carta—about a thousand years ago—and that was the last thing you were willing to commit to in writing! Write it down! Release me from this censorship!! C'mon—you're better than this! You gave us a great language, you built roads everywhere, and we are still watching reruns of *Benny Hill* every day in the U.S.A. The least you could do now is to allow an author to write what is on his mind instead of having to ask British citizens to escape the monarchy and travel into cyberspace (www.michaelmoore.com) to find out what I wasn't able to say on this page.)

On the evening of November 30, 2001, around 8:00 P.M., I received a call from HarperCollins.

"It seems as if no one is budging," my editor sadly told me. "You won't budge, they won't budge. It's a standoff. This book is not going to come out in this form."

I told him I would just take it to another publisher.

"You can't do that," he said. "Read your contract. We hold the rights for a year."

"So, if the book doesn't come out, what will you do with 50,000 copies sitting in the warehouse?"

"Well," he said, "I guess they would be pulped."

Pulped? Destroyed? I felt sick. I couldn't sleep that night. Where was I? I tried to cheer myself up by trying to make light of what I had just been told. "Hey, look at the bright side," I told my wife, "at least this shows how far our side has pushed the political agenda—now, even the Oppressor thinks of recycling!"

It was a lame attempt not to think too hard about just how deep my country was sinking into the Land of the Semi-Free. We all knew—and still know—that which we can't bring ourselves to admit: we are now in a budding police state formerly known as the U.S.ofA., a place that doesn't need the Orwellian thought police because we've got something better—The Corporate Police. As long as the government rounded up the Arab-looking people and locked them up for months—years—without any charges, the Corporate Elite would carry out the dirty work of keeping the rest of the public stupid and suppressed.

And so I thought it was over, over for me, over for my book, over for the country—until I awoke the next morning, December 1, 2001. The first of December should be a national holiday in America as it was on this day in 1955 that a seamstress refused to move to the back of a public bus in Montgomery, Alabama. The law said she had to move because her skin color was black. Her singular act of courage rocked the nation and started a revolution. This woman, Rosa Parks, who now resides in my home state of Michigan, is an important reminder that the great changes in society occur when one or two people of conscience act.

And so it was on this December 1, 2001, I found. myself somewhere off the New Jersey Turnpike in a room with about a hundred people whom I had promised to come speak to at their annual meeting of their citizens action council. As I stood on the makeshift stage, I told those gathered that I did not feel like giving the speech I had planned on giving. I told them instead what I had been told the night before and how I hadn't been able to sleep. I told them that I now thought no one would ever be able to read these words—*words!*—I had written. I asked them if they would mind if I read them a couple of my chapters—as they were probably going to be the only people ever to hear my work known as "Stupid White Men."

The room nodded the collective nod the way you'd expect the working class of Jersey to nod if given the chance to hear something those in power have deemed they are not allowed to hear. So I went ahead and read the dangerous, homeland-threatening chapters known as "Dear George" and "Kill Whitey." There was warm applause, and they asked afterward if I would sign some books. "What books?" I asked.

"Your first book," a woman responded.

"Sure," I said, and sat down to sign not the book I had just written in 2001, but the one I had cranked out nearly five years ago. As I affixed my signature to copy after copy of this old book, I thought about how I would have been signing my *new* book right now if only I had just given in, given in *a bit* . . . a lot . . . if only I had just given up instead of having to make my *point*.

When I was done I rushed out of the building because I did not want these people see me cry . . . the big, bad, brave Michael Moore! I headed back up the turnpike, convinced that my publishing "career" was over and that I was now living in a place that had sucked the soul right out of me. I wiped away the tears as the butchered skyline of the city came into view. Well, I thought to myself, at least I'm still here, unlike the firemen on my block, or the producer I had worked with in April who, on that day in September, was on the plane that slammed into the south tower of the World Trade Center. Yeah, I was still here.

And then something miraculous happened. Unbeknownst to me, there was a woman sitting in the back of that room off the New Jersey Turnpike that December 1 who, after hearing my tale of woe, decided to do something about it. She was a librarian from Englewood, New Jersey, and her name was Ann Sparanese. She went home and got on the Internet. She wrote a letter to her librarian friends and posted it on a couple of sites devoted to progressive librarian issues. She told them what HarperCollins was planning to do. She scolded me (in true librarian fashion!) that I should not be silent about this, that it was not my *right* to be silent because this pervasive climate of censorship and suppression was not just about me. It was affecting everyone. The new U.S.A. Patriot Act now made it illegal for librarians to refuse any police request to see what anyone was reading. Librarians could go to jail if they even contacted a lawyer for advice! Ann Sparanese asked that everyone write to HarperCollins and demand that they release Michael Moore's book.

And that is just what hundreds, and eventually thousands, did.

I had no clue this was happening. Not until I got a call from HarperCollins.

"WHAT DID YOU TELL THE LIBRARIANS?" the voice on the other end of the phone demanded.

"What are you talking about?" I asked, wondering what he was talking about.

"You were out in New Jersey and you told the librarians everything!"

"There weren't any librarians in New Jersey and how do you know what I told anybody?"

"We got it off the Internet. Some librarian is spreading the whole story. AND NOW WE'RE GETTING HATE MAIL FROM LIBRARIANS!"

Hmm, I thought, librarians are certainly one terrorist group you don't want to mess with.

"I'm sorry," I said, sheepishly. "I did check to make sure there was no press there."

"Well, it's all out in the open now. I'm getting calls from *Publishers Weekly*."

Within days, *PW* quoted my editor saying that I would, in fact, be rewriting the book (he later claimed he said no such thing). After months of silence to the press, hoping I could settle this crisis peacefully, I told *PW* the whole truth about the ordeal I had been through and how there were 50,000 copies of my book being held hostage in Scranton. The reporter told me about the librarian from New Jersey who had stirred the hornets' nest.

"I have never met this woman," I said, "but whoever she is I would like to thank her."

The following week, after being summoned to a meeting of the brass at HarperCollins—at which I was threatened again that my book, as it was written, "with this cover and this title, simply cannot be released"—I received a call from my agent telling me that the book would indeed be released as is, not a single word removed or changed.

The publisher was clearly pissed that the whole thing was now in the public arena and that they were being—properly—seen as censors. *Damn those librarians!* Thank God for librarians! Of course, it should have come as no surprise that the librarians were leading the charge. Most people think of them as all mousy and quiet and telling everyone to "SHHHHHH!" I'm now convinced that "shush" is just the sound of the steam coming out of their ears as they sit there plotting the revolution! You better believe they're mad. They aren't paid shit, their hours and benefits are continually being cut, their budgets are the first to be slashed, and they spend their days repairing the dilapidated forty-year-old books which fill their shelves. Of course it was a librarian who came to my aid! And it was proof to me once again just how big a difference one person can make.

The unhappy publisher had decided, though, that this book would die, one way or the other, librarians or no librarians. They ordered no further copies printed. I was told that there would be no ads taken out in the newspapers to promote the book and that my "book tour" would consist of three cities ("three and a half if you want to count the city you live in"): Ridgewood, NJ (home of the Republican congressman against whom our TV show, "The Awful Truth," had run a ficus tree in the 2000 election), Arlington, Virginia (home of the Pentagon), and Denver. I asked if they had torn this page out of the manual called, "How to Kill an Author's Book." As the release day finally approached, Harper-Collins had booked me on a total of **zero** broadcast network TV shows. There was to be no mention of the book on public radio or television, and I was informed that one bookstore chain had said they could not have me appearing in any of their stores "for security reasons."

The book appeared headed for an early burial when I decided to go on the Internet and send out a letter to my list about what I had been through. I wrote about how, in this new era of repression, words were now considered as dangerous as terrorists. I asked that people please buy my book and not let these words go unread.

Within hours, the first 50,000 copies were sold out. By the next day, *Stupid White Men* went to #1 on the Amazon.com bestseller list. HarperCollins was in a state of shock. How could this be happening? After all, they told me that my book was "out of touch with the American people."

By the fifth day, the book was already in its ninth printing. The publisher could not keep up with the demand. It shot to #1 on the *New York Times* bestseller list and every other bestseller list in the country. It was months before you could walk into any bookstore and be assured of finding a copy.

Stupid White Men is in its fifth month on the bestseller list as I write this, and still at #1 this week in the *New York Times*. There has still not been a single ad taken out for the book and I have appeared on only TWO broadcast network TV shows—one that comes on around 1:00 A.M. and the other at 7:00 A.M.

That's it. A virtual media blackout. But it has not mattered one bit. The American public, which has been portrayed to you by your media as being about as stupid as a slug, has risen to the occasion this time and I have no one other than George W. Bush to thank for this. His actions alone since September have sent a chill down every thinking American's spine. This book has sold more copies than any other non-fiction book in America this year. The last time I checked it was on its way to its twenty-fifth printing. Take heart, my fellow English-speaking citizens of our fair planet, there may be hope for us Americans after all.

What makes me happy to have an edition finally printed outside the U.S. is that I know from all the mail I receive from London to Liverpool, from Galway to Perth, that it's clear we do not have a lock on all the stupid white men in the world. After this book went to #1 in Canada (and is still there after four months), I began to get a lot of mail from Canadians about all the rogue bastards running their nation, from the arrogant (but ultimately U.S.A.ss-kissing) prime minister to the one guy who now owns virtually all the major dailies, a host of television networks, and 120 community newspapers in the country. Yes, the Canadians could easily relate.

But then something strange happened. My wife called me over to her computer one day and said, "Check this out." She had pulled up Amazon.co.uk. And there it was: *Stupid White Men* at #1 in the U.K. How could this be? The book wasn't even for sale there yet. Unable to buy it in Britain (my early and repeated requests to HarperCollins to publish a British edition were met with early and repeated "No"s), Brits and Irish were buying an overpriced import by the thousands. Realizing that there's quids in *dem der hills*, ReganBooks/HarperCollins quickly cranked up the printing presses in the U.S. and starting shipping over more overpriced imports to the British Isles. Within a week, the book went to #1 on the *Sunday Times* list.

Well, I am now free of the Murdoch machine—and to my aid have come the good people at Penguin Books in the U.K. with their offer to publish the foreign paperback edition of this book. Their letter to me was one of the most generous and powerful shows of commitment to my work that I have ever seen and I am very grateful for their support.

This is not the first time I have found a far better relationship outside the U.S. The BBC offered to produce my first TV series, *TV Nation*, after it was rejected by NBC in the United States. Once the BBC gave it its stamp of approval, NBC decided it had made a mistake and put us on American TV. The BBC then produced my documentary, *The Big One*. Channel Four U.K. produced the first season of our next series, *The Awful Truth*, and their Canadian partner, Salter Street Films, ended up funding my next feature film, *Bowling for Columbine*. It is both fortunate and sad that, in order for me to produce work that examines the American condition, I must leave America in order to find the money to bring that work back to the American public.

Clearly, it does not take much digging to find stupid white men in the U.S. But, as grateful as I am to those in your various nations who have helped me out, I would be remiss if I did not point out that America does not have a monopoly on *all* the stupid white men. There are plenty of these creatures who lurk throughout the Commonwealth and on the old sod of Cork and Tipperary that my great-grandparents called home.

In Britain, it seems that all the attention in recent years has been on the evils of Mad Cow—with little or no heed paid to the Mad Men! Just because you don't eat the Mad Men is no reason to ignore the serious safety issue here. British politicians and corporate executives are running amok, trying to catch up with the United States and show the world that your British SWM can go head to head with the best of any stupidity that the Americans can produce. You need only consider the state of the train system in Britain to see where following the American Way (in this case, of privatizing formerly well-run public entities) will get you.

There is nothing sadder than seeing leaders of other countries trying to mimic the leaders of our country. America decides to bomb some country—and your head of state joins right in. We accept a dumbed-down mass media—and your nightly newscasts soon start to resemble ours. We decide to eliminate the safety net for our poor, and your legislative bodies can't wait to start cutting numerous social services that have been in place for decades.

And that last one has been the real shock to this observer. To see you in your countries start to beat up on those who are less fortunate, to make life more difficult for them, I'm convinced that this will be the unraveling of your soul. If you get a kick out of watching Americans open fire in their schools and workplaces on a monthly basis, if you think it's progress to have infant mortality rates in your cities that are worse than Nairobi, if you'd like to live in a world with even less civil liberties than you now enjoy, just keep following our path. You'll not only end up being a Mini-Me-America, you'll get every invitation to join us in our attempts to exploit the poor in other countries so we can all have really cheap running shoes to wear! HOW CAN YOU PASS THIS UP?!

Well, maybe you can. Maybe there is still hope for you. It may be too late for us, I dunno. This book will provide you with a look at the U.S. in a way that is not normally presented to you even in your media. Consider this book as a mirror to what is happening now in your country. Consider it a warning of what is yet to come. When you're finished, put it down and commit to root out every stupid white guy from every position of power. You'll not only feel good, it may just get the trains back to running on time (and on track) again.

Michael Moore

July, 2002

A Very American Coup

THE FOLLOWING MESSAGE WAS INTERCEPTED BY U.N. FORCES ON 9/1/01, AT 0600 HOURS, FROM SOMEWHERE WITHIN THE NORTH AMERICAN CONTINENT:

I am a citizen of the United States of America. Our government has been overthrown. Our elected President has been exiled. Old white men wielding martinis and wearing dickies have occupied our nation's capital.

We are under siege. We are the United States Government-in-Exile.

Our numbers are not insignificant. There are over 154 million adults among us, and 80 million children. That's 234 million people who did not vote for, and are not represented by, the regime that has placed itself in power.

Al Gore is the elected President of the United States. He received 539,898 more votes than George W. Bush. But he does not sit tonight in the Oval Office. Instead our elected President roams the country without purpose or mission, surfacing only to lecture college students and replenish his stash of Little Debbie's Snack Cakes.

Al Gore won. Al Gore, President-in-Exile. Long live El Presidente Albertooooooo Gorrrrrrrrrrre!

So who, then, is the man that now occupies 1600 Pennsylvania Avenue? I'll tell you who:

He is George W. Bush, "President" of the United States. The Thief-in-Chief.

It used to be that politicians would wait until they were in office before they became crooks. This one came prepackaged. Now he is a trespasser on federal land, a squatter in the Oval Office. If I told you this was Guatemala, you'd believe it in a heartbeat, no matter what your political stripe. But because this coup was wrapped in an American flag, delivered in your choice of red, white, or blue, those responsible believe they're going to get away with it.

That's why, on behalf of 234 million Americans held hostage, I have requested that NATO do what it did in Bosnia and Kosovo, what America did in Haiti, what Lee Marvin did in *The Dirty Dozen*:

Send in the Marines! Launch the SCUD missiles! Bring us the head of Antonin Scalia!

I have sent a personal request to U.N. Secretary General Kofi Annan to hear our plea. We are no longer able to govern ourselves or to hold free and fair elections. We need U.N. observers, U.N. troops, U.N. resolutions!

Dammit, we need Jimmy Carter!

We are now finally no better than a backwater banana republic. We are asking ourselves why any of us should bother to get up in the morning to work our asses off to produce goods and services that only serve to make the junta and its cohorts in Corporate America (a separate, autonomous fiefdom within the United States that has been allowed to run on its own for some time) even richer. Why should we pay our taxes to finance their coup? Can we ever again send our sons off into battle to give their lives defending "our way of life"—when all that really means is the lifestyle of the gray old men holed up in the headquarters they seized by the Potomac?

Oh JesusMaryAndJoseph, I can't take it! Somebody pass me the universal remote! I need to switch back to the fairy tale that I was a citizen in a democracy with an inalienable right to life, liberty, and the pursuit of Happy Meals. The story I was told as a child said that I mattered, that I was equal to every one of my fellow citizens—and that not a single one of us was to be treated differently or unfairly, that no one was to wield power over others without their consent. The will of the people. America the Beautiful. Land that I love. Twilight's . . . last . . . gleaming. Oh, say, can you see—are the Belgian peacekeepers on their way? Hurry!

The coup began long before the shenanigans on Election Day 2000. In the summer of 1999 Katherine Harris, an honorary Stupid White Man who was both George W. Bush's presidential campaign cochairwoman *and* the Florida secretary of state in charge of elections, paid $4 million to Database Technologies to go through Florida's voter rolls and remove anyone "suspected" of being a former felon. She did so with the blessing of the governor of Florida, George W.'s brother Jeb Bush—whose own wife was caught by immigration officials trying to sneak $19,000 worth of jewelry into the country without declaring and paying tax on it . . . a felony in its own right. But hey, this is America. We don't prosecute felons if they're rich or married to a governing Bush.

The law states that ex-felons cannot vote in Florida. And sadly (though I'm confident that Florida's justice system was always unimpeachably fair), that means 31 percent of *all* black men in Florida are prohibited from voting because they have a felony on their record. Harris and Bush knew that removing the names of ex-felons from the voter rolls would keep thousands of black citizens out of the voting booth.

Black Floridians, overwhelmingly, are Democrats—and sure enough, Al Gore received the votes of more than 90 percent of them on November 7, 2000.

That is, 90 percent of those who were *allowed* to vote.

In what appears to be a mass fraud committed by the state of Florida, Bush, Harris, and company not only removed thousands of black felons from the rolls, they also removed thousands of black citizens *who had never committed a crime in their lives*—along with thousands of eligible voters who had committed only misdemeanors.

How did this happen? Harris's office told Database—a firm with strong Republican ties—to cast as wide a net as possible to get rid of these voters. Her minions instructed the company to include even people with "similar" names to those of the actual felons. They insisted Database check people with the same birth dates as known felons, or similar Social Security numbers; an 80 percent match of relevant information, the election office instructed, was sufficient for Database to add a voter to the ineligible list.

These orders were shocking, even to Bush-friendly Database. They would mean that thousands of legitimate voters might be barred from voting on Election Day just because they had a name that sounded like someone else's, or shared a birthday with some unknown bank robber. Marlene Thorogood, the Database project manager, sent an E-mail to Emmett "Bucky" Mitchell, a lawyer for Katherine Harris's election division, warning him that "Unfortunately, programming in this fashion may supply you with false positives," or misidentifications.

Never mind that, said ol' Bucky. His response: "Obviously, we want to capture more names that possibly aren't matches and let [county election] supervisors make a final determination rather than exclude certain matches altogether."

Database did as they were told. And before long 173,000 registered voters in Florida were permanently wiped off the voter rolls. In Miami-Dade, Florida's largest county, 66 percent of the voters who were removed were black. In Tampa's county, 54 percent of those who would be denied the right to vote on November 7, 2000, were black.

But culling names from Florida's records alone was not enough for Harris and her department. Eight thousand additional Floridians were thrown off the voting rolls because Database used a false list supplied by another state, a state which claimed that all the names on the list were former convicted felons who had since moved to Florida.

It turns out that the felons on the list had served their time and had all their voting privileges reinstated. And there were others on the list who had committed only misdemeanors—such as parking violations or littering. What state was it that offered Jeb and George a helping hand by sending this bogus list to Florida? Texas.

This entire incident stunk to the high heavens, but the American media ignored it. It took the British Broadcasting Corporation to dig deep into this story, running fifteen-minute segments on its prime-time news program revealing all the sordid details and laying responsibility for the scam right at the doorstep of Governor Jeb Bush. It's a sad day when we have to look to a country 5,000 miles away to find out the truth about our own elections. (Eventually the *Los Angeles Times* and the *Washington Post* picked up the story, but it received little attention.)

This assault on the voting rights of minorities was so widespread in Florida that it even affected people like Linda Howell. Linda received a letter informing her that she was a felon—and therefore advising her not to bother showing up on Election Day, because she would be barred from voting. The only problem was, Linda Howell wasn't a felon—in fact, she was the elections supervisor of Madison County, Florida! She and other local election officials tried to get the state to rectify the problem, but their pleas fell on deaf ears. They were told that everyone who complained about being prevented from voting should submit themselves for fingerprinting—and then let the state determine whether or not they were felons.

On November 7, 2000, as black Floridians flocked to the polls in record numbers, many were met at the ballot boxes with a blunt rebuke: "You cannot vote." In a number of precincts in Florida's inner cities, the polling locations were heavily fortified with police to block anyone on Katherine and Jeb's "felons list" from voting. Hundreds of law-abiding citizens looking to exercise their constitutional right to vote, mostly in black and Hispanic communities, were sent away—and threatened with arrest if they protested.

George W. Bush would officially be credited with receiving 537 more votes than Al Gore in Florida. Is it safe to assume that the thousands of registered black and Hispanic voters barred from the polls might have made the difference if they had been allowed to vote—and cost Bush the election? Without a doubt.

On election night, after the polls closed, there was much confusion over what was happening with the counting of the votes in Florida. Finally a decision was made by the man in charge of the election night desk for the Fox News Channel. He decided that Fox should go on the air and declare that Bush had won Florida and thus the election. And that's what happened. Fox formally declared Bush the winner.

But down in Tallahassee, the counting of the votes had not yet been completed; in fact, the Associated Press insisted it was still too close to call, and refused to follow Fox's lead.

Not so the other networks. They ran like lemmings after Fox made the call, afraid that they would be seen as slow or out of the loop—even though their own news reporters on the ground were insisting that it was too early to call the election. But who needs reporters when you're playing follow the leader—the leader, in this case, being John Ellis, the man in charge of Fox's election coverage. Who is John Ellis?

He's a first cousin of George W. and Jeb Bush.

Once Ellis made the call and everyone followed suit, there was no going back—and nothing was more psychologically devastating for Gore's chances of winning than the sudden perception that HE was being the spoiler by asking for recounts, withdrawing his concession of defeat, tying up the courts with lawyers and lawsuits. The truth is that during all of this, Gore actually was ahead—he had the most votes—but that was *never* how the news media played it.

The one moment from that election night I will never forget came earlier in the evening, after the networks had first—correctly—projected the state of Florida for Gore. The cameras cut to a hotel room in Texas. There sat George W. with his father, the former President, and his mother, Barbara. The old man appeared cool as a cucumber, even though it looked like curtains for Sonny. A reporter asked young Bush what he thought about the outcome.

"I'm not . . . conceding anything in Florida," Junior piped up, semicoherently. "I know you've all the projections, but people are actually counting the votes. . . . The networks called this thing awfully earlier and people are actually counting the votes have different perspective so . . ." It was an odd moment in that crazy night of election result coverage. The Bushes, with their relaxed smiles, looked like a family of cats that had just wolfed down a bunch of canaries—as if they knew something we didn't.

They did. They knew Jeb and Katherine had done their job months earlier. They knew cousin John was holding down the fort at Fox election central. And if all else failed, there was always that team Poppy could count on: the United States Supreme Court.

As we all know, that's exactly what happened for the next thirty-six days. The forces of the Empire struck back, and they did so without mercy. While Gore was stupidly concentrating on getting recounts in a few counties, the Bush team was going after the holy grail—the overseas absentee ballots. Many of these ballots would come from the military, which typically votes Republican, and would finally give Bush the lead that denying the vote to thousands of blacks and Jewish grandmothers hadn't.

Gore knew this, and tried to make sure the ballots underwent maximum scrutiny before they could be counted. Sure, this ran contrary to the "let every vote be counted" plea he'd made when calling for recounts. But he also had Florida law, which is pretty clear about this, on his side. It states that overseas absentee ballots can only be counted if they were cast and signed on or before election day, and mailed and postmarked from another country by election day.

But while Jim Baker was chanting his mantra—"It is not fair to change the rules and standards governing the counting or recounting of votes after it appears that one side has concluded that is the only way to get the votes it needs"—he and his operatives were doing just that.

A July 2001 investigation by the *New York Times* showed that of the 2,490 overseas ballots that ended up being included in the certified election results, 680 were considered flawed and questionable. Bush got the overseas vote by a ratio of 4 to 5. By that percentage, 544 of the votes that went to Bush should have been thrown out. Got the math? Suddenly Bush's "winning margin" of 537 votes is down to a chilly negative 7.

So how did all these votes end up being counted for Bush? Within hours of the election, the Bush campaign had launched their attack. The first step was to make sure that as many ballots got in as possible. Republican operatives sent out frantic E-mails to navy ships asking them to dig up any ballots that might be hanging around. They even put in a call to Clinton Defense Secretary William S. Cohen (a Republican) to ask him to put pressure on the military outposts. He declined, but it didn't matter: thousands of votes poured in—even some that were signed *after* election day.

Now all they had to do was make sure that as many of these votes as possible went to W. And so the real thievery began.

According to the *Times*, Katherine Harris had planned to send out a memo to her canvassing boards clarifying the procedure for counting overseas ballots. Included in this memo was a reminder that state law required all ballots to have been "postmarked or signed and dated" by election day. When it was clear that George's lead was rapidly shrinking, she decided not to send the memo. Instead she sent out a note that said ballots "are not required to be postmarked on or prior to" election day. Hmmm.

What caused her to change her mind—and the law? We may never know, since the computer records that showed what happened have been mysteriously erased—a possible violation of Florida's Sunshine Laws. Now, long after the horse has left the barn, Harris has turned over her hard drives to the media for inspection—but only after her own computer consultant "looked them over." This is a woman who is now planning to run for Congress. Can these people get any more shameless?

Armed with the blessing of the secretary of state, the Republicans launched an all-out campaign to make sure as broad a standard as possible was used in counting these absentee ballots. "Equal representation," Florida style, meant that the rules governing acceptance or denial of your absentee ballot depended on what county you were from. Perhaps that would explain why in counties where Gore won, only 2 out of 10 absentee ballots with unclear postmarks were counted; in Bush counties, predictably, 6 out of 10 such ballots made it into the final tally.

When the Democrats complained that ballots that didn't follow the rules shouldn't be counted, the Republicans launched a fierce public relations campaign to make it look as if the Democrats were trying to screw the men and women who were risking their lives for our country. A Republican city council member from Naples was typical in his hyperbole: "If they catch a bullet, or fragment from a terrorist bomb, that fragment does not have any postmark or registration of any kind." Republican Congressman Steve Buyer from Indiana even obtained (possibly illegally) the phone numbers and E-mail addresses of military personnel so that he could gather tales of ballot-denial woe to garner sympathy for "our fighting men and women." Even Stormin' Norman Schwarzkopf weighed in with the reflection that "it's a very sad day in our country" when Democrats start harassing military voters.

All the pressure worked on the wimpy, spineless Democrats. They choked. While appearing on *Meet the Press*, vice presidential candidate Joe Lieberman argued that the Democrats should stop creating a fuss and not be bothered that hundreds of military ballots were being counted, just because they weren't "postmarked."

Lieberman, like so many others among this new breed of Democrats, should have fought for principle instead of worrying about image. Why? Well, as the *New York Times* found out:

* 344 ballots had no evidence that they were cast on or before Election Day

* 183 ballots were postmarked in the United States

* 96 ballots lacked appropriate witness information

* 169 ballots came from unregistered voters, had envelopes that weren't signed properly, or came from people who hadn't requested a ballot

* 5 ballots came after the November 17 deadline

✳ 19 overseas voters voted on two ballots—and had both counted

All of these ballots violated Florida law, yet they all were counted. Can I say this any louder? *Bush didn't win! Gore did.* It has nothing to do with chads, or even the blatant repression of Florida's African-American community and their right to vote. It was a simple matter of breaking the law, all documented, all the evidence sitting there in Tallahassee, clearly marked without question—and all done purposefully to throw the election to Bush.

On the morning of Saturday, December 9, 2000, the Supreme Court got word that the recounts in Florida, in spite of everything the Bush camp had done to fix the elections, were going in favor of Al Gore. By 2 P.M., the unofficial tally showed that Gore was catching up to Bush—"only 66 votes down, and gaining!" as one breathless newscaster put it. It was critical to Bush that the words "Al Gore is in the lead" never be heard on American television: With only moments to spare, they did what they had to do. At 2:45 that afternoon, the Supreme Court stopped the recount.

On the Court sat Reagan appointee Sandra Day O'Connor and Nixon appointee Chief Justice William Rehnquist. Both in their seventies, they were hoping to retire under a Republican administration so that their replacements would share their conservative ideology. On election night, O'Connor was heard lamenting at a party in Georgetown that she couldn't hold out another four—or eight—years. Junior Bush was their only hope for securing a contented retirement in their home state of Arizona.

Meanwhile, two other justices with extremist right-wing viewpoints found themselves with a conflict of interest. Justice Clarence Thomas's wife, Virginia Lamp Thomas, worked at the Heritage Foundation, a leading conservative think tank in D.C.; now, she has just been hired by George W. Bush to help recruit people to serve in his impending administration. And Eugene

Scalia, the son of Justice Antonin Scalia, was a lawyer with the firm of Gibson, Dunn & Crutcher—the very law firm representing Bush before the Supreme Court!

But neither Thomas nor Scalia saw any conflict of interest, and they refused to remove themselves from the case. In fact, when the Court convened later, it was Scalia who issued the now-infamous explanation of why the ballot-counting *had* to be halted: "The counting of votes that are of questionable legality does, in my view, threaten irreparable harm to petitioner [Bush], and to the country, by casting a cloud upon what he [Bush] claims to be the legitimacy of his election." In other words, if we let all the votes be counted and they come out in Gore's favor, and Gore wins, well, that will impair Bush's ability to govern once we install him as "President."

True enough: if the ballots proved that Gore had won—which they eventually would—then I guess that *would* tend to dampen the country's feelings of legitimacy about a Bush presidency.

In their decision, the Court used the equal protection clause of the Fourteenth Amendment—the same amendment they've loudly disclaimed when used by blacks over the years to halt discrimination based on race—to justify the theft. Because of the variation in the recount methods, they argued, voters in each district weren't being treated equally, and therefore their rights were being violated. (Funny, but only the dissenters on the court mentioned that the antiquated voting equipment found disproportionately in poor and minority Florida neighborhoods had created an entirely different—and far more disturbing—inequality in the system.)

Eventually the press got around to conducting their own recounts of the votes, doing their best to spin the jumbled ball of public confusion into orbit. The headline in the *Miami Herald* read: "Review of ballots finds Bush's win would have endured manual recount." But if you read the *entire* story, buried deep inside was this paragraph: "Bush's lead would have vanished if the recount had been conducted under the severely restrictive standards that some

Republicans advocated. . . . The review found that the result would have been different if every canvassing board in every county had examined every undervote . . . [Under] the *most inclusive* standard [that is, a standard that sought to include the true will of ALL the people] Gore would have won by 393 votes. . . . On ballots that [suggested] a fault with either the machine or the voter's ability to use it . . . Gore would have won by 299 votes."

I did not vote for Al Gore, but I think any fair person would conclude that the will of the people in Florida clearly went his way. Whether it was the counting debacle or the exclusion of thousands of black citizens that corrupted the results, there is little doubt that Gore was the people's choice.

There was perhaps no worse example of the wholesale denial of the right of each voter to have his vote properly counted than in Palm Beach County. Much has been made of the "butterfly ballot," which made it easy to vote for the wrong person because candidates' names and punch holes were crammed unevenly onto facing pages. The media went out of its way to point out that the ballot was designed by one of the county's election commissioners, a Democrat, and then approved by the majority-Democrat local board. What right did Gore have to complain if his own party was responsible for the faulty design of the ballot?

Had anyone bothered to check, they would have discovered that one of the two "Democrats" on the committee—the ballot's designer, Theresa LePore—had actually been a registered Republican. She switched her affiliation to Democrat in 1996; then, just three months after Bush seized office, she resigned as a Democrat and switched her voter registration to Independent. No one in the press bothered to question what was really going on.

Thus, the *Palm Beach Post* estimates that more than 3,000 voters, mostly elderly and Jewish, who thought they were voting for Al Gore ended up punching the wrong hole—for Pat Buchanan. Even Buchanan went on TV to declare that no way in hell did those Jewish voters vote for him.

* * *

On January 20, 2001, George W. Bush, positioned with his junta
on the Capitol steps, stood in front of Chief Justice Rehnquist
and took the oath that *Presidents* take at their inaugurations. A
cold and steady rain fell over Washington throughout the day.
Dark clouds obscured the sun, and the parade route, usually
jammed with tens of thousands of citizens all the way to the
White House, was eerily bare.

Except for the 20,000 protesters who jeered Bush every inch
of the way. Holding signs denouncing Bush for stealing the election, the rain-soaked demonstrators were the conscience of the
nation. Bush's limousine could not avoid them. Instead of cheer-
ing crowds of supporters, he was greeted by good people moved
to remind this illegitimate ruler that he did not win the election—
and that the people would never forget.

At the traditional point where Presidents since Jimmy Carter
have stopped their limos and emerged to walk the last four blocks
(as a reminder that we are a nation ruled not by kings but by,
uh, equals), Bush's triple-armored black car with its dark-tinted
windows—favored by mobsters everywhere—came to an abrupt
halt. The crowd grew louder—"HAIL TO THE THIEF!" You
could see the Secret Service and Bush's advisers huddling in the
freezing rain, trying to figure out what to do. If Bush got out and
walked, he would be booed, shouted down, and pelted with eggs
the rest of the way. The limousine sat there for what must have
been five minutes. The rain poured. Eggs and tomatoes hit the
car. The protesters dared Bush to step out and face them.

Then, suddenly, the President's car bolted and tore down the
street. The decision had been made—hit the gas and get past this
rabble as quickly as possible. The Secret Service agents running
beside the limo were left behind, the car's tires splashing dirty rain
from the street onto the men who were there to protect its passenger. It might have been the finest thing I have ever witnessed in

Washington, D.C.—a pretender to the American throne forced to turn tail and run from thousands of American citizens armed only with the Truth and the ingredients of a decent omelet.

Once the American Lie put the pedal to the metal, it ran for cover to the bulletproof reviewing stand in front of the White House. Many of Bush's family and invited guests had already left to get dry. But George stood there and waved proudly at the marching bands, their instruments disabled by the rain, the long parade of floats wilted and crumbled by the time they arrived at the 1600 block of Pennsylvania Avenue. Every so often a lucky convertible passed by, carrying the few dampened celebrities Bush had convinced to honor him—Kelsey Grammer, Drew Carey, Chuck Norris. By parade's end Bush stood alone in the stands, drenched, even his parents having deserted him for shelter. It was a pathetic sight—the poor little rich boy who came in second showing up to claim his prize, with no one there to cheer him on.

Sadder still were the 154 million of us who had not voted for him. In a nation of 200 million voters, I would say we constitute the majority.

And yet what could George W. have been thinking, other than "What, me worry?" There were plenty of hired hands to be installed in the White House, pulling the strings for their puppet President. With Daddy's old buddies called back to D.C. to lend a hand, Georgie could sit back and tell the public he was "delegating." The puppetmasters moved in, and the business of running the world could easily be left to them.

And who are these fine, patriotic pillars of the Bush junta? They represent the modest and selfless ranks of corporate America, and they are listed below, for easy reference, to help the United Nations and NATO forces round them up when they arrive to restore order and democracy. Grateful citizens will line the boulevards and avenues and cheer their arrival.

Personally, I will settle for nothing less than multiple show trials and their immediate deportation to a real banana republic. God Bless America!

WHO'S WHO IN THE COUP

Acting President/"Vice President"—Dick Cheney

I'm not sure yet where the "compassionate" part of "compassionate conservatism" comes from, but I do know where the conservatism resides. For six terms Dick Cheney was a congressman representing Wyoming, and he had one of the most conservative voting records of all 435 members of Congress. Cheney voted against the Equal Rights Amendment, against funding the Head Start program, against a House resolution calling for South Africa to release Nelson Mandela from prison, and against federal funding for abortions *even in cases of rape or incest*. And his record doesn't stop there. Cheney has had his hand in all of the recent Republican administrations, including that of Richard Nixon, when he was deputy White House counsel under Don "Rummy" Rumsfeld. He replaced Rumsfeld as President Ford's chief of staff. Under George Bush I, Cheney was defense secretary, leading the country in two of the largest military campaigns in recent history: the invasion of Panama and the war against Iraq.

In between Bush regimes, Cheney was CEO of Halliburton Industries, an oil services company that has dealings with repressive governments like Burma and Iraq. During the 2000 campaign, Cheney denied that Halliburton had a business relationship with Saddam Hussein. Then, in June 2001, the *Washington Post* revealed that in fact two Halliburton subsidiaries *were* doing business with Iraq. Can you imagine the field day Republicans would have had if they'd ever discovered such a thing about

Clinton or Gore? And Alaska isn't the only place Cheney has suggested we dig up: Halliburton has a major construction deal in the development of Mexico's Cantarell offshore oil fields in the Gulf of Mexico. When nominated for the vice presidency, Cheney hemmed and hawed about divesting himself of his Halliburton stock. I guess he knew that good times were still to come.

Attorney General—John Ashcroft

The man in charge of overseeing our justice system is a man who has opposed all abortion, even in cases of rape or incest; who is against providing job discrimination protection for homosexuals; who voted to limit the death penalty appeals process (and then oversaw seven executions as governor); and who has been a staunch supporter of out-of-control, over-the-top drug laws. Perhaps this record could explain why he lost his Senate reelection bid against a dead man. For his efforts, however, Ashcroft received substantial donations from AT&T, Enterprise Rent-A-Car, and Monsanto. The Schering-Plough pharmaceutical company contributed $50,000—perhaps as a thank-you for the bill he had introduced that would have extended the company's patent on the allergy pill Claritin. (The bill ultimately failed.) All this pharmaceutical funding may also explain why Ashcroft has voted against including prescription drugs under the Medicare program. Another campaign contributor, Microsoft, gave Ashcroft $10,000 through his joint fund-raising committee with the National Republican Senatorial Committee. Lucky for them he lost the Senate race, so that he can turn his full attention to running the Justice Department—or, that is, standing back while the software giant, newly freed of the court ruling that would have split the company in two, is allowed to run amok under his watchful eye.

Ashcroft is also to the right (if such a thing is possible) of the

National Rifle Association when it comes to gun control. His first pro-gun act as attorney general was to announce that *within twenty-four hours of a purchase and background check*, all background-check files on persons who purchase guns will be destroyed by the Justice Department (leaving the government with NO record of who has a gun or what kind of gun they have).

Secretary of the Treasury—Paul O'Neill

This champion of the abolition of corporate taxes served as president and CEO of Alcoa, the world's largest aluminum manufacturer (and one of the biggest polluters in Texas) before joining the Bush administration. Alcoa no longer has its own Political Action Committee (PAC) but instead does its lobbying through the law firm of Vinson & Elkins. That firm, the third largest contributor to Bush's campaign, was able to work a loophole into Texas environmental regulations that allowed Alcoa to emit 60,000 tons of sulfur dioxide each year. Alcoa has also been a big contributor to O'Neill's pockets. O'Neill recently sold off his shares in Alcoa—which make up a large portion of his $62 million in assets—but did so only begrudgingly and very slowly, first watching them rise 30 percent during his time in office. As Treasury chief, O'Neill has said that Social Security and Medicare are not necessary. Perhaps that's because he receives an annual pension from Alcoa of $926,000.

Secretary of Agriculture—Ann Veneman

Like many in the Bush cabinet, Agriculture Secretary Ann Veneman has a long career within Republican administrations. She worked for both Ronald Reagan and Poppy Bush and then served as director of California's Food and Agriculture

Department under Governor Pete Wilson. In California she encouraged policies that have helped giant corporate farms squeeze out family-owned farms—so that now, for example, a mere four companies process 80 percent of American-produced beef. One of the least wealthy of the cabinet members (worth a mere $680,000), Veneman supplemented her income by serving on the board of Calgene—the first company to market genetically engineered foods to stores. Calgene was bought out by Monsanto, the nation's leading biotech company. Monsanto was then bought by Pharmacia. Monsanto, which gave $12,000 to Bush's presidential campaign, is trying to block legislation that would require food labels to identify biotech ingredients. Veneman has also served on the International Policy Council on Agriculture, Food and Trade, a group funded by major food manufacturers such as Nestlé and Archer Daniels Midland.

Secretary of Commerce—Don Evans

Before coming to the Bush administration, Evans was chairman and CEO of Tom Brown, Inc., a $1.2 billion oil and gas company. Evans also sat on the board of TMBR/Sharp Drilling. As finance chair for Bush's campaign, he set a fund-raising record of more than $190 million. The National Oceanic and Atmospheric Administration—which controls the country's coastlines—falls within this oil man's domain.

Secretary of Defense—Don Rumsfeld

Don Rumsfeld is an old-school Republican hawk. He was White House counsel to Richard Nixon, where he worked alongside Dick Cheney. While serving as President Ford's secretary of defense and then as Ford's chief of staff, Rumsfeld was able, almost single-handedly, to kill the SALT II treaty with the Soviet Union. He has consistently opposed any arms control, calling the ABM treaty "ancient history" during his 2001 confirmation hearing. A longtime supporter of "Star Wars" defense schemes, Rumsfeld oversaw a 1998 commission that measured the ballistic missile threat to the United States. Rumsfeld, aka Chicken Little, claimed that the United States would feel such threats from rogue nations within five years (half the amount of time the CIA predicted). When not pushing B-1 bombs or MX missiles, Rumsfeld has been CEO of the G. D. Searle pharmaceutical company (now owned by Pharmacia) and General Instrument (now owned by Motorola). Before joining the Bush administration, he sat on several boards, including Kellogg's, Sears, Allstate, and the Tribune Company (which publishes the *Chicago Tribune* and *Los Angeles Times* and owns a chain of TV stations, including New York's Channel 11).

Secretary of Energy—Spencer Abraham

As a senator from Michigan, Abraham had such a strong antienvironment record that the League of Conservation Voters gave him a zero rating. He opposed research into renewable energy, wanted to repeal the federal gas tax, and thought oil drilling in Alaska was a good idea. Perhaps that's why he voted in 2000 to abolish the department he now leads. Abraham received more from the automotive industry—$700,000—than any other candidate. One of the largest contributors was DaimlerChrysler, which is part of the Coalition for Vehicle Choice, a trade group trying to stop an increase in fuel economy standards. This year DaimlerChrysler has plans to introduce a longer-body SUV that gets about 10 miles per gallon. No worries: when he was a senator, Abraham also voted against increasing fuel-efficiency requirements for SUVs.

Secretary of Health and Human Services— Tommy Thompson

The man who will have perhaps the greatest role in dealing with the tobacco industry should have no trouble being objective about policy. After all, just because Thompson served on the advisory board of the Washington Legal Fund as it filed briefs on behalf of those who would promote smoking—or because as governor he received about $72,000 in campaign contributions from Philip Morris, or because Philip Morris paid for several trips abroad that Thompson made to promote free trade—is no reason to think he won't be able to act impartially on this health issue. Too bad he recently sold his Philip Morris stock for an amount between $15,000 and $50,000—as these should be very good years for Big Tobacco.

Good times ahead for wire hanger manufacturers, too. Tommy T is what they like to call "pro-life," putting up as many roadblocks to a women's right to an abortion as possible. As governor of Wisconsin he required women to seek counseling and wait three days before having the procedure.

Secretary of the Interior—Gale Norton

Gale Norton is already following in the footsteps of her mentor and predecessor, James Watt. She started her legal career with the Mountain States Legal Foundation, a conservative environmental think tank funded by oil companies and founded by Watt. Working closely with this group, Norton helped the state of Alaska challenge an Interior Department fisheries law. She has declared the Endangered Species Act unconstitutional and written legal opinions against the National Environmental Protection Act. As a lawyer with Brownstein, Hyatt & Farber,

Norton represented Delta Petroleum and lobbied for NL Industries (formerly known as National Lead) while it defended itself in lawsuits over children's exposure to lead paint. She was also national chairwoman of the Coalition of Republican Environmental Advocates, a group funded by Ford Motor Company and BP Amoco.

Secretary of Labor—Elaine Chao

Chao has worked primarily in the nonprofit sector, with United Way and the Peace Corps, but has also sat on the boards of Dole Food, Clorox, and health care companies C. R. Bard (who pleaded guilty in the 1990s to manufacturing faulty heart catheters and conducting illegal experiments on the devices) and the behemoth Hospital Corporation of America (HCA). She also sat on the board of Northwest Airlines. She is married to conservative Senator Mitch McConnell (R-KY).

Secretary of State—Colin Powell

When not fighting wars, Powell sat on the boards of Gulfstream Aerospace and AOL. Gulfstream makes jets for both Hollywood honchos and foreign governments like Kuwait and Saudi Arabia. During his time at AOL the company merged with Time Warner, and Powell's stock rose in value by $4 million. At the time, Colin's son, Michael Powell, had been the only Federal Communications Commission (FCC) member who advocated that the AOL/Time Warner merger go through without question. Powell's son has since been named chairman of the FCC by George W. Bush; part of his job is to oversee the activities of AOL/Time Warner. He will also oversee any regulation of AOL's monopolistic "instant messaging" technology.

Secretary of Transportation—Norman Y. Mineta

A leftover from the Clinton administration, the only "Democrat" in Bush's cabinet, Mineta has his own corporate connections. When he was a congressman representing Silicon Valley, he received campaign contributions from Northwest Airlines, United Airlines, Greyhound, Boeing, and Union Pacific. After retiring from the House, he went to work at Lockheed Martin. What better place to park himself now than at the cabinet department that "oversees" all of them?

White House Chief of Staff—Andrew H. Card Jr.

Card was General Motors's chief lobbyist before leaving to work in the Bush administration. He was also CEO of the now-defunct American Automobile Manufacturers Association, which lobbied against stricter fuel emissions standards and fought over trade issues with Japan. Card testified before Congress on behalf of the U.S. Chamber of Commerce Lobbying Group against the "Passenger's Bill of Rights." He personally contributed $1,000 each to the losing campaigns of John Ashcroft and Spencer Abraham.

Director of the Office of Management and Budget— Mitch Daniels Jr.

Daniels was formerly a senior vice president of Eli Lilly pharmaceuticals. In his present position, Daniels will oversee the drafting of the federal budget, including how much money (if any) will be earmarked for a prescription drug benefit for Medicare patients—a provision Eli Lilly and other pharmaceutical companies are lobbying against. Daniels also owns stock worth between $50,000 and $100,000 in GE, Citigroup, and Merck. The chances of this administration allowing a prescription drug benefit for seniors to pass in the next year are about as good as those of me setting myself on fire in front of a Rite Aid.

National Security Adviser—Condoleezza Rice

For her service on Chevron's board of directors, Rice had a 130,000-ton oil tanker named after her. She was also a director at Charles Schwab and Transamerica, and has served as an adviser for J. P. Morgan; she also served on Bush the Elder's National Security team.

Senior Adviser to the President—Karl Rove

A longtime supporter and friend of Bush, Rove was once an adviser to Philip Morris. For five years, while he was an adviser to Governor Bush, the tobacco company paid him $3,000 a month to get his inside opinion on what was happening in the elections and with the candidates. Since Rove took the job at the White House, he has been under constant fire for using his position to further the interests of companies in which he owns stock. Recently Rove was criticized for holding meetings with Intel executives about a prospective merger while at the same time he held Intel stock (part of an overall portfolio valued at between $1 million and $2.5 million). The merger was approved two months after the meetings, and Rove sold his stock a month later.

Shadow Adviser to the President—Kenneth L. Lay

Lay is the head of Enron, the largest electricity trader in the United States and a top contributor to the Bush presidential campaign. Lay has used his close relationship with the President to pressure the chairman of the Federal Energy Regulatory Commission to speed up energy deregulation. Lay has apparently provided Bush with a list of preferred candidates for key commission posts. Thanks in part to the California energy crisis, Enron has quickly grown into a $100 billion company. Bush and Cheney rely on Lay for advice; some administration appointees must first be "interviewed" by Lay before getting the job.

As you can see, friends and neighbors, this is a regime that is intent on lining its pockets—and who won't leave office without a fight. It is their mission to combine their economic and (newly acquired) political power to rule the country and help their friends get even richer along the way.

These Stupid White Men must be stopped. I have informed Kofi Annan of the various locations where these (mostly) men can be found and apprehended by U.N. troops. Mr. Annan, I beseech you. You have invaded other countries for less grievous offenses. Do not ignore our plight. We plead with you: Save the United States of America! Demand that new, clean elections be held. Give the junta forty-eight hours to agree—and, if they don't, then treat them to a U.S. Air Force–style laser light show!

HOW TO STAGE THE COUNTERCOUP

We, the people, can start a groundswell that will eventually topple the Bush/Cheney Junta—with a commitment of only a couple of hours a week. Here's how:

1. **Contact your representatives on a weekly basis, and get three friends to do the same.** Senators, members of congress, and other elected officials PAY CAREFUL ATTENTION to the calls, letters, and telegrams they receive. Each day they receive a tally of their constituents' messages. Take just a few minutes each week, and let your thoughts be known.

   The Bush agenda can be brought to a grinding halt by a

public outcry—and even a few hundred letters can constitute an outcry. Several Bush policies have already been
shelved after public disapproval. IT WORKS! We all
whine too much; why not put it to good use? Pick an issue
you care about and do the following today:

   a. Call 202-224-3121—the U.S. Capitol switchboard.
       Just tell them your zip code, and they'll transfer you
       to your representative.
   b. Write to: Office of Senator [Name], United States
       Senate, Washington, DC 20510; or to: Office of
       Representative [Name], United States House of
       Representatives, Washington DC, 20515.
   c. E-mail: For Senators, go to www.senate.gov/
       contacting/index_by_state.cfm; for Representatives,
       go to www.house.gov/writerep/
   d. Send a telegram: call Western Union—1-800-325-
       6000—or visit their Web site: www.westernunion.
       com

2. **Dog Bush Wherever He Goes.** If you hear Junior's coming to town, organize a group of friends to protest the
   event. Remind the media that Bush doesn't govern by the
   will of the people. Be loud. Be *funny*. Signs, street theater,
   mock trials—show him there's no safe haven from the
   Truth.

3. **Force the Democrats to do their job.** Obviously, the eas-
   iest way to counter the coup is to get the "opposition" to
   fight the good fight. But it won't be easy: today's
   Democrats have little time for those who can't make their
   $1,000-a-plate dinners. So here's how to start a little
   Democratic behavior modification program:

* **Take the Pledge.** Go to my Web site (www. michaelmoore.com) and sign the on-line petition that challenges the Democrats in Congress to stand up to Bush/Cheney *and fast*—or we'll work to deny them Congressional leadership next year by running Greens in close races where the Democrat's just a Republican in a bad suit.

* **Take over your local Democratic Party.** In most counties the local Democratic Party is run by just a few people, 'cause most citizens would never think of showing up. Go the next county or town Party meeting, and bring ten friends. In most cases your bunch will constitute a majority. Use the rules and the state party by-laws (which can often be found on the Web) and seize control.

4. **YOU must run for office.** That's right—YOU, the person reading this book. It's the only way things are ever going to change. Unless normal, decent people run for government office, the job is left to rascals. How can we carp about crooked politicians if we won't do the job ourselves? It's time for YOU to throw your hat in the ring—and to do it next year. You can run for school board, city council, county treasurer, drain commissioner, city or county clerk, state representative, state senate, state board of education, secretary of state, governor, member of Congress, U.S. Senator, even dogcatcher—or any number of other offices. The one you should *definitely* run for is precinct delegate. Every precinct in America elects delegates from each party; it may be the lowliest office, but it's also the foundation on which the whole house of cards is built. Selected delegates attend the national party conventions to nomi-

nate the presidential candidates; you should be among
them.

And I'm not just saying this—I'm doing it, this year, and
getting a dozen friends to run in their precincts too. It
requires collecting enough signatures to get your name on
the ballot, and qualifications vary. But so few people vote in
primaries—and so many precincts end up with no candidates—that often getting elected isn't much harder than
just showing up. So head down to your board of elections
or county clerk's office and pick up some petitions before
the deadline passes.

These are only a few of the measures we can take to
stage our countercoup. Whether you do it as a Democrat,
or a Green, or just one pissed-off citizen, the important
thing is to rise up and do it.

TWO

Dear George

Dear Governor Bush:

You and I—we're like family. Our personal connection goes back many years. Neither of us has cared to publicize it, for all the obvious reasons—mostly because no one would believe it. But because of something personal, something the Bush family did, my life was profoundly affected.

Let's come clean and admit it: it was your cousin Kevin who shot *Roger & Me*.

At the time I made the movie, I didn't know that your mother and Kevin's mother were sisters. I just thought Kevin, whom I'd met when he was shooting his own film at a cross burning in Michigan, was one of those bohemian artist types who lived in Greenwich Village. Kevin had made a great film, *Atomic Café*, and on a lark I asked him if he would come to Flint, Michigan, and teach me how to make a movie. To my astonishment he said yes, and so for one week in February of 1987 Kevin Rafferty and Anne Bohlen traipsed around Flint with me, showing me how to work the equipment, giving me invaluable tips on how to make a documentary. Without your cousin's generosity, I don't know if *Roger & Me* would have ever been made.

I remember the day your dad was inaugurated as President. I was editing the film in a ratty old editing room in D.C. and decided to go down to watch him be sworn in on the Capitol steps. How weird it was to see your cousin Kevin, my mentor, sitting next to you up on the dais! I remember also walking down The Mall and seeing the Beach Boys playing "Wouldn't It Be Nice" at a free inaugural concert in honor of your father. Back in the editing room, my friend Ben was on the screen, all choked up about going crazy on the assembly line and singing the same Beach Boys song over scenes of Flint in shreds.

Months later, when the film was released, your dad, the President, ordered a print of *Roger & Me* sent to Camp David one weekend for the family to watch. Oh, to have been a fly on the wall as you all viewed the havoc and despair that had been visited upon my hometown—thanks, in large part, to the actions of Mr. Reagan and your father. Here's something I've always wanted to know: At the end of the film, as the deputy sheriff was tossing the homeless kids' presents and Christmas tree out on the curb because they were $150 behind in their rent, were there any tears in the room? Did anyone feel responsible? Or did you all just think, "Nice camerawork, Kev!"?

Well, that was the late eighties. You'd just given up your hard drinking; after being sober for a few years, you were trying to "find yourself" with Dad's help—an oil venture here, a baseball team there. It's been clear to me for some time that you never had any intention of being President yourself. We all stumble into jobs we don't want at one time or another—who hasn't done that?

For you, though, it must be different. After all, it's not just that you don't want to be there: now that you're there, you're surrounded by the same gang of geezers who used to run the world with Pops. All those men roaming around the White House—Dick, Rummy, Colin—not a single one is a pal of *yours!* It's all the old farts Poppy used to have over to the house for a good cigar and vodka as they dreamed up plans to carpet bomb the civilians of Panama.

But you're one of us—a Boomer, a C student, a partier! What the hell are you doing with that crowd? They're eating you alive and spitting you out like a bad pork rind.

They probably didn't tell you that the tax cut they drew up for you to sign was a swindle to take money from the middle class and give it to the super-rich. I know you don't need the extra money; you're already set for life, thanks to Grandpappy Prescott Bush and his smart trading with the Nazis before and during World War II.*

But all those dudes who gave you a record-breaking $190 million to run your campaign (two-thirds of which came from just over seven hundred individuals!), they want it all back—and more. They're going to hound you like dogs in heat, making sure you do exactly as they say. Your predecessor may have been renting out the Lincoln bedroom to Barbra Streisand, but that ain't nothin': before you know it, your pal, Acting President Cheney, will be turning over the keys of the West Wing to the chairmen of AT&T, Enron, and ExxonMobil.

----

*During the late 1930s and through the 1940s, Prescott Bush, George I's father and W's grandfather, was one of seven directors in the Union Banking Corporation, owned by Nazi industrialists. After filtering their money through a Dutch bank, they hid an estimated $3 million in Bush's bank. As a principal player, it's unlikely that Bush would have been unaware of the Nazi connection. The government eventually seized the assets and the bank dissolved in 1951, after which Prescott Bush—and *his* father, Sam Bush—received $1.5 million.

Your critics berate you for taking naps in the middle of the day and ending your workday around 4:30 P.M. You should just tell them you're starting a new American tradition—lunchtime naps for all, and everybody home by five! Do that, and trust me, you'll be remembered as our greatest President.

How dare they suggest you're not getting anything done in office? Not true! I have never seen a new President busier than you. It's almost as if you think your days as The Man are numbered. With the Senate already gone to the Democrats and the House on its way in 2002—well, hey, look at the bright side, you'll still have two more years before all those sore winners who voted for Gore give you the boot.

Your list of accomplishments—in just your first few months in office—is brutally impressive.

You have:

* Cut $39 million from federal spending on libraries

* Cut $35 million in funding for advanced pediatric training for doctors

* Cut funding for research into renewable energy sources by 50 percent

* Delayed rules that would reduce "acceptable" levels of arsenic in drinking water

* Cut funding for research into cleaner, more efficient cars and trucks by 28 percent

* Revoked rules strengthening the power of the government to deny contracts to companies that violate federal laws, environmental laws, and workplace safety standards

* Allowed Secretary of the Interior Gale Norton to request suggestions for opening up national monuments for foresting, coal mining, and oil and gas drilling

* Broken your campaign promise to invest $100 million per year in rain forest conservation

* Reduced by *86 percent* the Community Access Program, which coordinated care for people without health insurance among public hospitals, clinics, and other health care providers

* Nullified a proposal to increase public access to information about the potential ramifications of chemical plant accidents

* Cut funding for the Girls and Boys Clubs of America programs in public housing by $60 million

* Pulled out of the 1997 Kyoto Protocol agreement on global warming, ultimately signed by 178 other countries

* Rejected an international accord to enforce the 1972 treaty banning germ warfare

* Cut $200 million from workforce training programs for dislocated workers

* Cut $200 million from the Childcare and Development grant, a program that provides child care to low-income families as they are forced from welfare to work

* Eliminated prescription contraceptive coverage to federal employees (though Viagra is still covered)

* Cut $700 million in funds for public housing repairs

* Cut half a *billion* dollars from the Environmental Protection Agency's budget

* Overturned workplace ergonomic rules designed to protect workers' health and safety

* Abandoned your campaign pledge to regulate carbon dioxide emissions, a major contributor to global warming

* Prohibited any federal aid from going to international family planning organizations that provide abortion counseling, referrals, or services with their own funds

* Nominated former mining company executive Dan Lauriski as Assistant Secretary of Labor for Mine Safety and Health

* Appointed Lynn Scarlett, a global warming skeptic and an opponent of stricter standards on air pollution, as Undersecretary of the Interior

* Approved Interior Secretary Gale Norton's controversial plan to auction off areas close to Florida's eastern shore for oil and gas development

* Announced your plans to allow oil drilling in Montana's Lewis and Clark National Forest

* Threatened to shut down the White House AIDS office

* Decided no longer to seek guidance from the American Bar Association on federal judicial appointments

* Denied college financial aid to students convicted of misdemeanor drug charges (though convicted murderers are still eligible for financial aid)

* Allocated only 3 percent of the amount requested by Justice Department lawyers in the government's continued litigation against tobacco companies

* Pushed through your tax cut, 43 percent of which goes to the wealthiest 1 percent of Americans

* Pushed for a bill making it harder for poor and middle-class Americans to file for bankruptcy, even when facing overwhelming medical bills

* Appointed affirmative action opponent Kay Cole James to direct the Office of Personnel Management

* Cut $15.7 million from programs dealing with child abuse and neglect

* Proposed elimination of the "Reading Is Fundamental" program, which gives free books to poor children

* Pushed for development of "mini-nukes," designed to attack deeply buried targets—a violation of the Comprehensive Test Ban Treaty

* Tried to reverse regulation protecting sixty million acres of national forest from logging and road building

* Appointed John Bolton, an opponent of nonproliferation treaties and the United Nations, as Undersecretary of State for Arms Control and International Security

* Made Monsanto executive Linda Fisher deputy administrator of the Environmental Protection Agency

* Nominated Michael McConnell, a leading critic of the separation of church and state, to a federal judgeship

* Nominated civil rights opponent Terrence Boyle to a federal judgeship

* Canceled the 2004 deadline for auto makers to develop prototype high-mileage cars

* Named John Walters, an ardent opponent of prison drug *treatment* programs, as drug czar

* Appointed oil and coal lobbyist J. Steven Giles as Deputy Secretary of the Interior

* Named Bennett Raley, who has called for the repeal of the Endangered Species Act, as Assistant Secretary of the Interior for Water and Science

* Sought the dismissal of a class-action lawsuit filed in the United States against Japan by Asian women forced to work as sex slaves in World War II

* Appointed as solicitor general Ted Olson, your chief lawyer in the Florida voting debacle

* Proposed to ease the permit process for constructing refineries and nuclear and hydroelectric dams, including lowering environmental standards

* Proposed the selling of oil and gas tracts in the Alaska Wildlife Preserve

Whew! I'm tired just typing this list! Where do you get the energy? (It is the naps, isn't it?)

Of course, a lot of the above is supported by many Democrats (and I'll have a few words for them later in the book).

But right now, I'm concerned about you. Think back—what was your first act as "President"? You remember: before you would get in the car to ride down Pennsylvania Avenue in your inaugural parade, you insisted someone get a screwdriver and take the D.C. license plates off the limo because they contained the words "Support D.C. Statehood." Here it is, the biggest day of your life, and you're pissed at the license plates? You have GOT to relax!

I guess, though, I started worrying about you long before that day. A number of disturbing revelations regarding your behavior surfaced during the campaign. Eventually they went away, but I continue to have concerns about your ability to function on the job. Please don't take this as prying or moralizing—we'll leave that to Cheney! It is simply an honest attempt at intervention from a close friend of the family.

Let me be blunt: I'm afraid you may be a threat to our national security.

That may seem a bit strong, but I don't make this statement lightly. It has nothing to do with our minor disagreements regarding executing innocent people on death row, or how much of Alaska to carve up with oil rigs. And I'm not questioning your patriotism—I'm sure you'd love any country that's been this good to you.

Rather, it has to do with a number of behaviors many of us who care for you have witnessed over the years. Some of these habits are a little surprising; some you can't control; and others are, unfortunately, all too common among us Americans.

Because you have your finger on The Button (you know, the one that could blow up the world), and because decisions you make have vast and far-reaching consequences for the stability of said world, I would like to ask you three pointed questions—and I would like you to give me, and the American people, three honest answers:

1. George, are you able to read and write on an adult level?

It appears to me and many others that, sadly, you may be a functional illiterate. This is nothing to be ashamed of. You have lots of company (just count the typoes in this book. In fact, isn't *that* a typo?). Millions of Americans cannot read and write above a fourth-grade level. No wonder you said "leave no child behind"—you knew what it felt like.

But let me ask this: if you have trouble comprehending the complex position papers you are handed as the Leader of the Mostly-Free World, how can we entrust something like our nuclear secrets to you?

All the signs of this illiteracy are there—and apparently no one has challenged you about them. The first clue was what you named as your favorite childhood book. *"The Very Hungry Caterpillar,"* you said.

Unfortunately, that book wasn't even published until a year after you graduated from college.

Then there's the question of your college transcripts, if those really are your transcripts. How *did* you get into Yale when other applicants in 1964 had higher SATs and much better grades?

During the campaign, when asked to name the books you were currently reading, you answered gamely—but when quizzed about the books' contents, you didn't know what to say. No wonder your aides stopped letting you hold press conferences with two months left in the campaign. Your handlers were scared to death of what you might get asked—and how you might answer.

One thing is clear to everyone—you can't speak the English language in sentences we can comprehend. At first, the way you mangled words and sentences seemed cute, almost charming. But after a while it became worrisome. Then in an interview you broke America's decades-long policy toward Taiwan, saying we were willing to do "whatever it took" to defend Taiwan, even suggesting we might deploy troops there. Jeez, George, the whole world flipped out; before you knew it, everyone was at Defcon 3.

If you're going to be Commander-in-Chief, you *have* to be able to communicate your orders. What if these little slipups keep happening? Do you know how easy it would be to turn a little faux pas into a national-security nightmare? No wonder you want to increase the Pentagon budget. We'll need all the firepower we can get after you accidentally order the Russians "wiped out," when what you meant to say was, "I need to wipe the Russian dressing off my tie."

Your aides have said that you don't (can't?) read the briefing papers they give you, and that you ask them to read them for you or to you. Your mother was passionately committed to reading programs as First Lady. Should we assume she knew firsthand the difficulty of raising a child who couldn't read?

Please don't take any of this personally. Perhaps it's a learning disability. Some sixty million Americans have learning disabilities. There's no shame in this. And yes, I believe a dyslexic can be President of the United States. Albert Einstein was dyslexic; so is Jay Leno. (Hey, I finally found a way to work Leno and Einstein into the same sentence! See, language can be fun.)

But if you refuse to seek help with this problem, I'm afraid you may be too great a risk for the country. You need help. You need Hooked on Phonics, not just another Oval Office briefing.

Tell us the truth, and I'll come read to you every night at bedtime.

2. **Are you an alcoholic, and if so, how is this affecting your performance as Commander-in-Chief?**

Again, there is no finger being pointed here, no shame or disrespect intended. Alcoholism is a huge problem; it affects millions of American citizens, people we all know and love. Many are able to recover and live normal lives. Alcoholics can be, and have been, President of the United States. I greatly admire anyone who can deal with this addiction. You have told us that you cannot handle drinking, and that you haven't touched a drop of alcohol since you were forty. Congratulations.

You have also told us that you used to "drink too much" and that you eventually "realized that alcohol was beginning to crowd out my energies and could crowd, eventually, my affections for other people." That is the definition of an alcoholic. This does not disqualify you from being President, but it does require that you answer some questions, especially after you spent years covering up the fact that in 1976 you were arrested for drunk driving.

Why won't you use the word *alcoholic*? That is, after all, the First Step to recovery. What support system have you set up to make sure you don't fall off the wagon? Being President is perhaps the most stressful job in the world. What have you done to ensure you can handle the pressure and the anxiety associated with being the most powerful man on earth?

How do we know you won't turn to the bottle when faced with a serious crisis? You've never had a job like this. For twenty years, from what I can tell, you had no job at all. When you stopped "drifting," your dad set you up in the oil business with some ventures that failed, and then he helped you get a major league baseball team, which required you to sit in a box seat and watch a lot of long, slow baseball games.

As governor of Texas, you couldn't have had much stress; there just isn't enough to do. Being governor of Texas is a relatively ceremonial job. How will you deal with some unexpected new threat to world security? Do you have a sponsor you can call? Is there a meeting you can attend? You don't have to tell me the answers to these questions; you just have to promise me you've thought them out for yourself.

I know this is very personal, but the public has a right to know. For those who say, "Well, c'mon, it's his personal life—that was twenty-four years ago," I have this to say: I was hit by a drunk driver twenty-eight years ago, and to this day I cannot completely extend my right arm. I'm sorry, George, but when you go out on a public highway drunk, it's no longer just your PERSONAL life we're talking about. It's *my* life, and the lives of my family.

Your campaign people—the enablers—tried to cover for you, lying to the press about the nature of your arrest for driving under the influence. They said the cop pulled you over because you were "driving too slowly." But the arresting officer said it was because you had swerved off on the shoulder of the road.

You yourself joined in the denial when asked about the evening you spent in jail.

"I didn't spend time in jail," you insisted. The officer told the local reporter that in fact you were handcuffed, taken to the station, and held in custody for at least an hour and a half. Could it be that you truly don't remember?

This is not just some simple traffic ticket. I can't believe your enablers actually implied your drunk driving conviction wasn't as offensive as Clinton's transgressions. Lying about consensual sex you had with another adult while you are married is wrong, but it is NOT the same as getting behind the wheel of a car when you are drunk and endangering the lives of others (including, George, *the life of your own sister*, who was with you in the car that night).

It is also NOT the same, despite what your defenders said before the election, as Al Gore volunteering that he smoked pot in his youth. Unless he was driving while stoned, his actions endangered no life but his own—and *he* wasn't trying to cover it up.

You've tried to dismiss the incident by saying "it was back in my youth." But you were NOT a "youth"; you were in your *thirties*.

The night your conviction was finally revealed to the nation, just days before the election, it was painful to watch you swagger as you tried to chalk up your "irresponsible" action as the mere "youthful indiscretion" of having a few beers with the boys (smirk, smirk). I really felt for the families of the *half a million* people who have been killed by drunks like yourself in the twenty-four years since your "little adventure." Thank God you kept drinking for *only another several years* after you "learned your lesson." I think, too, of what you must have put your wife, Laura, through. She knew all too well how dangerous it is when any of us get behind the wheel. At seventeen she killed a high school friend of hers when she ran through a stop sign and collided with his car. I'm hopeful that you can look to her for guidance if ever you feel the pressures of the job getting to you. (Whatever you do, don't turn to Dick Cheney for help: he's had two drunk driving arrests on *his* record for more than twenty-five years!)

Finally, I have to tell you how distressed I was when, back in that crazy week before the election, you hid behind your daughters as your excuse for covering up this conviction. You said you were worried that your history of drunkenness would set a bad example for them. A lot of good that secrecy has done, as proven by the twins' various arrests this year for alcohol possession. In some ways, I admire their rebellion. They asked you, they begged you, they told you: "Please, Dad, *don't* run for President and ruin our lives!" You did. It did. Now, like all good teenagers, it's payback time.

Perhaps the news anchor on *Saturday Night Live* put it best: "George Bush said he didn't reveal the drunk driving charge because of what his daughters might think of him. He had preferred that they think of him as a man with numerous failed business ventures who now executes people."

Here's what I suggest: Get help. Join AA. Take your daughters to Al-Anon. You will all be welcomed with open arms.

3. Are you a felon?

When you were asked in 1999 about your alleged cocaine use, you replied that you had committed "no felonies in the last twenty-five years." With all we've learned about tricky answers in the last eight years, that kind of response could only lead a reasonable observer to believe that the years before that were a different story.

What felonies did you commit before 1974, George?

Believe me, I'm not asking this in order to seek punishment for anything you did. I am concerned that if there is some deep,

dark secret you are hiding, you may in effect be providing
ammunition for anyone who uncovers that secret—be it a foreign power (your current favorite, the Chinese) or domestic
(like—oh, pick one—say, R.J. Reynolds). If they discover your
history of a felony or felonies, they'll have something to hold
over you, putting them in a position to blackmail you. That
makes you, George, a national security threat.

Trust me, *someone* will find out what you are hiding—and
when they do, we'll all be at risk. You have a duty to disclose the
nature of whatever felony you imply that you may have committed. Only by revealing it can you neutralize its potential use as a
weapon against you—or us.

Also, you recently made it a requirement for any young person seeking financial aid for college to answer a question on
the application form that reads: "Have you ever been convicted
for any drug offense?" If they have, they are denied student
aid—which means that many of them will not be going to college. (Or, to put it another way, according to your new orders
Sirhan Sirhan can still receive student aid, but a kid with a joint
can't.)

Doesn't this move on your part strike you as a little hypocrit-
ical? You would deny a college education to thousands of kids
who only did *exactly* what you have implied you did as a young
person? Man, that takes some chutzpah! As you'll be receiving
$400,000 a year from us until 2004—from the same federal kitty
that pays out the college aid—it seems only fair to make you
answer the same question: "Have you ever been convicted of
selling or possessing drugs (not including alcohol or tobacco)?"

We do know, George, that you have been arrested *three* times.
Other than some peace-activist friends of mine, I don't personally
know anyone who has been arrested *three* times in their life.

In addition to the drunk driving, you were arrested with some
fraternity brothers for stealing a Christmas wreath as a prank.
What was *that* all about?

Your third arrest was for disorderly conduct at a football game. Now this I *really* don't get. *Everyone* conducts themselves in a disorderly manner at a football game! I've been to many football games and have had many a beer spilled on my head, but to this day I've never seen anyone arrested. You've gotta work pretty hard to get noticed in a crowd of drunken football fans.

George, I have a theory about why and how all this has happened to you.

Instead of having to earn it, you have been handed the presidency, the same way you've come by everything else in your life. Money and name alone have opened every door for you. Without effort or hard work or intelligence or ingenuity, you have been bequeathed a life of privilege.

You learned at an early age that, in America, all someone like you has to do is show up. You found yourself admitted to an exclusive New England boarding school simply because your name was Bush. You did not have to EARN your place there. It was bought for you.

When they let you into Yale, you learned you could bypass more deserving students who had worked hard for twelve years to qualify for admission to college. You got in because your name was Bush.

You got into Harvard Business School the same way. After screwing off during your four years at Yale, you took the seat that rightfully belonged to someone else.

You then pretended to serve a full stint in the Texas Air National Guard. But one day, according to the *Boston Globe*, you just skipped out and failed to report back to your unit—*for a year and a half*! You didn't have to fulfill your military obligation, because your name was Bush.

Following a number of "lost years" that don't appear in your official biography, you were given job after job by your daddy and other family members. No matter how many of your business ventures failed, there was always another one waiting to be handed to you.

Finally, you got to be a partner in a major league baseball team—another gift—even though you put up only one one-hundredth of the money for the team. And then you conned the taxpayers of Arlington, Texas, into giving you another perk—a brand-new multimillion-dollar stadium that *you* didn't have to pay for.

So it's no wonder you think you deserved to be named President. You didn't earn it or win it—therefore it must be yours!

And you see nothing wrong with this. Why should you? It is the only life you have ever known.

On election night, as the vote swayed back and forth across the nation, you told the press that your brother had assured you Florida was yours. If a Bush said it was so, it was so.

But it ain't so. And when it dawned on you that the presidency had to be earned and won by a vote of the people—yes, the people!—you went berserk. You sent in hatchet man James Baker ("Fuck the Jews, they don't vote for us anyway" was his advice to Poppy in '92) to tell lies to the American people and stoke the nation's fears. When that didn't seem to work, you went to federal court and sued to stop the votes from being counted—because you knew how the vote would turn out. If you were truly sure you had the vote of the people, you wouldn't have minded all those votes being counted.

What startles me is how you turned to the big bad federal government for help. Your mantra during every campaign stop was the following: "My opponent trusts the federal government. *I trust you, the people!*"

Well, we soon learned the truth. You didn't trust the people at all. You went straight to the *federal* court to get your handout (trust the voting machines, not the people!). At first the judges in Florida didn't buy it—and for perhaps the first time in your life, someone told you no.

But as we've already seen, Daddy's friends on the U.S. Supreme Court were there to take care of everything.

In short, you've been a drunk, a thief, a possible felon, an unconvicted deserter, and a crybaby. You may call that statement cruel. I call it "tough love."

For the sake of all that is decent and sacred, good God, man, take leave immediately and bring some honor to your all-important family name! Make those of us who know there's a thread of decency in your family proud once again to claim that a Bush in the hand is better than a handout to a Bush.

Yours,

Michael Moore

THREE

Dow Wow Wow

AS I'M SITTING in a Michigan airport waiting for my American Airlines flight to Chicago, a man in a uniform sits down beside me and strikes up a conversation.

I learn that he is actually a pilot, for American Airlines—or more precisely American Eagle, the commuter airline of American Airlines, which like all commuters these days is now adding jets to its fleets for flights of under two hours. This saves the parent company lots of money, I guess.

The pilot who has approached me is not scheduled to fly the plane I'm on. He's hoping to grab an empty seat for the flight across Lake Michigan.

"Do you have to pay to fly if it's a personal trip?" I asked.

"No," he replied. "It's about the only fringe benefit we have."

He then revealed that the starting pay for a pilot at American Eagle was $16,800 a year.

"What?" I asked, sure that I had misheard the figure. "Sixteen grand *per year*?"

"That's right," the captain responded. "And that's high. At Delta's commuter airline, starting pay is $15,000 for a pilot; at Continental Express, it's around $13,000."

"*Thirteen thousand*? For the captain of a commercial airliner? Are you messing with me?"

"No, I'm not messin' with anyone. It gets worse. That first year as a pilot, you have to pay for your own flight training and your own uniforms. After that's all deducted, you end up with about $9,000."

He paused so that could sink in. Then he added: "*Gross.*"

"I can't believe what I'm hearing." My voice was now getting to a level where others around us began listening in.

"Believe it," he assured me. "One of our pilots last month went down to the welfare office and applied for food stamps. No kidding. With four kids, at his level of pay as a pilot, he was legally eligible for assistance. The front office at American found out about this and sent out a memo that said no pilot was to apply for food stamps or welfare—even if they were eligible for it! Anyone who did apply would be let go.

"So now my buddy just goes down to the food bank on his way home. They don't ask for anything from you that would get back to American Airlines."

I thought I'd heard everything by now. But this story was beyond frightening. I did *not* want to get on that plane. You see, there's something about us humans and our basic animal instincts for survival—and one of those instincts, probably traceable back to the caveman days, is: *Never, ever let someone fly you up in the air who's making less than the kid at Taco Bell.*

I got on the plane, but only after I convinced myself the guy must have been feeding me a line. How else could I justify risking my life like that? The following week, though, I made some calls and did some research. Much to my horror, that pilot's figures were right. While captains who had been with these commuter airlines for a number of years were pulling in the big money ($40,000/year!), first-year rookies in many cases were living below the poverty level.

I don't know about you, but I want the people taking me with them to defy nature's most powerful force—gravity—to be happy, content, confident, and well paid. Even on the big jets for the major airlines, the flight attendants—another group of employees whose training may one day be critical to saving your life—start out at somewhere between $15,000 and $17,000 a year. When I'm at 30,000 feet I do *not* want the minds of the pilots or the attendants to be occupied with how they're going to get the heat and lights turned back on once they get home tonight, or which Bob's Big Boy they're going to have to stick up in order to make the monthly rent. And what's the lesson for the flying public? Be nice to people on welfare—they may be flying you to Buffalo.

For the first half of 2001, the pilots for Delta Connection were on strike. The greedy bastards at the union were demanding $20,000 for their pilots' starting pay. But Delta refused, and the work stoppage went on for months. You'd think that considering the booming economy—especially for the well-to-do who fly often—there would be little problem giving the pilots a wage that allows them to subsist on something besides dog food. (When boarding a plane, I used to do a "sniff check" to see if the pilots had been drinking; now I'll be looking for stray Kibbles or Bits as I pass by the cockpit.) After begging for scraps from the table, the Delta Connection pilots finally got their $20,000 a year.

These pilots—and the rest of the public—are being told that the economy isn't doing so well, that there's been a huge downturn, that profits are off, that the stock market has taken a beating, and that no matter how far Mr. Greenspan lowers the interest rates, nothing seems to be helping.

They certainly have numbers to back up their claim. An average of 403,000 Americans are filing new unemployment claims every week. Hundreds of companies are announcing massive lay-offs. Thousands of start-ups in the new high-tech-dot-com fields have gone belly-up. Car sales are down. Retailers had a horrible Christmas. From Silicon Alley to Silicon Valley, the belts are being tightened.

And we've fallen for it.

There *is* no recession, my friends. No downturn. No hard times. The rich are wallowing in the loot they've accumulated in the past two decades, and now they want to make sure you don't come a-lookin' for your piece of the pie.

The wealthy are doing everything they can to convince you that you'd better not be asking for your share, because—well, suddenly, *there's not enough to go around*! Night after night, the media they own tell you one sad story after another, about the latest Internet company that went down, or mutual fund that lost everything, or NASDAQ investor who went belly-up. Today the Dow Jones Industrial Average lost over 300 points. Lucent Technologies announced another fifteen thousand layoffs. The merger between United and U.S. Airways is off, General Motors is killing off Oldsmobile, and there are now reports that even your personal 401K is not safe. Pretty scary stuff, eh?

Oh, it's all true. They wouldn't lie to you. At least not about these puny details they use to manipulate your fears.

But what about the bigger lie? The one about how horrible the larger world economy is today? I mean, on one level, it appears to be true. If you're middle class or lower, you have every right to be fearful. Why? Because those on top are even more afraid. They're scared silly that you're going to want to participate in the party they've been having. They're afraid you're going to say, "OK, you got your yachts and your homes in the south of France—now what about me? How 'bout a little something for me so I can get a new garage door?" The only thing bigger than this fear of theirs is their astonishment that none of you have demanded a raise, or a vacation, or a co-paid visit to the dentist, or any share in the excessive wealth that's been generated in the past ten years. Can it really be that you're content to spend four nights a week wondering who wants to be a millionaire, but never actually answer "*ME!*"? The corporate poobahs have been waiting for you to drop the other shoe.

Yes, those in charge know it's inevitable: one day you're going to want your share. And because *that* must never happen, the long knives are drawn—and they've decided to perform a preemptive strike in the hope that you'll never even *think* of eyeing their piles of cash.

So that's why they're laying you off, or pleading poverty. That's why they've removed the free coffee pot—not because they can't afford the coffee but because they need to fuck with your mind. They need you in a constant state of stress, suspicion, and fear. *YOU COULD BE NEXT!* Forget about the Maxwell House—save yourselves! The bosses must be sitting back having one of the biggest laughs of their lives.

Now how do I know all this, you ask? Well, you see, I walk among them. I live on the island of Manhattan, a three-mile-wide strip of land that is luxury home and corporate suite to America's elite. Much of the suffering you experience as an American emanates from this piece of platinum real estate nestled between two polluted rivers. Those who run your lives live in my neighborhood. I walk the streets with them each day. I see their children being raised by Haitian immigrants, and I watch them pass by the Invisible Men who clean the grouting on the marble floors without saying a word, always in a hurry to get to wherever they're going—most likely to reduce your insurance benefits or put your workplace on the chopping block. They are fit, coifed, and hungry to make a killing—and the next body they drop could be yours!

I listen to them talk about how well they've done—the new home in the Berkshires, the trip they just took to Easter Island. They couldn't be happier.

When I first moved into my building, it was occupied by artists and playwrights and half the cast of *Saturday Night Live*. There were hockey guys from the Rangers, a retired NFL player, a cameraman, a few college professors, and some senior citizens. Now it's pretty much just us, one of the Rangers, and my crazy friend Barry, the cinematographer; everyone else, it seems, is either rich enough to do without a job, or busy reaping huge profits from the various properties they own in poor neighborhoods, or living off some trust fund, or working on Wall Street, or from another country (here in New York overseeing the family's foreign investments). The Fortune 500 corporations are their bread and butter. And I'm here to tell you, they're loaded, and they're not cutting back one bit for themselves.

If you don't want to take my word alone, then let me offer you some neutral, objective statistics about just how well those at the top are doing:

* From 1979 until now, the richest 1 percent in the country have seen their wages increase by 157 percent; those of you in the bottom 20 percent are actually making $100 *less* a year (adjusted for inflation) than you were at the dawn of the Reagan era.

* The world's richest two hundred companies have seen their profits grow by 362.4 percent since 1983; their combined sales are now higher than the combined gross domestic product of all but ten nations on earth.

* Since the recent mergers of the top four U.S. oil companies, their profits have soared by 146 percent— during what we were told was an "energy crisis."

* In the most recent year for which there are figures, forty-four of the top eighty-two companies in the United States did not pay the standard rate of 35 percent in taxes

that corporations are expected to pay. In fact, 17 percent of them paid NO taxes at all—and seven of those, including General Motors, played the tax code like a harp, juggling business expenses and tax credits until the government actually owed *them* millions of dollars!

∗ Another 1,279 corporations with assets of $250 million or more also paid NO taxes and reported "no income" for 1995 (the most recent year for which statistics were available).

We are getting bilked in so many ways that listing them all might get me charged with inciting a riot. But who cares? Mercedes Benz, which has continually refused to meet American mileage and pollution standards, was being fined for its lawbreaking when it came up with an ingenious plan. For the years 1988 and 1989, the company deducted from their taxes the $65 million it had paid in fines as "ordinary expenses incurred . . . in carrying on its trade or business." That means that you and I paid $65 million so that a bunch of rich people could drive around in big, fancy cars and ruin our lungs. Fortunately, the IRS was on to this scam and denied their claim.

Halliburton, the oil company, set up a subsidiary in the Cayman Islands in the early nineties. Problem is, there *is* no oil in the Cayman Islands. Nor are there any oil refineries or distribution centers. So what was that Halliburton subsidiary doing there? Evidently the government was suspicious. From 1996 until 1998, fourteen separate tax actions were filed against Halliburton entities. In one case, the government contended that Halliburton used these subs to avoid $38 million in taxes. Most of these cases have been resolved.

They aren't the only ones interested in defrauding the federal government. A half-dozen major U.S. insurance companies now call Bermuda their "headquarters," including insurance giants Chubb, Hartford, Kemper, Liberty Mutual, and others. Accenture, which used to be known as Andersen Consulting, recently "moved" its company to Bermuda in order to avoid paying taxes. It's really just a paper move—they still have all their offices around the country, and everyone shows up to work every day doing what they always did for Andersen. It's just their "headquarters" that have moved. Wouldn't you love to wake up tomorrow and declare that you've "moved" yourself to Fiji, even though you still have to look at Topeka outside your window?

Forbes magazine estimates that corporate tax shelters cost us average Americans over $10 billion dollars a year (and we have to make up the difference, by paying more taxes or by losing services). Next time you can't afford to fix the furnace or replace the computer, you can thank all those fat cats who've got you repeating the line "the economy isn't doing too well right now."

Instead of collecting this money that's being stolen from us, how is the IRS spending its time these days? They've decided to go after *you*. That's right. They've thrown up the white flag; they're surrendering their efforts to get the rich to pay their taxes. Their new policy is to focus on squeezing those who make the least. According to the General Accounting Office, those who earn less than $25,000 a year have seen their IRS audits double—while those earning over $100,000 have seen their audits drop by over 25 percent.

What does this mean on the balance sheet? It's resulted in a drop of 26 percent in the amount of taxes corporations pay, while you, the average American, have seen your taxes go up by at least 13 percent. In the 1950s, taxes from corporations made up 27 percent of the revenues for the federal government; today that number has dropped to less than 10 percent. Who has made up the difference? You and your second job.

Part of the reason you're hearing so much about how bad the economy is these days is that many of those who are getting their pink slips are the friends and family of those reporting the bad news. Unlike the massive layoffs of the eighties, which were all but ignored by those who went to good colleges and made good money, the layoff massacres today are mostly white-collar and professional. Lay off a few hundred thousand of these people, and you're gonna hear about it. Why? Well, because it's . . . it's . . . it's SO UNFAIR! I mean, these high-tech guys paid their dues! They played by the rules, gave their heart and soul and first marriage to the company. They were there for every company retreat, never missed a late-night "think session," attended every charity event the chairman and his friends threw. And then one day . . . "Bob, this is an employment counselor we've hired to help you with your transition, which we'd like to make as easy for you as possible. Please hand me your keys, and this gentleman with the badge and gun will escort you to your cubicle so you can collect your personal belongings and leave the building in the next twelve minutes."

There is no downturn. Are businesses earning less than last year? Absolutely. How could they not? The nineties saw these corporations post surreal, over-the-top profits, a once-in-a-lifetime bonanza that had nothing to do with reality. Compare any year's figures to those, and you're comparing apples and windfalls. There was a headline the other day that said GM's profits were down 73 percent from last year. That sounds bad—but last year was nothing short of a profit orgy. Even with that 73 percent drop, GM will still pocket over $800 million profit in the first half of 2001.

Are dot-coms folding left and right? Of course they are! Big deal. That's what happens with any new, revolutionary invention—a ton of entrepreneurs hop on board to find their fortune, and in the end only the mediocre but ruthless few are still standing. It's called C-A-P-I-T-A-L-I-S-M. In 1919, twenty years after the invention of the automobile, there were 108 automobile manufacturers in the United States. Ten years later the number had whittled down to the Big 44 U.S. auto companies. By the end of the fifties it had dropped to 8, and today we have a grand total of 2½ U.S. car manufacturers. That's the way it works in our system. You don't like it, you can move to . . . to . . . um . . . damn, where *do* you move to these days?

Oh, of course—Bermuda!

FOUR

Kill Whitey

I DON'T KNOW what it is, but every time I see a white guy walking toward me, I tense up. My heart starts racing, and I immediately begin to look for an escape route and a means to defend myself. I kick myself for even being in this part of town after dark. Didn't I notice the suspicious gangs of white people lurking on every street corner, drinking Starbucks and wearing their gang colors of Gap Turquoise or J. Crew Mauve? What an idiot! Now the white person is coming closer, closer—and then—*whew*! He walks by without harming me, and I breathe a sigh of relief.

White people scare the crap out of me. This may be hard for you to understand—considering that I *am* white—but then again, my color gives me a certain insight. For instance, I find *myself* pretty scary a lot of the time, so I know what I'm talking about. You can take my word for it: if you find yourself suddenly surrounded by white people, you better watch out. *Anything* can happen.

As white people, we've been lulled into thinking it's safe to be around other white people. We've been taught since birth that it's the people of that *other color* we need to fear. *They're* the ones who'll slit your throat!

Yet as I look back on my life, a strange but unmistakable pattern seems to emerge. *Every* person who has ever harmed me in my lifetime—the boss who fired me, the teacher who flunked me, the principal who punished me, the kid who hit me in the eye with a rock, the other kid who shot me with his BB gun, the executive who didn't renew *TV Nation*, the guy who was stalking me for three years, the accountant who double-paid my taxes, the drunk who smashed into me, the burglar who stole my stereo, the contractor who overcharged me, the girlfriend who left me, the next girlfriend who left even sooner, the pilot of the plane I was on who hit a truck on the runway (he probably hadn't eaten in days), the other pilot who decided to fly through a tornado, the person in the office who stole checks from my checkbook and wrote them out to himself for a total of $16,000—every one of these individuals has been a white person! Coincidence? I think not!

I have never been attacked by a black person, never been evicted by a black person, never had my security deposit ripped off by a black landlord, never *had* a black landlord, never had a meeting at a Hollywood studio with a black executive in charge, never seen a black agent at the film/TV agency that used to represent me, never had a black person deny my child the college of her choice, never been puked on by a black teenager at a Mötley Crüe concert, never been pulled over by a black cop, never been sold a lemon by a black car salesman, never *seen* a black car salesman, never had a black person deny me a bank loan, never had a black person try to bury my movie, and I've never heard a black person say, "We're going to eliminate ten thousand jobs here—have a nice day!"

I don't think I'm the only white guy who can make these claims. Every mean word, every cruel act, every bit of pain and suffering in my life has had a Caucasian face attached to it.

So, um, why is it *exactly* that I should be afraid of black people?

I look around at the world I live in—and, folks, I hate to tell tales out of school, but it's not the African-Americans who have made this planet such a pitiful, scary place to inhabit. Recently a headline on the front page of the Science section of the *New York Times* asked the question "Who Built the H-Bomb?" The article went on to discuss a dispute that has arisen between the men who claim credit for making the first bomb. Frankly, I could have cared less—because I already know the only pertinent answer: "IT WAS A WHITE GUY!" No black guy ever built or used a bomb designed to wipe out hordes of innocent people, whether in Oklahoma City, Columbine, or Hiroshima.

No, my friends, it's *always* the white guy. Let's go to the tote board:

* Who gave us the black plague? A white guy.

* Who invented PBC, PVC, PBB, and a host of chemicals that are killing us? White guys.

* Who has started every war America has been in? White men.

* Who is responsible for the programming on FOX? White men.

* Who invented the punch card ballot? A white man.

* Whose idea was it to pollute the world with the internal combustion engine? Whitey, that's who.

* The Holocaust? That guy *really* gave white people a bad name (that's why we prefer to call him a Nazi and his little helpers Germans).

* The genocide of Native Americans? White man.

* Slavery? Whitey!

* So far in 2001, American companies have laid off over 700,000 people. Who ordered the layoffs? White CEOs.

* Who keeps bumping me off the Internet? Some friggin' white guy, and if I find him, he's a dead white guy.

You name the problem, the disease, the human suffering, or the abject misery visited upon millions, and I'll bet you ten bucks I can put a white face on it faster than you can name the members of 'N Sync.

And yet when I turn on the news each night, what do I see again and again? *Black* men alleged to be killing, raping, mugging, stabbing, gangbanging, looting, rioting, selling drugs, pimping, ho-ing, having too many babies, dropping babies from tenement windows, father-less, motherless, Godless, penniless. "The suspect is described as a black male ... the suspect is described as a black male ... THE SUSPECT IS DESCRIBED AS A BLACK MALE. ..." No mat-ter what city I'm in, the news is always the same, the suspect always the same unidentified black male. I'm in Atlanta tonight, and I swear the police sketch of the black male suspect on TV looks just like the black male suspect I saw on the news *last* night in Denver and the night before in L.A. In every sketch he's frowning, he's menacing—and he's wearing the same knit cap! Is it possible that it's the same black guy committing every crime in America?

I believe we've become so used to this image of the black man as predator that we are forever ruined by this brainwashing. In my first film, *Roger & Me*, a white woman on Social Security clubs a bunny rabbit to death so that she can sell him as "meat" instead of as a pet. I wish I had a nickel for every time in the last ten years someone has come up to me and told me how "horrified" and "shocked" they were when they saw that "poor little cute bunny" bonked on the head. The scene, they say, made them physically sick. Some had to turn away or leave the theater. Many wondered why I would include such a scene. The Motion Picture Association of America (MPAA) gave *Roger & Me* an R rating in response to that rabbit killing (which compelled *60 Minutes* to do a story on the stupidity of the rating system). Teachers write me and say they have to edit that part out of the film so they won't get in trouble for showing my movie to their students.

But less than two minutes after the bunny lady does her deed, I included footage of a scene in which the police in Flint opened fire and shot a black man who was wearing a Superman cape and holding a plastic toy gun. Not once—not *ever*—has anyone said to me, "I can't believe you showed a black man being shot in your movie! How horrible! How disgusting! I couldn't sleep for weeks." After all, he was just a black man, not a cute, cuddly bunny. There is no outrage at showing a black man being shot on camera (least of all from the MPAA ratings board, who saw absolutely nothing wrong with that scene).

Why? Because a black man being shot is no longer shocking. Just the opposite—it's *normal*, natural. We've become so accustomed to seeing black men killed—in the movies and on the evening news—that we now accept it as standard operating procedure. *No big deal, just another dead black guy!* That's what blacks do—kill and die. Ho-hum. Pass the butter.

It's odd that, despite the fact that most crimes are committed by whites, black faces are usually attached to what we think of as "crime." Ask any white person who they fear might break into their home or harm them on the street, and if they're honest, they'll admit that the person they have in mind doesn't look much like them. The imaginary criminal in their heads looks like Mookie or Hakim or Kareem, not little freckle-faced Jimmy.

How does the brain process a fear like this, when everything it sees says the opposite? Are white people's brains hardwired to see one thing but believe the opposite because of race? If that's the case, then do all white people suffer from some shared low-grade mental illness? If every time the sun was out it was nice and bright and clear, but your brain told you to stay inside because it definitely looked like a storm was brewing, well, we might encourage you to seek some professional help. Are white people who see black boogeymen around every corner any different?

Obviously, no matter how many times their fellow whites make it clear that the white man is the one to fear, it simply fails to register. Every time you turn on the TV to news of another school shooting, it's always a white kid who's conducting the massacre. Every time they catch a serial killer, it's a crazy white guy. Every time a terrorist blows up a federal building, or a madman gets four hundred people to drink Kool-Aid, or a Beach Boys songwriter casts a spell causing half a dozen nymphets to murder "all the piggies" in the Hollywood Hills, you know it's a member of the white race up to his old tricks.

So why don't we run like hell when we see whitey coming toward us? Why don't we ever greet the Caucasian job applicant with, "Gee, uh, I'm sorry, there aren't any positions available right now"? Why aren't we worried sick about our daughters marrying white guys?

And why isn't Congress trying to ban the scary and offensive lyrics of Johnny Cash ("I shot a man in Reno / just to watch him die"), the Dixie Chicks ("Earl had to die"), or Bruce Springsteen (". . . I killed everything in my path / I can't say that I'm sorry for the things that we done"). Why all the focus on rap lyrics? Why doesn't the media print rap lyrics like these and tell the truth?

I sold bottles of sorrow, then chose poems and novels.
—WU-TANG CLAN

People use yo' brain to gain. —ICE CUBE

A poor single mother on welfare . . . tell me how ya did it.
—TUPAC SHAKUR

I'm trying to change my life, see I don't wanna die a sinner.
—MASTER P

African-Americans have been on the lowest rung of the economic ladder since the day they were beaten and dragged here in chains—and they have *never made it* off that rung, not for a single damn day. Every other immigrant group who has landed here has been able to advance from the bottom to the middle and upper levels of our society. Even Native Americans, who are among the poorest of the poor, have fewer children living in poverty than African-Americans.

You probably thought things had gotten better for blacks in this country. I mean, after all, considering all the advances we've made eliminating racism in our society, one would think our black citizens might have seen their standard of living rise. A survey published in the *Washington Post* in July 2001 showed that 40 to 60 percent of white people thought the average black person had it as good or better than the average white person.

Think again. According to a study conducted by the economists Richard Vedder, Lowell Gallaway, and David C. Clingaman, the average income for a black American is 61 percent less per year than the average white income. *That is the same percentage difference as it was in 1880!* Not a damn thing has changed in more than 120 years.

Want more proof? Consider the following:

* About 20 percent of young black men between the ages of sixteen and twenty-four are neither in school nor working—compared with only 9 percent of young white men. Despite the "economic boom" of the nineties, this percentage has not fallen substantially over the last ten years.

* In 1993, white households had invested nearly three times as much in stocks and mutual funds and/or IRA and Keogh accounts as black households. Since then, the stock market has more than doubled its value.

* Black heart attack patients are far less likely than whites to undergo cardiac catheterization, a common and potentially lifesaving procedure, regardless of the race of their doctors. Black and white doctors together referred white patients for catheterization about 40 percent more often than black patients.

* Whites are five times more likely than blacks to receive emergency clot-busting treatment for stroke.

* Black women are four times more likely than white women to die while giving birth.

* Black levels of unemployment have been roughly twice those of whites since 1954.

Does this make anyone angry besides me and the Reverend Farrakhan? To what do African-Americans owe this treatment, considering that they are responsible for so little of the suffering our society faces? Why are they the ones who are being punished? Damned if I know.

So how have we white people been able to get away with this without all ending up like Reginald Denny?*

Caucasian ingenuity! You see, we used to be real dumb. Like idiots, we wore our racism on our sleeve. We did really obvious things, like putting up signs on rest room doors that said WHITES ONLY. Over a drinking fountain we'd hang a sign that said COLOREDS. We made black people sit at the back of the bus. We prevented them from attending our schools or living in our neighborhoods. They got the crappiest jobs (those advertised for NEGROES ONLY), and we made it clear that if you weren't white you were going to be paid a lower wage.

---

*The white truck driver who was dragged from his rig and beaten nearly to death by blacks during the L.A. riots in 1992.

Well, this overt, over-the-top segregation got us into a heap of trouble. A bunch of uppity lawyers went to court—citing, of all things, our very own Constitution! They pointed out that the Fourteenth Amendment doesn't allow for *anyone* to be treated differently because of their race.

Eventually, after a long procession of court losses, demonstrations, and riots, we got the message: if we didn't wise up, we were going to have to start sharing some of the pie. We learned an important lesson: if you're going to be a successful racist, better find a way to do it with a smile on your face!

So white people got smart and took down the signs, stopped lynching black men who might have stopped on the street to talk with our women, passed a bunch of civil-rights laws, and ceased saying words like *nigger* in public. We even got magnanimous enough to say, *Sure, you can even live here in our neighborhood; your kids can go to our kids' school. Why the hell not? We were just leaving anyway*. We smiled, gave black America a pat on the back—and then ran like the devil to the suburbs. Now we get to have things

---

CLIP 'N CARRY

Excerpt from the Fourteenth Amendment

Section 1. All persons born or naturalized in the United States, and subject to the jurisdiction thereof, are citizens of the United States and of the state wherein they reside. No state shall make or enforce any law which shall abridge the privileges or immunities of citizens of the United States; nor shall any state deprive any person of life, liberty, or property, without due process of law; nor deny to any person within its jurisdiction the equal protection of the laws.

just the way we always used to have them in the cities. When we walk out to pick up the paper in the morning, we look one way down the street and see white people; look the other way, and guess what?—more white people!

At work, we whites still get the plum jobs, double the pay, and a seat in the front of the bus to happiness and success. Look back down the aisle, though, and you'll see the blacks sitting where they've always been, picking up after us, waiting on us, serving us from behind the counter.

In order to create a cover for this continued discrimination, we hold "diversity seminars" at our workplaces and appoint "urban relations" people to help us "connect with the community." When we advertise for a job opening we gleefully include the words "An Equal Opportunity Employer." It feels so good—and it's good for a chuckle, 'cause we know there's no way in hell a black guy's going to get the job. Only 4 percent of the African-American population have a graduate degree (compared with 9 percent of whites and 15 percent of Asian-Americans). We've rigged the system from birth, guaranteeing that black people will go to the worst public schools, thus preventing them from admission to the best colleges, and paving their way to a fulfilling life making our lattés, servicing our BMWs, and picking up our trash. Oh, sure, a few slip by—but they pay an extra tariff for the privilege: the black doctor driving his BMW gets pulled over continually by the cops; the black Broadway actress can't get a cab after the standing ovation; the black broker is the first to be laid off because of "seniority."

We whites really deserve some kind of genius award for this. We talk the talk of inclusion, we celebrate the birthday of Dr. King, we frown upon racist jokes; thanks to that rat bastard Mark Fuhrman blowing our cover, we've even coined a new term—"the N-word"—to replace the real Nigger McCoy. Trust me, you'll NEVER catch any of us saying that word out loud—not these days, no-sir-ree-bob! The only time it's acceptable is when we're singing along with a rap song—and boy, do we suddenly love to rap!

We never fail to drop a mention of "my friend—he's black . . ." We give money to the United Negro College Fund, recognize Black History Month, and make sure we put our lone black employee up at the front reception desk so we can say things like "See—we don't discriminate! We *hire* black people."

Yes, we are a very crafty, cagey race—and damn if we haven't gotten away with it!

We're also very adept at learning—and lifting—from black culture. We co-opt it, put it through a white blender, and make it ours. Benny Goodman did it, Elvis did it, Lenny Bruce did it. Motown created a whole new sound, and then was seduced to move to L.A., where it withdrew and made way for the Great White Pop Stars. Eminem admits he owes a lot to Dr. Dre, Tupac, and Public Enemy. The Backstreet Boys and 'N Sync are indebted to Smokey Robinson and the Miracles, the Temptations, and the Jackson Five.

Blacks invent it, we appropriate it. Comedy, dance, fashion, language—we love the way black people express themselves, whether it's talking about giving your girlfriend "props" for a tasty dinner, or hanging out with your "peeps," or trying your darndest to "Be Like Mike." Of course the operative word there is *like*, because no matter how many millions he makes, to *be* Mike would mean spending an awful lot of time pulled over on the New Jersey Turnpike.

Professional sports (other than hockey) has been dominated by African-Americans for the past three decades. We've been very generous in turning over all that hard work and training and exertion to young black men, because let's face it, it's more fun to sit in your La-Z-Boy eating chips and dip and watching them chase that ball. If we need exercise, we can always work up a sweat calling in to sports talk radio to whine about how "overpaid" those athletes are. Seeing black people end up with so much money just kind of makes us feel . . . uneasy.

Where are the rest of the black-skinned people these days, the ones who don't shoot hoop or wait on us? Working in film and television, I rarely see them. When I leave New York to go to Los Angeles for a few days to work and meet with people in the business, and from the plane I fly out on to the hotel I'm staying at, to my visit at the old talent agency, to the executives I meet, to the drinks I must have with a producer in Santa Monica, and then the dinner I enjoy with friends in West Hollywood—I can go days and never encounter a single African-American unless it's someone to whom I'm handing a tip. How can that happen? To pass the time, I now play a game with myself, trying to clock how long it will be before I spot a black man or woman who isn't wearing a uniform or sitting at a receptionist's desk (they do the Negro-at-the-reception-desk trick in L.A., too). During my last three trips to Los Angeles the clock never stopped: the black head count was zero. That I could exist for days at a time in the second largest city in America and encounter only whites, Asians, and Hispanics but no blacks at all—now THAT's an incredible feat, testimony to the strength of our commitment to be a segregated society. Think of how much energy has to go into something like this, so that I don't have to be troubled by any black people! How did the white people out there keep the one million black citizens of Los Angeles county hidden from my view? Sheer, unadulterated genius!

I know it's easy to pick on L.A. You can have the hear-no-black-people, see-no-black-people experience in most parts of America. And it's not just the TV and film world. I'd be surprised if any black hands have touched the manuscript of this book since it left my office (other than to messenger it to the publisher across town).

For once I'd love to see a black person in the seat next to me at a Knicks game—or within twenty rows of me in any direction (players and Spike Lee excluded). For once I'd like to walk onto an airplane and see it filled with only black passengers instead of a bunch of complaining white jerks who feel a sense of entitlement in demanding that I give up my lap so they can put their seat in it.

Now don't get me wrong. I'm not a self-hating Caucasian. It's not the white skin color of others that gives me the creeps. What galls me is that my fellow white people have become so conniving they've figured out a way to turn black people *into* white people! When I first heard Clarence Thomas speak I thought, "For crying out loud, don't white people have enough people already?" Now the airwaves are filled with blacks who are trotted out to push the white agenda. I am stumped as to where the networks dig these individuals up. They speak out against affirmative action, even though many of them got into college *thanks* to affirmative action. They blast welfare mothers, even though that's who their own mother was, struggling for years in poverty so her son could grow up to debase her and her kind. They speak out against homosexuals, even though AIDS has devastated black gay men more than any other group. They despise Jesse Jackson, even though he spent years being arrested and risking his life so they would have the freedom to sit down in any restaurant and order lunch, let alone voice any opinion they wished. I'm not saying that black America must speak with one political voice; I'm just repulsed by the venom some of these "conservatives" spew.

It's the saddest thing to watch, this Uncle Tom porn. How much are these freaks being paid? I wonder, when the red light on the camera goes off, does Bill O'Reilly or Chris Matthews or Tucker Carlson ever say to these sellouts, "Hey, there's a house next to mine for sale—you oughta move in!" or "Hey, my sister's single now, and so are you—how 'bout it?" I don't know, maybe they do. Maybe O'Reilly will have me over for Kwanzaa this December.

I wonder how long we'll have to live with the legacy of slavery. That's right. I brought it up. SLAVERY. You can almost hear the groans of white America whenever you bring up the fact that we still suffer from the impact of a government-approved and supported slave system.

Well, I'm sorry, but the roots of most of our social ills can be traced straight back to this sick chapter of our history. African-Americans *never* got a chance to have the same fair start the rest of us got. Their families were willfully destroyed. Their language and culture and religion were stripped from them. Their poverty was institutionalized so that our cotton could get picked, our wars could be fought, our convenience stores could remain open all night. The America we've come to know would never have come to pass if not for the millions of slaves who built it and created its booming economy—and for the millions of their descendants who do the same dirty work for whites today.

"Mike, Why are you bringing up slavery? No black person living today was ever a slave. *I* didn't enslave anyone. Why don't you quit blaming all this on some past injustice, and make them take responsibility for their own actions?"

Well, it's not like we're talking ancient Rome here, folks. My grandfather was born just *three years* after the Civil War.

That's right, my *grandfather*. My great-uncle was born *before* the Civil War. And I'm only in my forties. Sure, people in my family seem to marry late and have their babies even later, but the truth remains: I'm just two generations from slave times. That, my friends, is NOT a "long time ago." In the vast breadth of human history, it was only yesterday. Until we realize that, and accept that we *do* have a responsibility to correct an immoral act that still has repercussions today, we will never remove the single greatest stain on the soul of our country.

The day after the L.A. riots began in 1992, when the mayhem had spread into the white neighborhoods near Beverly Hills and Hollywood, white people went into urgent survival mode. Thousands who live in the hills above Los Angeles fled. Thousands more stayed and brought out their guns. It appeared as if the racial Armageddon many had feared was upon us.

I was working out of a Warner Bros. office in Rockefeller Center in New York City. Word was passed throughout the building that everyone was to evacuate and head for home by 1:00 P.M. It was feared that blacks in New York might catch "riot fever" and go berserk. At 1:00 P.M. I went out on the street, and what I saw I believe (and hope) I may never see again—tens of thousands of white people running down the sidewalks to get the next commuter train or bus out of town. It was like a scene from *The Day of the Locust*, wall-to-wall humans in a collective panic, moving as one, in fear for their lives.

Within half an hour, the streets were deserted. Empty. It was eerie, creepy. New York City, in the middle of the day, in the middle of the week—and it looked like five A.M. on a Sunday morning.

I walked home to my neighborhood. Not really concerned about anything other than the fact that my pen had run out of ink, I stopped by the stationery store across the street from my apartment. It was one of the few businesses still open (most had closed and shuttered their windows). I picked up a couple of pens and some paper and went up to the counter to pay. There, at the cash register, stood the elderly owner—with a baseball bat on the counter in front of him. I asked him what the bat was for.

"Just in case," he replied, eyes darting around to see what was happening outside on the street.

"Just in case of what?" I asked.

"You know, in case *they* decide to riot here."

He wasn't referring to L.A. rioters hopping on a plane and bringing their Molotovs here to toss around the Big Apple. What he had in mind—like everyone who was running to catch the last train home to the white suburbs—was the fact that our race problem has never really been solved, and that black America was harboring a lot of pent-up anger over the incredible disparity between the lives of blacks and whites in this country. That bat on the counter spoke volumes about the one basic unspoken fear all whites have: that sooner or later, the blacks are going to rise up and get their revenge. We are all sitting on a racial tinderbox, and we know we better be ready when the victims of our greed come calling.

Well, hey, why wait for *that* to happen? Do you really want to let it get to *that* point? Wouldn't you rather fix the problem than have to flee for your life as your house burns behind you? I know *I* would!

So I've put together some easy-to-follow survival tips that might help save your honky ass. Sooner or later—you know it and I know it—there are going to be millions of Rodney Kings knocking on your door, and this time they aren't going to be the ones taking the beating.

If we are unwilling to take serious action to correct our race problem, chances are we'll all end up having to live in a gated neighborhood, armed with semiautomatic weapons and a private security force. Now what fun is that?

SURVIVAL TIPS FOR WHITE AMERICA

1. Hire only black people.

I'm done hiring white people. Nothing against them personally, of course. They're a dependable, hardworking lot. Those I've hired for my films and TV shows have been a great bunch.

But they *are* white.

How can I write what I've already written in this chapter when I've done little or nothing to correct the problem in my own backyard? Oh, sure, I could give you a hundred excuses for why it's so hard to find African-Americans in this business—and they'd all be true. So what? So it's hard? Does that absolve me of responsibility? I oughta be leading a picket of myself!

By giving jobs to white people—for many of them, their first job in this medium—I've enabled them to go on and have successful careers on shows like *Politically Incorrect, Dharma and Greg*, David Letterman's show, *The Daily Show with Jon Stewart*, and more. A dozen other former staffers have gone on to make their own independent films. One became an executive at

Comedy Central, and two others created shows for that network. Some of our editors have worked at HBO, and one of them has gone on to edit many of Ang (*Crouching Tiger, Hidden Dragon*) Lee's films.

I'm happy for them all, but there's a question that gnaws away inside my head: What if I'd done the same for a hundred *black* writers, editors, field producers, and cinematographers on my projects over the years? Where would *they* be today? My guess— using their talent to affect a hundred shows or movies, having their voices heard. And we'd all be better off for it.

The more I think about it, white employees can be a lot of trouble. Right now, the white person in the office next to me is playing an Eagles CD. That person's got to go. They can also be a pretty lazy bunch—especially those who grew up with a lot of money and went to the nicer schools. They're the ones who've spilled crap all over our carpets, leaving huge, ugly stains, and who've scratched up all our furniture. Their genetically encoded sense of privilege whispers in their ears, "Someone else (someone black?) will pick up after you." Another employee just came in and told me she wants to take Friday off "to go out to the Hamptons." Sure—and why don't you take the rest of your life off while you're at it?

So they've all gotta go. From now on, whitey don't work here no more.

I suppose some government agency is going to pay me a visit over this, as I'm legally prohibited from denying employment to an entire race of people. I don't care. Bring it on! And you better not send me some white guy, or I'll have him fetching me burgers and scrubbing my toilet.

So if you're African-American and you'd like to work in the media—or already do but haven't been able to get out from behind that damn reception desk—then I encourage you to drop me a line and send me your résumé.

Our lone white receptionist will be happy to answer any questions you may have.

2. If you own a business, pay people a living wage, provide day care, and make sure all your employees have health insurance.

This survival tip is for those of you who consider yourselves conservative and are great believers in capitalism. If being conservative is all about looking out for number one, I have a radical, but simple, idea that will guarantee you larger profits, a more productive workforce, and no labor problems.

Our black citizens are disproportionately our poorest citizens. Yet without them to do the hard labor, white society would be crippled. You want them to work even harder? You want them to help you make more money?

Here's what you need to do:

> **Make sure the amount you pay your employees is enough for them to own their own home, have reliable transportation, take a vacation, and send their kids to college.**

How does paying people more money make *you* more money?

It works like this. The more you pay workers, the more they spend. Remember, they're not just your workers—they're your consumers, too. The more they spend their extra cash on your products, the more your profits go up. Also, when employees have enough money that they don't have to live in constant fear of bankruptcy, they're able to focus more on their work—and be more productive. With fewer personal problems and less stress hanging over them, they'll lose less time at work, meaning more profits for *you*. Pay them enough to afford a late-model car (i.e., one that works), and they'll rarely be late for work. And knowing that they'll be able to provide a better life for their children will not only give them a more positive attitude, it'll give them hope—and an incentive to do well for the company, because the better the company does, the better they'll do.

Of course, if you're like most corporations these days—announcing mass layoffs right after posting record profits—then you're already hemorrhaging the trust and confidence of your remaining workforce, and your employees are doing their jobs in a state of fear. Productivity will drop. That will hurt sales. You will suffer. Ask the people at Firestone: Ford has alleged that the tire company fired its longtime union employees, then brought in untrained scab workers who ended up making thousands of defective tires—and 203 dead customers later, Firestone is in the toilet.

Open an on-site day care center for employees with children ages two to five.

Now, I can hear your first reaction already: "No way I'm having a bunch of little brats running around here—THIS IS A PLACE OF BUSINESS!" I understand. Those little ones can cause quite a distraction, especially when you're trying to close a big deal with that German bank and little LaToya speeds by, dragging Kasheem around by the hair like a stuffed animal.

But here's a greater distraction to consider: if your employees are spending all their time at work worrying about their kids, they won't be as productive as they should be. Parents will always worry about their children before their jobs. That's just human nature. And single parents? They've got no help. When somebody needs to cut out of work to go pick up their sick kid at the babysitter's, or needs to split the second the clock strikes five because the day care center charges a penalty for late pickups, they've got no choice but to drop what they're doing.

Imagine if your workers didn't have to spend time on the job worrying about the kids, and instead focused 100 percent on *making you money*? If they no longer had to miss work just because the babysitter flaked out, and got to spend all day long *making you money*?

A day care center on the premises doesn't cost that much—and most parents would be willing to share that cost with you if it meant a reprieve from worrying about the kids. Think of how relaxed it would make your workers, knowing that their children were safe and secure—and nearby! Man, they'll be working their butts off!

Translation: More dough for YOU!!

Provide good health care insurance for everyone, and give workers enough paid sick days.

Do I even need to explain this one? How much efficiency is sacrificed every year by employees who come to work sick because they can't afford to go to the doctor or avoid doing so until they're near collapse? With no other choice, they bring their viruses to work—and infect everyone in their path. It's far more profitable to pay for health insurance for your workers, so they can get better quick and start busting their humps for you again—at full speed. A healthy workforce is a productive workforce. With health insurance, it's one afternoon off work to see the doctor, a speedy diagnosis and prescription, and—look!—back to work in *a couple of days*, instead of lingering at home for a week or two waiting for the condition to clear up.

The good news is, all of the above is in the interest of your own bottom line—no bleeding-heart, bleeding-money liberalism required. You can stay as regressive and greedy as you want—I don't care. If it means life will get better for some of the millions of African-Americans who work hard for little pay, scanty benefits, and no security, then I'll be happy.

3. Don't buy a handgun.

What sense does it make to have a gun in the house? If it's for hunting, then it's simple: keep your rifle or shotgun unloaded and locked up in the attic until hunting season.

If you're thinking of buying a handgun for protection, on the other hand, let me give you a few statistics. A member of your family is twenty-two times more likely to die from gunfire if you have a gun in your house than if you don't.

The idea that having a gun is the only way to ensure "home protection" is a myth. Fewer than 1 out of 4 violent crimes is committed while the victim is at home. Among all the instances when guns are fired during a break-in while the owner is at home, in only 2 percent are guns used to shoot the intruder. The other 98 percent of the time, residents accidentally shoot a loved one or themselves—or the burglars take the gun and kill them with it.

Nonetheless, we have almost a *quarter-billion* guns in our homes.

The vast majority of guns in America are purchased and owned—that is, introduced into society—by white people. Each year about 500,000 guns are stolen, mostly from these same white people in the suburbs. And the vast majority of those guns end up in the inner city, sold cheaply or traded for legal or illegal goods and services.

These white guns have caused an enormous amount of death and suffering among African-Americans. Gunfire is the number one cause of death among young blacks. Black men between the ages of fifteen and twenty-four are almost six times more likely to be shot to death than white men in that same age group.

No African-American owns a gun company. Cruise through the part of your town where African-Americans live: there are no gun factories there. At prices that range from several hundred to several thousand dollars, most African-Americans can't afford to buy a Glock, Beretta, Luger, Colt, or Smith & Wesson. No black guy owns a plane that's smuggling automatic weapons into the country.

All of this is done by whites. But sooner or later, thousands of these legally purchased guns end up in the hands of desperate people who live in poverty and who live with their own set of fears. To introduce guns into this volatile environment—which we white people have done little to improve—is a deadly proposition.

So if you're white, and you'd like to help reduce the number one cause of death among young black men, here's the answer: Don't buy a gun. Don't keep one in your house or car. No guns laying around means no guns stolen to be resold in poor black neighborhoods. Wherever you live, chances are that crime is at an all-time low. Chill out, sit back, and enjoy the good life an unlevel playing field has given you. If you're truly concerned about your protection, get a dog. Bad guys generally don't want to tussle with a crazy barking animal with sharp teeth.

You don't need a gun.

4. Lose all the liberal "concern" for black people.

Really. Black people are onto us. They know we say and do things to make it look as if progress has been made. They see us working hard to show how not-prejudiced we are. Skip it. We haven't made real progress. We're still bigots—and they know it.

Cut the crap about all your "black friends." You don't *have* black friends. A friend is someone you have over for dinner regularly, someone you go on vacation with, someone you ask to be in your wedding party, someone you go to church with on Sunday, someone you call often to share your most intimate secrets. *That* kind of friend.

Your black "friends" know that the chances of your dropping your toddler off with *them* in *their* part of town while you go on a weekend trip is about as good as your inviting them to go on the trip with you.

I've heard liberals say dumb things like, "There are no black people on *Friends*." I *like* it that there are no black friends on

Friends, because in real life friends like that *don't* have black friends. It's an honest, believable show.

So let's dispense with this ruse that blacks and whites are now all part of that big multi-cultural quilt we call America. We live in our world, they live in theirs. And that's what we've grown comfortable with, like it or not. This wouldn't be so bad if their world existed on a financially and socially parallel plane. If it did, then we could just mix and mingle however we saw fit—as equals, the way we already do with other white people. For instance, I don't have much desire to hang out with Young Republicans. That's okay, because they're going to do just fine without me, and my decision not to associate with them doesn't affect their standard of living or quality of life. (In fact, it probably improves it.)

Isn't it better not to coddle each other with the delusion that African-Americans are finally part of the mainstream? Isn't it smarter to lift the veil of false hope we give African-Americans, so that we don't waste any time fooling ourselves? The next time you're talking to one of your "black friends," instead of telling him how you're really "down" with the new Jay-Z CD, why not put your arm around him and say, "I love ya, bro, you know that, so I gotta tell you a little secret we white people have: Your people aren't ever going to have it as good as we do. And if you think working hard and trying to fit in is going to get you a seat on the board of directors when we've already got our black seat filled— well, friend, if it's equality and advancement you seek, try Sweden."

The sooner we all start talking like that, the more honest a society we'll all be living in.

5. Look in the mirror.

If you're white, and you really want to help change things, why not start with yourself? Spend time with your fellow whiteys talking about what you can do to make the world a little better for whites and African-Americans alike. Stop the next white person you hear make a stupid racist comment and set him straight. Quit your whining about affirmative action. No black person is ever going to ruin your life by getting the job you "deserve." The door will always open for you. Your only duty is to hold it open for those who have less of a chance simply because they aren't white.

6. Don't marry whitey.

If you're white and you don't like any of the above ideas, or you think they're impractical, then there's always one surefire way to help create a colorblind world—marry a black person and have yourselves some babies! Blacks and whites making love with each other—instead of whites just screwing blacks—will eventually give us a nation of one color. (And Hispanics and Asians can play, too!) Who's your daddy? Everybody!

And when we're all one color, we won't have anything to hate each other for—other than who gets stuck at that damn reception desk.

SURVIVAL TIPS FOR BLACK PEOPLE

1. Driving While Black:

* Make yourself a less likely target for drive-by racial profiling by placing a life-size, inflatable white doll in the passenger seat (the kind people use so they can drive in carpool-only express lanes). The cops will probably think you're a chauffeur and leave you alone.

* Try to avoid drawing any additional attention to yourself when Driving While Black. Keep your hands in the classic "10 and 2" position on the wheel. Buckle your seat belt; in fact, buckle *all* seatbelts, whether or not there's anyone else in the car. Remove any "Honk If You're Black Too!" bumper stickers; replace them with "I ❤ Hockey!"

✳ Avoid renting or driving any car with New Hampshire, Utah, or Maine license plates—these states have virtually no black residents, and it will of course be assumed that you're driving a *stolen* vehicle and/or running drugs and/or carrying weapons. On second thought, cops make the same assumptions about black drivers in states with sizable black populations. Better idea: take the bus.

2. Shopping While Black:

✳ If you want to avoid being followed by shopkeepers who assume you're going to shoplift or hold a gun to their heads while emptying the cash drawer, the solution is simple: *catalogs and on-line shopping*! The beauty part? No need to leave the comforts of your home—and no more long waits for a parking spot at the mall!

✳ If you must enter a store, for God's sake leave your coat outside! All those pockets will *surely* end up getting searched for stolen goods—you're just asking to be arrested. Needless to say, lose the purses, shopping bags, and backpacks, too. Better yet, do your shopping in the nude. Sure, you might be subjected to the occasional body cavity search, but that's a small price to pay to exercise your God-given right as a black American to buy stuff and contribute some of the $572 billion in your pockets that goes to the white economy every year.

3. Voting While Black:

✳ Because whites have rigged our elections by ensuring that the most ancient, ill-functioning voting machines all find their way to the black precincts in town, don't leave the polling place unless you've personally seen your ballot marked the way you intended and placed in the locked ballot box. If you use a voting machine, ask the poll worker to check the machine after you've voted to make sure your vote gets counted.

Bring whatever tools you think you may need to see that your vote is recorded: No. 2 pencil, black marker, knitting needle (to make sure you don't just impregnate the ballot but actually punch the holes all the way out), 3-in-1 Oil, pliers, the rest of your Sears Craftsman tools, a magnifying glass, a copy of the local election laws, a copy of your voter registration card, a copy of your birth certificate, a copy of your second grade report card, any other proof that you're still alive, a camera to record any funny business, a local reporter to show her firsthand that you weren't kidding when you said your polling place was shipped in from Bolivia, duct tape, string, paraffin wax, a Bunsen burner, Wite-Out, Shout stain remover, a lawyer, a minister, a Justice of the Supreme Court. Get all those ducks in a row, and there's half a chance your vote will be counted.

✳ In the 2002 elections, vote for the Democratic or Green candidate for Congress. If just five seats change party hands in favor of the Democrats, the Democrats will not only control the House, but through seniority nineteen black congressmen and women will become chair of their House committee or subcommittee. Nineteen! That's a black takeover of the House of Representatives! (Where Green Party candidates have a chance of winning, or in districts where the Democrat behaves like a Republican, an elected Green Party congresswoman will caucus with the Democrats to make up the majority.) Don't tell too many white people about this one—the idea of a "Black House" might really spook them out!

4. Having a Good Laugh While Black:

* Bring back those Whites Only signs from the 1950s. When nobody's looking, place them on the doors of businesses that don't hire blacks.

* Nonchalantly put one on the front-row seat in First Class next time you get on a plane.

* Hang one on the front office of any major league team, or anywhere in the better seats at any NBA game.

* Plant one in the lawn in front of the United States Supreme Court, and when Clarence Thomas walks by, just throw up your hands and say, "What?"

CLIP 'N CARRY

Excerpt from the Federal Voting Rights Act of 1965 (suitable for laminating and carrying in your wallet)

Section 2: No voting qualification or prerequisite to voting, or standard, practice, or procedure shall be imposed or applied to any State or political subdivision to deny or abridge the right of any citizen of the United States to vote on account of race or color.

5. Breathing While Black:

You may just get to the point where you can't take it any-more—the harassment, the discrimination, the resentment, the utter sense that you don't belong in a nation so deeply rooted in intolerance. You may just feel like it's time to get the hell out and move to a place where being black doesn't make you a minority—a place that feels like home.

Africa? Better think twice.

Here's what Amnesty International has to say about Africa: "Armed conflict, mass displacement of people, torture, ill-treatment and endemic impunity continue to be rife in the African region." And 52 percent of the people in sub-Saharan Africa live on less than $1 a day. In 1998 the average monthly expenditure was only $14 a person. That IS worse than living in Detroit.

Life expectancy in the region is, at best, fifty-seven years—that is, if you live in Ghana. If you're stuck in Mozambique, you get to live to the ripe old age of thirty-seven and a half.

Couple this with seemingly never-ending droughts and famine and an overwhelming percentage of the world's AIDS cases (and deaths), and suddenly it might look a lot easier just to dig up some old naked photos of Trent Lott at a men's-only Ol' Miss mixer and force his resignation (photos of Orrin Hatch, Tom DeLay, and others would do just as well).

Amy McCampbell, one of the numerous African-Americans I've hired since I started writing this chapter (five of my last five hires have been black—hey, take this book out of the humor sec-tion, I ain't kidding around!), suggests that for those who want to return to their "black roots," there's only one way to go—the Caribbean! She says: "How about Barbados? It's a tropical para-dise; the people are peaceful, and crime is nonexistent. Life expectancy is well into the seventies. Eighty percent of the population is African, so we'd feel right at home. They even speak English! And here's the weird part—we'd get to call Queen Elizabeth our head of state. Whoa!"

Sounds nice, huh?

It'd be nicer, though, if we could make Amy and others feel more at home right here where they were born. I'm open for suggestions. . . .

FIVE

Idiot Nation

DO YOU FEEL like you live in a nation of idiots?

I used to console myself about the state of stupidity in this country by repeating this to myself: *Even if there are two hundred million stone-cold idiots in this country, that leaves at least eighty million who'll get what I'm saying—and that's still more than the populations of the United Kingdom and Iceland combined!*

Then came the day I found myself sharing an office with the ESPN game show *Two-Minute Drill.* This is the show that tests your knowledge of not only who plays what position for which team, but who hit what where in a 1925 game between Boston and New York, who was rookie of the year in 1965 in the old American Basketball Association, and what Jake Wood had for breakfast the morning of May 12, 1967.

I don't know the answer to any of those questions—but for some reason I do remember Jake Wood's uniform number: 2. Why on earth am I retaining that useless fact?

I don't know, but after watching scores of guys waiting to audition for that ESPN show, I think I do know something about intelligence and the American mind. Hordes of these jocks and lunkheads hang out in our hallway awaiting their big moment, going over hundreds of facts and statistics in their heads and challenging each other with questions I can't see why anyone would be able to answer other than God Almighty Himself. To look at these testosterone-loaded bruisers you would guess that they were a bunch of illiterates who would be lucky if they could read the label on a Bud.

In fact, they are geniuses. They can answer all thirty obscure trivia questions in less than 120 seconds. That's four seconds a question—including the time used by the slow-reading celebrity athletes who ask the questions.

I once heard the linguist and political writer Noam Chomsky say that if you want proof the American people aren't stupid, just turn on any sports talk radio show and listen to the incredible retention of facts. It is amazing—and it's proof that the American mind is alive and well. It just isn't challenged with anything interesting or exciting. *Our* challenge, Chomsky said, was to find a way to make politics as gripping and engaging as sports. When we do that, watch how Americans will do nothing but talk about who did what to whom at the WTO.

But first, they have to be able to read the letters *WTO*.

There are forty-four million Americans who cannot read and write above a fourth-grade level—in other words, who are functional illiterates.

How did I learn this statistic? Well, I *read* it. And now you've read it. So we've already eaten into the mere 99 hours a *year* an average American adult spends reading a book—compared with 1,460 hours watching television.

I've also read that only 11 percent of the American public bothers to *read* a daily newspaper, beyond the funny pages or the used car ads.

So if you live in a country where forty-four million can't read—and perhaps close to another two hundred million can read but usually don't—well, friends, you and I are living in one very scary place. A nation that not only churns out illiterate students BUT GOES OUT OF ITS WAY TO REMAIN IGNORANT AND STUPID is a nation that should not be running the world—at least not until a majority of its citizens can locate Kosovo (or any other country it has bombed) on the map.

It comes as no surprise to foreigners that Americans, who love to revel in their stupidity, would "elect" a president who rarely reads *anything*—including his own briefing papers—and thinks Africa is a nation, not a continent. An idiot leader of an idiot nation. In our glorious land of plenty, less is always more when it comes to taxing any lobe of the brain with the intake of facts and numbers, critical thinking, or the comprehension of anything that isn't . . . well, sports.

Our Idiot-in-Chief does nothing to hide his ignorance—he even brags about it. During his commencement address to the Yale Class of 2001, George W. Bush spoke proudly of having been a mediocre student at Yale. "And to the C students, I say you, too, can be President of the United States!" The part where you also need an ex-President father, a brother as governor of a state with missing ballots, and a Supreme Court full of your dad's buddies must have been too complicated to bother with in a short speech.

As Americans, we have quite a proud tradition of being represented by ignorant high-ranking officials. In 1956 President Dwight D. Eisenhower's nominee as ambassador to Ceylon (now Sri Lanka) was unable to identify either the country's prime minister or its capital during his Senate confirmation hearing. Not a problem—Maxwell Gluck was confirmed anyway. In 1981 President Ronald Reagan's nominee for deputy secretary of state, William Clark, admitted to a wide-ranging lack of knowledge about foreign affairs at his confirmation hearing. Clark had no

idea how our allies in Western Europe felt about having American nuclear missiles based there, and didn't know the names of the
prime ministers of South Africa or Zimbabwe. Not to worry—he
was confirmed, too. All this just paved the way for Baby Bush,
who hadn't quite absorbed the names of the leaders of India or
Pakistan, two of the seven nations that possess the atomic bomb.

And Bush went to Yale *and* Harvard.

Recently a group of 556 seniors at fifty-five prestigious American universities (e.g., Harvard, Yale, Stanford) were given a
multiple-choice test consisting of questions that were described
as "high school level." Thirty-four questions were asked. These
top students could only answer 53 percent of them correctly. And
only one student got them all right.

A whopping 40 percent of these students did not know when the
Civil War took place—even when given a wide range of choices:
A. 1750–1800; B. 1800–1850; C. 1850–1900; D. 1900–1950; or E.
after 1950. (*The answer is C, guys.*) The two questions the college
seniors scored highest on were (1) Who is Snoop Doggy Dog? (98
percent got that one right), and (2) Who are Beavis and Butt-head?
(99 percent knew). For my money, Beavis and Butt-head represented some of the best American satire of the nineties, and
Snoop and his fellow rappers have much to say about America's
social ills, so I'm not going down the road of blaming MTV.

What I *am* concerned with is why politicians like Senators Joe
Lieberman of Connecticut and Herbert Kohl of Wisconsin want
to go after MTV when *they* are the ones responsible for the massive failure of American education. Walk into any public school,
and the odds are good that you'll find overflowing classrooms,
leaking ceilings, and demoralized teachers. In 1 out of 4 schools,
you'll find students "learning" from textbooks published in the
1980s—or earlier.

Why is this? Because the political leaders—and the people
who vote for them—have decided it's a bigger priority to build

List of Leaders of Fifty Largest Countries

(in order of country's size)

1. CHINA
President Jiang Zemin

2. INDIA
President Kocheril Raman Narayanan

3. UNITED STATES
"President" George W. Bush

4. INDONESIA
President Megawati Sukarnoputri

5. BRAZIL
President Fernando Henrique Cardoso

6. RUSSIA
President Vladimir Putin

7. PAKISTAN
General Pervez Musharraf

8. BANGLADESH
President A. Q. M. Badruddoza
Chowdhury

9. JAPAN
Prime Minister Junichiro Koizumi

10. NIGERIA
President Olusegun Obasanjo

11. MEXICO
President Vicente Fox Quesada

12. GERMANY
Chancellor Gerhard Schroder

13. PHILIPPINES
President Gloria Macapagal-Arroyo

14. VIETNAM
President Tran Duc Luong

15. EGYPT
President Mohammed Hosni Mubarak

16. TURKEY
President Ahmet Necdet Sezer

17. IRAN
Ayatollah Ali Hoseini-Khamenei,
President Mohammad Khatami

18. ETHIOPIA
President Girma Woldegiorgis

19. THAILAND
Prime Minister Thaksin Chinnawat

20. UNITED KINGDOM
Prime Minister Anthony C. L. Blair

21. FRANCE
President Jacques Chirac

22. ITALY
Prime Minister Silvio Berlusconi

23. CONGO (KINSHASA)
President Joseph Kabila

24. UKRAINE
President Leonid D. Kuchma

25. SOUTH KOREA
President Kim Dae-jung

continued

List of Leaders of Fifty Largest Countries

(in order of country's size)

26. SOUTH AFRICA
President Thabo Mbeki

27. BURMA
Prime Minister Than Shwe

28. SPAIN
Prime Minister Jose Maria Aznar

29. COLOMBIA
President Andres Pastrana

30. POLAND
President Aleksander Kwasniewski

31. ARGENTINA
President Eduardo Alberto Duhalde

32. TANZANIA
President Benjamin William Mkapa

33. SUDAN
President Lt. Gen. Omar el-Bashir

34. CANADA
Prime Minister Jean Chretien

35. ALGERIA
President Abdelaziz Bouteflika

36. KENYA
President Daniel arap Moi

37. MOROCCO
Prime Minister Abderrahmane Youssoufi

38. PERU
President Alejandro Toledo

39. AFGHANISTAN
President Hamid Karzai

40. UZBEKISTAN
President Islom Karimov

41. NEPAL
King Gyanendra, Prime Minister
Sher Bahadur Derba

42. VENEZUELA
President Hugo Chavez Frias

43. UGANDA
President Lt. Gen. Yoweri Museveni

44. IRAQ
President Saddam Hussein

45. ROMANIA
President Ion Iliescu

46. TAIWAN
President Shui-bian Chen

47. SAUDI ARABIA
King Fahd bin Abd al-Aziz Al Saud

48. MALAYSIA
Prime Minister Dr. Mahathir bin
Mohamad

49. NORTH KOREA
President Kim Jong Il

50. GHANA
President John Agyekum Kufuor

Note to Australian readers: Although it may seem like Australia belongs on this list, it doesn't. Ghana, at #50, has a population of 20,244,000 (2002), while Australia's is 19,546,000 (2002).

another bomber than to educate our children. They would rather hold hearings about the depravity of a television show called *Jackass* than about their own depravity in neglecting our schools and children and maintaining our title as Dumbest Country on Earth.

I hate writing these words. I *love* this big lug of a country and the crazy people in it. But when I can travel to some backwater village in Central America, as I did back in the eighties, and listen to a bunch of twelve-year-olds tell me their concerns about the World Bank, I get the feeling that *something* is lacking in the United States of America.

Our problem isn't just that our kids don't know nothin' but that the adults who pay their tuition are no better. I wonder what would happen if we tested the U.S. Congress to see just how much our representatives know. What if we were to give a pop quiz to the commentators who cram our TVs and radios with all their nonstop nonsense? How many would *they* get right?

A while back, I decided to find out. It was one of those Sunday mornings when the choice on TV was the *Parade of Homes* real estate show or *The McLaughlin Group*. If you like the sound of hyenas on Dexedrine, of course, you go with *McLaughlin*. On this particular Sunday morning, perhaps as my punishment for not being at Mass, I was forced to listen to magazine columnist Fred Barnes (now an editor at the right-wing *Weekly Standard* and co-host of the Fox News show *The Beltway Boys*) whine on and on about the sorry state of American education, blaming the teachers and their evil union for why students are doing so poorly.

"These kids don't even know what *The Iliad* and *The Odyssey* are!" he bellowed, as the other panelists nodded in admiration at Fred's noble lament.

The next morning I called Fred Barnes at his Washington office. "Fred," I said, "tell me what *The Iliad* and *The Odyssey* are."

He started hemming and hawing. "Well, they're . . . uh . . . you know . . . uh . . . okay, fine, you got me—I don't know what they're about. Happy now?"

No, not really. You're one of the top TV pundits in America, seen every week on your own show and plenty of others. You gladly hawk your "wisdom" to hundreds of thousands of unsuspecting citizens, gleefully scorning others for their ignorance. Yet you and your guests know little or nothing yourselves. Grow up, get some books, and go to your room.

Yale and Harvard. Princeton and Dartmouth. Stanford and Berkeley. Get a degree from one of those universities, and you're set for life. So what if, on that test of the college seniors I previously mentioned, 70 percent of the students at those fine schools had never heard of the Voting Rights Act or President Lyndon Johnson's Great Society initiatives? Who needs to know stuff like that as you sit in your Tuscan villa watching the sunset and checking how well your portfolio did today?

So what if *not one* of these top universities that the ignorant students attend requires that they take even one course in American history to graduate? Who needs history when you are going to be tomorrow's master of the universe?

Who cares if 70 percent of those who graduate from America's colleges are not required to learn a foreign language? Isn't the rest of the world speaking English now? And if they aren't, hadn't all those damn foreigners better GET WITH THE PROGRAM?

And who gives a rat's ass if, out of the seventy English Literature programs at seventy major American universities, only twenty-three now require English majors to take a course in Shakespeare? Can somebody please explain to me what Shakespeare and English have to do with each other? What good are some moldy old plays going to be in the business world, anyway?

Maybe I'm just jealous because I don't have a college degree. Yes, I, Michael Moore, am a college dropout.

Well, I never *officially* dropped out. One day in my sophomore year, I drove around and around the various parking lots of our commuter campus in Flint, searching desperately for a parking

Important Dates in History

June 19, 1865: "Juneteenth." Although the Emancipation Proclamation had pronounced the slaves of the Confederacy free more than two years earlier, the word hadn't gotten to everyone in the South. On this day in Galveston, Texas, a Union general arrived and officially informed the slaves of their freedom.

December 29, 1890: Massacre at Wounded Knee. As part of one last effort to quell the one remaining Indian rebellion, U.S. troops were sent out to arrest Big Foot, the chief of the Sioux Indian tribe. Members of the tribe were captured, forced to give up their arms, and moved into a camp surrounded by the U.S. troops. On the morning of December 29, the soldiers opened fire on the Indian camp and three hundred mostly unarmed Sioux, including Big Foot, were killed. It was the last battle in the four-hundred-year campaign of genocide against the Native Americans.

May 18, 1896: In *Plessy* v. *Ferguson*, the U.S. Supreme Court decided that inferior accommodations for blacks on railroad cars did not constitute a violation of the equal protection clause of the Fourteenth Amendment. The decision paved the way for the "separate but equal" policies that resulted in Jim Crow laws.

April 14, 1914: The Ludlow Massacre. Colorado coal miners who had been trying for years to unionize went on strike. After being kicked out of their company-owned

continued

homes, the strikers and their families set up tent colonies on public property. On the morning of the April 14, Colorado militiamen and other strikebreakers fired their guns into the camp and burned down the tents, killing twenty— mostly women and children.

March 22, 1947: President Truman issued Executive Order 9835 to identify the "infiltration of disloyal persons" within the government. This ushered in an era of fear and paranoia about alleged Communists that led to more than six million people being investigated and five hundred being dismissed from their jobs for "questionable loyalty."

December 1, 1955: A tired seamstress and local civil rights activist in Montgomery, Alabama, Rosa Parks, refused to give up her seat on a bus to a white passenger. This quiet act launched the Montgomery bus boycott, which lasted for 381 days and established Martin Luther King Jr. as the movement's leader. The boycott was ended after the Supreme Court ruled that segregation laws on public transportation were illegal.

April 30, 1975: The fall of Saigon. Although American ground troops had officially pulled out of Vietnam two years earlier, this day represents the end of the brutal war. Several weeks of chaos over the impending Communist takeover culminated in a desperate scene as the last of the U.S. rescue helicopters took off from the American embassy's rooftop with the few refugees they could carry.

space. There simply was no place to park—every spot was full, and no one was leaving. After a frustrating hour spent circling around in my '69 Chevy Impala, I shouted out the window, "That's it, I'm dropping out!" I drove home and told my parents I was no longer in college.

"Why?" they asked.

"Couldn't find a parking spot," I replied, grabbing a Redpop and moving on with the rest of my life. I haven't sat at a school desk since.

My dislike of school started somewhere around the second month of first grade. My parents—and God Bless Them Forever for doing this—had taught me to read and write by the time I was four. So when I entered St. John's Elementary School, I had to sit and feign interest while the other kids, like robots, sang, "A-B-C-D-E-F-G . . . Now I know my ABCs, tell me what you think of me!" Every time I heard that line, I wanted to scream out, "Here's what I think of you—quit singing that damn song! Somebody get me a Twinkie!"

I was bored beyond belief. The nuns, to their credit, recognized this, and one day Sister John Catherine took me aside and said that they had decided to skip me up to second grade, effective immediately. I was thrilled. When I got home I excitedly announced to my parents that I had already advanced a grade in my first month of school. They seemed underwhelmed by this new evidence of my genius. Instead they let out a "WHAT THE—," then went into the kitchen and closed the door. I could hear my mother on the phone explaining to the Mother Superior that there was *no way* her little Michael was going to be attending class with kids bigger and older than him, so please, Sister, put him back in first grade.

I was crushed. My mother explained to me that if I skipped first grade I'd always be the youngest and littlest kid in class all through my school years (well, inertia and fast food eventually proved her wrong on that count). There would be no appeals to my father, who left most education decisions to my mother, the valedictorian of her high school class. I tried to explain that if I was sent back to first grade it would appear that I'd *flunked* second grade on my first day—putting myself at risk of having the crap beaten out of me by the first graders I'd left behind with a rousing "See ya, suckers!" But Mom wasn't falling for it; it was then I learned that the only person with higher authority than Mother Superior was Mother Moore.

The next day I decided to ignore all instructions from my parents to go back to first grade. In the morning, before the opening bell, all the students had to line up outside the school with their classmates and then march into the building in single file. Quietly, but defiantly, I went and stood in the second graders' line, praying that God would strike the nuns blind so they wouldn't see which line I was in. The bell rang—and no one had spotted me! The second grade line started to move, and I went with it. *Yes!* I thought. *If I can pull this off, if I can just get into that second grade classroom and take my seat, then nobody will be able to get me out of there.* Just as I was about to enter the door of the school, I felt a hand grab me by the collar of my coat. It was Sister John Catherine.

"I think you're in the wrong line, Michael," she said firmly. "You are now in first grade again." I began to protest: my parents had it "all wrong," or "those weren't *really* my parents," or . . .

For the next twelve years I sat in class, did my work, and remained constantly preoccupied, looking for ways to bust out. I started an underground school paper in fourth grade. It was shut down. I started it again in sixth. It was shut down. In eighth grade I not only started the paper again, I convinced the good sisters to let me write a play for our class to perform at the Christmas pageant. The play had something to do with how many rats occupied the parish hall and how all the rats in the country had descended on St. John's Parish Hall to have their annual "rat convention." The priest put a stop to that one—and shut down the paper again. Instead, my friends and I were told to go up on stage and sing three Christmas carols and then leave the stage without uttering a word. I organized half the class to go up there and utter nothing. So we stood there and refused to sing the carols, our silent protest against censorship. By the second song, intimidated by the stern looks from their parents in the audience, most of the protesters joined in on the singing—and by the third song, I, too, had capitulated, joining in on "O Holy Night," and promising myself to live to fight another day.

High school, as we all know, is some sort of sick, sadistic punishment of kids by adults seeking vengeance because they can no longer lead the responsibility-free, screwing-around-24/7 lives young people enjoy. What other explanation could there be for those four brutal years of degrading comments, physical abuse, and the belief that you're the only one not having sex?

As soon as I entered high school—and the public school system—all the grousing I'd done about the repression of the Sisters of St. Joseph was forgotten; suddenly they all looked like scholars and saints. I was now walking the halls of a two-thousand-plus-inmate holding pen. Where the nuns had devoted their lives to teaching for no earthly reward, those running the public high school had one simple mission: "Hunt these little pricks down like dogs, then cage them until we can either break their will or ship them off to the glue factory!" Do this, don't do that, tuck your shirt in, wipe that smile off your face, where's your hall pass, THAT'S THE WRONG PASS! *YOU—DETENTION!!*

One day I came home from school and picked up the paper. The headline read: "26th Amendment Passes—Voting Age Lowered to 18." Below that was another headline: "School Board President to Retire, Seat Up for Election."

Hmm. I called the county clerk.

"Uh, I'm gonna be eighteen in a few weeks. If I can vote, does that I mean I can also run for office?"

"Let me see," the lady replied. "That's a new question!"

Guide to Student Rights

As an American student you probably haven't learned much about the U.S. Constitution or about your civil rights, so here's a handy guide based on information from the American Civil Liberties Union (ACLU). For more facts about student rights, on subjects including dress codes, your school records, and discrimination based on sexual orientation, contact your state chapter of the ACLU or check their Web site at www.aclu.org/students/slfree.html.

* The First Amendment to the Constitution guarantees the right to free expression and free association. And according to the United States Supreme Court, these rights even apply to you, the lowly student—at least some of the time.

* In 1969, the Supreme Court (in *Tinker* v. *Des Moines Independent Community School District*) ruled that the First Amendment applies to students in public schools. Private schools have more leeway to set their own rules on free expression because they are not operated by the government.

* Public school students can express their opinions orally and in writing (in leaflets or on buttons, armbands or T-shirts), as long as they do not "materially and substantially" disrupt classes or other school activities.

✷ School officials can probably prohibit students from using "vulgar or indecent language," but they cannot censor only one side of a controversy.

✷ If you and other students produce your own newspaper and want to hand it out in school, administrators cannot censor you or prohibit distribution of the paper (unless it is "indecent" or handing it out disrupts school activities).

✷ But administrators *can* censor what appears in the official school paper (the one that is published with school money). In the 1988 decision *Hazelwood School District* v. *Kuhlmeier,* the United States Supreme Court held that public school administrators can censor student speech in official school publications or activities (like a school play, art exhibit, yearbook, or newspaper) if the officials think students are saying something inappropriate or harmful—even if it is not vulgar and does not disrupt any activity.

✷ Some states—including Colorado, California, Iowa, Kansas, and Massachusetts—have "High School Free Expression" laws that give students expanded free speech rights. Check with your local ACLU to find out if your state has such laws.

She ruffled through some papers and came back on the phone. "Yes," she said, "you can run. All you need to do is gather twenty signatures to place your name on the ballot."

Twenty signatures? That's it? I had no idea running for elective office required so little work. I got the twenty signatures, submitted my petition, and started campaigning. My platform? "Fire the high school principal and the assistant principal!"

Alarmed at the idea that a high school student might actually find a legal means to remove the very administrators he was being paddled by, five local "adults" took out petitions and got themselves added to the ballot, too.

Of course, they ended up splitting the older adult vote five ways—and I won, getting the vote of every single stoner between the ages of eighteen and twenty-five (who, though many would probably never vote again, relished the thought of sending their high school wardens to the gallows).

The day after I won, I was walking down the hall at school (I had one more week to serve out as a student), and I passed the assistant principal, my shirt tail proudly untucked.

"Good morning, Mr. Moore," he said tersely. The day before, my name had been "Hey-You!" Now I was his boss.

Within nine months after I took my seat on the school board, the principal and assistant principal had submitted their "letters of resignation," a face-saving device employed when one is "asked" to step down. A couple of years later the principal suffered a heart attack and died.

I had known this man, the principal, for many years. When I was eight years old, he used to let me and my friends skate and play hockey on this little pond beside his house. He was kind and generous, and always left the door to his house open in case any of us needed to change into our skates or if we got cold and just wanted to get warm. Years later, I was asked to play bass in a band that was forming, but I didn't own a bass. He let me borrow his son's.

I offer this to remind myself that all people are actually good at their core, and to remember that someone with whom I grew to have serious disputes was also someone with a free cup of hot chocolate for us shivering little brats from the neighborhood.

Teachers are now the politicians' favorite punching bag. To listen to the likes of Chester Finn, a former assistant secretary of education in Bush the Elder's administration, you'd think all that has crumbled in our society can be traced back to lax, lazy, and incompetent teachers. "If you put out a Ten-Most-Wanted list of who's killing American education, I'm not sure who you would have higher on the list: the teachers' union or the education school faculties," Finn said.

Sure, there are a lot of teachers who suck, and they'd be better suited to making telemarketing calls for Amway. But the vast majority are dedicated educators who have chosen a profession that pays them less than what some of their students earn selling Ecstasy, and for that sacrifice we seek to punish them. I don't know about you, but I want the people who have the direct attention of my child more hours a day than I do treated with tender loving care. Those are my kids they're "preparing" for this world, so why on earth would I want to piss them off?

You would think society's attitude would be something like this:

Teachers, thank you so much for devoting your life to my child. Is there ANYTHING I can do to help you? Is there ANYTHING you need? I am here for you. Why? Because you are helping my child—MY BABY—learn and grow. Not only will you be largely responsible for her ability to make a living, but your influence will greatly affect how she views the world, what she knows about other people in this world, and how she will feel about herself. I want her to believe she can attempt anything— that no doors are closed and that no dreams are too distant. I am entrusting the most valuable person in my life to you for seven hours each day. You, are thus, one of the most important people in my life! Thank you.

No, instead, this is what teachers hear:

* "You've got to wonder about teachers who claim to put the interests of children first—and then look to milk the system dry through wage hikes." (*New York Post*, 12/26/00)

* "Estimates of the number of bad teachers range from 5 percent to 18 percent of the 2.6 million total." (Michael Chapman, *Investor's Business Daily*, 9/21/98)

* "Most education professionals belong to a closed community of devotees . . . who follow popular philosophies rather than research on what works." (Douglas Carminen, quoted in the *Montreal Gazette*, 1/6/01)

* "Teachers unions have gone to bat for felons and teachers who have had sex with students, as well as those who simply couldn't teach." (Peter Schweizen, *National Review*, 8/17/98)

What kind of priority do we place on education in America? Oh, it's on the funding list—somewhere down between OSHA and meat inspectors. The person who cares for our child every day receives an average of $41,351 annually. A Congressman who cares only about which tobacco lobbyist is taking him to dinner tonight receives $145,100.

Considering the face-slapping society gives our teachers on a daily basis, is it any wonder so few choose the profession? The national teacher shortage is so big that some school systems are recruiting teachers outside the United States. Chicago recently recruited and hired teachers from twenty-eight foreign countries, including China, France, and Hungary. By the time the new term begins in New York City, seven thousand veteran teachers will have retired—and 60 percent of the new teachers hired to replace them are uncertified.

But here's the kicker for me: 163 New York City schools opened the 2000–2001 school year *without a principal*! You heard right—school, with *no one in charge*. Apparently the mayor and the school board are experimenting with chaos theory—throw five hundred poor kids into a crumbling building, and watch nature take its course! In the city from which most of the wealth in the world is controlled, where there are more millionaires per square foot than there is gum on the sidewalk, we somehow can't find the money to pay a starting teacher more than $31,900 a year. And we act surprised when we can't get results.

And it's not just teachers who have been neglected—American schools are *literally* falling apart. In 1999 one-quarter of U.S. public schools reported that the condition of at least one of their buildings was inadequate. In 1997 the entire Washington, D.C., school system had to delay the start of school for three weeks because nearly *one-third* of the schools were found to be unsafe.

Almost 10 percent of U.S. public schools have enrollments that are more than 25 percent greater than the capacity of their permanent buildings. Classes have to be held in the hallways, outdoors, in the gym, in the cafeteria; one school I visited even held classes in a janitor's closet. It's not as if the janitor's closets are being used for anything related to cleaning, anyway—in New York City almost 15 percent of the eleven hundred public schools are without full-time custodians, forcing teachers to mop their own floors and students to do without toilet paper. We already send our kids out into the street to hawk candy bars so their schools can buy band instruments—what's next? Car washes to raise money for toilet paper?

Further proof of just how special our little offspring are is the number of public and even school libraries that have been shut down or had their hours cut back. The last thing we need is a bunch of kids hanging out around a bunch of books!

Apparently "President" Bush agrees: in his first budget he

proposed cutting federal spending on libraries by $39 million, down to $168 million—a nearly 19 percent reduction. Just the week before, his wife, former school librarian Laura Bush, kicked off a national campaign for America's libraries, calling them "community treasure chests, loaded with a wealth of information available to everyone, equally." The President's mother, Barbara Bush, heads the Foundation for Family Literacy. Well, there's nothing like having firsthand experience with illiteracy in the family to motivate one into acts of charity.

For kids who are exposed to books at home, the loss of a library is sad. But for kids who come from environments where people don't read, the loss of a library is a tragedy that might keep them from ever discovering the joys of reading—or from gathering the kind of information that will decide their lot in life. Jonathan Kozol, for decades an advocate for disadvantaged children, has observed that school libraries "remain the clearest window to a world of noncommercial satisfactions and entice-ments that most children in poor neighborhoods will ever know."

Kids deprived of access to good libraries are also being kept from developing the information skills they need to keep up in workplaces that are increasingly dependent on rapidly changing information. The ability to conduct research is "probably the most essential skill [today's students] can have," says Julie Walker, executive director of the American Association of School Librari-ans. "The knowledge [students] acquire in school is not going to serve them throughout their lifetimes. Many of them will have four to five careers in a lifetime. It will be their ability to navigate information that will matter."

Who's to blame for the decline in libraries? Well, when it comes to school libraries, you can start by pointing the finger (yes, *that* finger) at Richard Nixon. From the 1960s until 1974, school libraries received specific funding from the government. But in 1974 the Nixon administration changed the rules, stipulat-

Literacy Programs

Barbara Bush Foundation for Family Literacy
1112 16th Street NW
Suite 340
Washington, DC 20036
202-955-6183
www.barbarabushfoundation.com

Literacy Volunteers of America
635 James Street
Syracuse, NY 13203-2214
315-472-0001
www.literacyvolunteers.org

Even Start Family Literacy Program
U.S. Department of Education
400 Maryland Avenue SW
Washington, DC 20202
202-260-0991
www.ed.gov/offices/OESE/CEP/programs.html#prog3

America Reads Challenge
U.S. Department of Education
400 Maryland Avenue SW
Washington, DC 20202
202-401-0596
www.ed.gov/inits/americareads/

National Center for Family Literacy
Waterfront Plaza, Suite 200
325 W. Main Street
Louisville, KY 40202-4251
502-584-0172
www.famlit.org

ing that federal education money be doled out in "block grants" to be spent by states however they chose. Few states chose to spend the money on libraries, and the downslide began. This is one reason that materials in many school libraries today date from the 1960s and early 1970s, before funding was diverted. ("No, Sally, the Soviet Union isn't our enemy. The Soviet Union has been kaput for ten years. . . .")

This 1999 account by an *Education Week* reporter about the "library" at a Philadelphia elementary school could apply to any number of similarly neglected schools:

> Even the best books in the library at T. M. Pierce Elementary School are dated, tattered, and discolored. The worst—many in a latter stage of disintegration—are dirty and fetid and leave a moldy residue on hands and clothing. Chairs and tables are old, mismatched, or broken. There isn't a computer in sight. . . . Outdated facts and theories and offensive stereotypes leap from the authoritative pages of encyclopedias and biographies, fiction and nonfiction tomes. Among the volumes on these shelves a student would find it all but impossible to locate accurate information on AIDS or other contemporary diseases, explorations of the moon and Mars, or the past five U.S. presidents.

The ultimate irony in all of this is that the very politicians who refuse to fund education in America adequately are the same ones who go ballistic over how our kids have fallen behind the Germans, the Japanese, and just about every other country with running water and an economy not based on the sale of Chiclets. Suddenly they want "accountability." They want the teachers held responsible and to be tested. And they want the kids to be tested—over and over and over.

There's nothing terribly wrong with the concept of using standardized testing to determine whether kids are learning to read and write and do math. But too many politicians and education bureaucrats have created a national obsession with testing, as if everything that's wrong with the educational system in this country would be magically fixed if we could just raise those scores.

The people who really should be tested (besides the yammering pundits) are the so-called political leaders. Next time you see your state representative or congressman, give him this pop quiz—and remind him that any future pay raises will be based on how well he scores:

1. What is the annual pay of your average constituent?

2. What percent of welfare recipients are children?

3. How many known species of plants and animals are on the brink of extinction?

4. How big is the hole in the ozone layer?

5. Which African countries have a lower infant mortality rate than Detroit?

6. How many American cities still have two competing newspapers?

7. How many ounces in a gallon?

8. Which do I stand a greater chance of being killed by: a gun shot in school or a bolt of lightning?

9. What's the only state capital without a McDonald's?

10. Describe the story of either *The Iliad* or *The Odyssey*.

ANSWERS

1. $28,548

2. 67 percent

3. 11,046

4. 10.5 million square miles

5. Libya, Mauritius, Seychelles

6. 34

7. 128 ounces

8. You're twice as likely to be killed by lightning as by a gun-shot in school.

9. Montpelier, Vermont

10. *The Iliad* is an ancient Greek epic poem by Homer about the Trojan War. *The Odyssey* is another epic poem by Homer recounting the ten-year journey home from the Trojan War made by Odysseus, the king of Ithaca.

Chances are, the genius representing you in the legislature won't score 50 percent on the above test. The good news is that you get to flunk him within a year or two.

There is one group in the country that isn't just sitting around carping about all them lamebrain teachers—a group that cares deeply about what kinds of students will enter the adult world. You could say they have a vested interest in this captive audience of millions of young people . . . or in the billions of dollars they spend each year. (Teenagers alone spent more than $150 billion last year.) Yes, it's Corporate America, whose generosity to our nation's schools is just one more example of their continuing patriotic service.

Just how committed are these companies to our children's schools?

According to numbers collected by the Center for the Analysis of Commercialism in Education (CACE), their selfless charity has seen a tremendous boom since 1990. Over the past ten years, school programs and activities have seen corporate sponsorship increase by 248 percent. In exchange for this sponsorship, schools allow the corporation to associate its name with the events.

For example, Eddie Bauer sponsors the final round of the National Geography Bee. Book covers featuring Calvin Klein and Nike ads are distributed to students. Nike and other shoemakers, looking for early access to tomorrow's stars, sponsor inner-city high school basketball teams.

Pizza Hut set up its "Book-It!" program to encourage children to read. When students meet the monthly reading goal, they are rewarded with a certificate for a Pizza Hut personal pan pizza. At the restaurant, the store manager personally congratulates the children and gives them each a sticker and a certificate. Pizza Hut suggests school principals place a "Pizza Hut Book-It!" honor roll list in the school for everyone to see.

General Mills and Campbell's Soup thought up a better plan. Instead of giving free rewards, they both have programs rewarding schools for getting parents to buy their products. Under General Mills's "Box Tops for Education" program, schools get ten cents for each box top logo they send in, and can earn up to $10,000 a year. That's 100,000 General Mills products sold. Campbell's Soup's "Labels for Education" program is no better. It touts itself as "Providing America's children with FREE school equipment!" Schools can earn one "free" Apple iMac computer for only 94,950 soup labels. Campbell's suggests setting a goal of a label a day from each student. With Campbell's conservative estimate of five labels per week per child, all you need is a school of 528 kids to get that free computer.

It's not just this kind of sponsorship that brings these schools and corporations together. The 1990s saw a phenomenal 1,384 percent increase in exclusive agreements between schools and soft-drink bottlers. Two hundred and forty school districts in thirty-one states have sold exclusive rights to one of the big three soda companies (Coca-Cola, Pepsi, Dr. Pepper) to push their products in schools. Anybody wonder why there are more over-weight kids than ever before? Or more young women with calcium deficiencies because they're drinking less milk? And even though federal law prohibits the sale of soft drinks in schools until lunch periods begin, in some overcrowded schools "lunch" begins in midmorning. Artificially flavored carbonated sugar water—the breakfast of champions! (In March 2001 Coke responded to public pressure, announcing that it would add water, juice, and other sugar-free, caffeine-free, and calcium-rich alternatives to soda to its school vending machines.)

I guess they can afford such concessions when you consider their deal with the Colorado Springs school district. Colorado has been a trailblazer when it comes to tie-ins between the schools and soft drink companies. In Colorado Springs, the district will receive $8.4 million over ten years from its deal with Coca-Cola—and more if it exceeds its "requirement" of selling seventy thousand cases of Coke products a year. To ensure the levels are met, school district officials urged principals to allow students unlimited access to Coke machines and allow students to drink Coke in the classroom.

But Coke isn't alone. In the Jefferson County, Colorado, school district (home of Columbine High School), Pepsi con-tributed $1.5 million to help build a new sports stadium. Some county schools tested a science course, developed in part by Pepsi, called "The Carbonated Beverage Company." Students taste-tested colas, analyzed cola samples, watched a video tour of a Pepsi bottling plant, and visited a local plant.

The school district in Wylie, Texas, signed a deal in 1996 that shared the rights to sell soft drinks in the schools between Coke and Dr. Pepper. Each company paid $31,000 a year. Then, in 1998, the county changed its mind and signed a deal with Coke worth $1.2 million over fifteen years. Dr. Pepper sued the county for breach of contract. The school district bought out Dr. Pepper's contract, costing them $160,000—plus another $20,000 in legal fees.

It's not just the companies that sometimes get sent packing. Students who lack the proper corporate school spirit do so at considerable risk. When Mike Cameron wore a Pepsi shirt on "Coke Day" at Greenbrier High School in Evans, Georgia, he was suspended for a day. "Coke Day" was part of the school's entry in a national "Team Up With Coca-Cola" contest, which awards $10,000 to the high school that comes up with the best plan for distributing Coke discount cards. Greenbrier school officials said Cameron was suspended for "being disruptive and trying to destroy the school picture" when he removed an outer shirt and revealed the Pepsi shirt as a photograph was being taken of students posed to spell out the word *Coke*. Cameron said the shirt was visible all day, but he didn't get in trouble until posing for the picture. No slouch in the marketing department, Pepsi quickly sent the high school senior a box of Pepsi shirts and hats.

If turning the students into billboards isn't enough, schools and corporations sometimes turn the school itself into one giant neon sign for corporate America. Appropriation of school space, including scoreboards, rooftops, walls, and textbooks, for corporate logos and advertising is up 539 percent.

Colorado Springs, not satisfied to sell its soul only to Coca-Cola, has plastered its school buses with advertisements for

Burger King, Wendy's, and other big companies. Free book covers and school planners with ads for Kellogg's Pop-Tarts and pictures of FOX TV personalities were also handed out to the students.

After members of the Grapevine-Colleyville Independent School District in Texas decided they didn't want advertisements in the classrooms, they allowed Dr. Pepper and 7-Up logos to be painted on the rooftops of two high schools. The two high schools, not coincidentally, lie under the Dallas airport flight path.

The schools aren't just looking for ways to advertise; they're also concerned with the students' perceptions of various products. That's why, in some schools, companies conduct market research in classrooms during school hours. Education Market Resources of Kansas reports that "children respond openly and easily to questions and stimuli" in the classroom setting. (Of course, that's what they're *supposed* to be doing in a classroom—but for their own benefit, not that of some corporate pollsters.) Filling out marketing surveys instead of learning, however, is probably *not* what they should be doing.

Companies have also learned they can reach this confined audience by "sponsoring" educational materials. This practice, like the others, has exploded as well, increasing 1,875 percent since 1990.

Teachers have shown a Shell Oil video that teaches students that the way to experience nature is by driving there—after filling your Jeep's gas tank at a Shell station. ExxonMobil prepared lesson plans about the flourishing wildlife in Prince William Sound, site of the ecological disaster caused by the oil spill from the Exxon *Valdez*. A third-grade math book features exercises involving counting Tootsie Rolls. A Hershey's-sponsored curriculum used in many schools features "The Chocolate Dream Machine," including lessons in math, science, geography—and nutrition.

In a number of high schools, the economics course is supplied by General Motors. GM writes and provides the textbooks and the course outline. Students learn from GM's example the benefits of capitalism and how to operate a company—like GM.

And what better way to imprint a corporate logo on the country's children than through television and the Internet beamed directly into the classroom. Electronic marketing, where a company provides programming or equipment to schools for the right to advertise to their students, is up 139 percent.

One example is the ZapMe! Corporation, which provides schools with a free computer lab and access to pre-selected Web sites. In return, schools must promise that the lab will be in use at least four hours a day. The catch? The ZapMe! Web browser has constantly scrolling advertisements—and the company gets to collect information on students' browsing habits, information they can then sell to other companies.

Perhaps the worst of the electronic marketers is Channel One Television. Eight million students in 12,000 classrooms watch Channel One, an in-school news *and advertising* program, every day. (That's right: EVERY day.) Kids are spending the equivalent of six full school days a year watching Channel One in almost 40 percent of U.S. middle and high schools. Instructional time lost to the ads alone? One entire day per year. That translates into an annual cost to taxpayers of more than $1.8 billion.

Sure, doctors and educators agree that our kids can never watch enough TV. And there's probably a place in school for some television programs—I have fond memories of watching astronauts blasting off on the television rolled into my grade school auditorium. But out of the daily twelve-minute Channel One broadcasts, only 20 percent of the airtime is devoted to stories about politics, the economy, and cultural and social issues.

That leaves a whopping 80 percent for advertising, sports, weather, features, and Channel One promotions.

Channel One is disproportionately shown in schools in low income communities with large minority populations, where the least money is available for education, and where the least amount is spent on textbooks and other academic materials. Once these districts receive corporate handouts, government's failure to provide adequate school funding tends to remain unaddressed.

Are You A Potential School Shooter?

The following is a list of traits the FBI has identified as "risk factors" among students who may commit violent acts. Stay away from any student showing signs of:

* Poor coping skills
* Access to weapons
* Depression
* Drug and alcohol abuse
* Alienation
* Narcissism
* Inappropriate humor
* Unlimited, unmonitored television and Internet use

Since this includes all of you, drop out of school immediately. Home schooling is not a viable option, because you must also stay away from yourself.

For most of us, the only time we enter an American high school is to vote at our local precinct. (There's an irony if there ever was one—going to participate in democracy's sacred ritual while two thousand students in the same building live under some sort of totalitarian dictatorship.) The halls are packed with burned-out teenagers shuffling from class to class, dazed and confused, wondering what the hell they're doing there. They learn how to regurgitate answers the state wants them to give, and any attempt to be an individual is now grounds for being suspected to be a member of the trench coat mafia. I visited a school recently, and some students asked me if I noticed that they and the other students in the school were all wearing white or some neutral color. Nobody dares wear black, or anything else wild and distinct. That's a sure ticket to the principal's office—where the school psychologist will be waiting to ascertain whether that Limp Bizkit shirt you have on means that you intend to shoot up Miss Nelson's fourth hour geometry class.

So the kids learn to submerge any personal expression. They learn that it's better to go along so that you get along. They learn that to rock the boat could get them rocked right out of the school. Don't question authority. Do as you're told. Don't think, just do as I say.

Oh, and have a good and productive life as an active, well-adjusted participant in our thriving democracy!

HOW TO BE A STUDENT SUBVERSIVE INSTEAD OF A STUDENT SUBSERVIENT

There are many ways you can fight back at your high school—and have fun while doing it. The key thing is to learn what all the rules are, and what your rights are by law and by school district policy. This will help to prevent you getting in the kind of trouble you don't need.

It may also get you some cool perks. David Schankula, a college student who has helped me on this book, recalls that when he was in high school in Kentucky, he and his buddies found some obscure state law that said any student who requests a day off to go to the state fair must be given the day off. The state legislature probably passed this law years ago to help some farm kid take his prize hog to the fair without being penalized at school. But the law was still on the books, and it gave any student the right to request the state fair day off—regardless of the reason. So you can imagine the look on the principal's face when David and his city friends submitted their request for their free day off from school—and there was nothing the principal could do.

Here's a few more things you can do:

1. Mock the Vote.

Student council and class elections are the biggest smokescreen the school throws up, fostering the illusion that you actually have any say in the running of the school. Most students who run for these offices either take the charade too seriously—or they just think it'll look good on their college applications.

So why not run yourself? Run just to ridicule the whole ridiculous exercise. Form your own party, with its own stupid name. Campaign on wild promises: *If elected, I'll change the school mascot to an amoeba,* or *If elected, I'll insist that the principal must first eat the school lunch each day before it is fed to the students.* Put up banners with cool slogans: "Vote for me—a real loser!"

If you get elected, you can devote your energies to accomplishing things that will drive the administration crazy, but help out your fellow students (demands for free condoms, student evaluations of teachers, less homework so you can get to bed by midnight, etc).

2. Start a School Club.

You have a right to do this. Find a sympathetic teacher to sponsor it. The Pro-Choice Club. The Free Speech Club. The Integrate Our Town Club. Make every member a "president" of the club, so they all can claim it on their college applications. One student I know tried to start a Feminist Club, but the principal wouldn't allow it because then they'd be obliged to give equal time to a Male Chauvinist Club. That's the kind of idiot thinking you'll encounter, but don't give up. (Heck, if you find yourself in that situation, just say *fine*—and suggest the that principal could sponsor the Chauvinist Club.)

3. Launch Your Own Newspaper or Webzine.

You have a constitutionally protected right to do this. If you take care not to be obscene, or libelous, or give them any reason to shut you down, this can be a great way to get the truth out about what's happening at your school. Use humor. The students will love it.

4. Get Involved in the Community.

Go to the school board meetings and inform them what's going on in the school. Petition them to change things. They will try to ignore you or make you sit through a long, boring meeting before they let you speak, but they have to let you speak. Write letters to the editor of your local paper. Adults don't have a clue about what goes on in your high school. Fill them in. More than likely you'll find someone there who'll support you.

Any or all of this will raise quite a ruckus, but there's help out there if you need it. Contact the local American Civil Liberties Union if the school retaliates. Threaten lawsuits—school administrators HATE to hear that word. Just remember: there's no greater satisfaction than seeing the look on your principal's face when you have the upper hand. Use it.

And Never Forget This:

There Is No Permanent Record!

SIX

Nice Planet, Nobody Home

I'D LIKE TO begin this chapter by revealing what I believe is one of the greatest threats currently facing our environment.

Me.

That's right—I'm a walking ecological nightmare.

I am the Mother of All Bhopals!

Let's start with this: I don't recycle.

I think recycling is like going to church—you show up once a week, it makes you feel good, and you've done your duty. Then you can get back to all the fun of sinning!

Let me ask you this: do you honestly know where all those newspapers go after you drop them off at the recycling center, or where your soda pop bottles end up after you put them in the blue recycling containers? To some facility that will recycle them? Says who? Have you ever followed the truck that picks up your recyclables to see where it goes? Do you care? Is it enough for you to separate your glass from your plastic, your paper from your metals—and then leave the follow-though to someone else?

I will never cease to be amazed at the lemminglike nature of human beings and our unquestioning obedience to authority. If the sign says Recycle, we do our part, and assume everything we put in there will be recycled. If the trash can is blue, we figure that's a surefire guarantee that the glass jars we place in there will be crushed, melted down, and made into new bottles of Ragu.

Well, think again.

One night, coming home late from work, I witnessed the garbage men tossing those earnestly clear blue garbage bags full of glass into their truck's crusher along with all the other garbage. I asked the guy who works in our building if that was normal.

"They got a lot of garbage to pick up," he said. "Sometimes they don't have time to separate everything."

I wondered if this was just an anomaly—or the norm. Here's a few things I found out:

In the mid-1990s, Indian environmental activists discovered that Pepsi was creating a complicated waste disposal problem in their country. Used plastic from Pepsi bottles turned in for recycling in the United States was being shipped over to India to be recycled back into Pepsi bottles or other plastic containers. But the senior manager of the Futura Industry factory outside of Madras, where most of the waste was being dumped, admitted that much of it was never actually recycled. To make matters worse, at around the same time the truth about the recycling was revealed, the company announced that it was going to open a company in India that would manufacture—of course—single-use disposable bottles for export to the United States and Europe, leaving toxic byproducts behind in India. So while India has been bearing the environmental and health burdens, consumers in industrialized countries continue using plastic products without suffering any of the drawbacks. And all the while we consumers cruise blissfully along, confident that we're improving the environment by "recycling."

In another instance, a magazine in San Francisco contracted with a paper recycler to pick up all its white waste paper each month. When one employee followed the trash out the door one day, he saw that the paper intended for recycling was being tossed in with the discarded McDonald's wrappers and Starbucks cups. When confronted about it, the waste recycling company denied it.

In 1999 an investigation of what happens to all the waste created by Congress (insert your own joke here) discovered that 71 percent of the 2,670 tons of paper used that year by the legislative branch was not recycled because it had been mixed in with food waste and other nonrecyclable materials. That same year up to 5,000 tons of glass bottles, aluminum cans, cardboard, and other recyclable waste on Capitol Hill was simply dumped in a landfill, no questions asked. Had Congress properly recycled these products, it could have saved taxpayers up to $700,000.

In instance after instance, I found the same thing. No real recycling was taking place. We were being conned.

So I stopped recycling. I came to the conclusion that when I recycled, what I was really doing was letting myself off the hook. As long as I did my little paper-glass-metal separation duty, I wasn't required to do anything else to save Planet Earth. Once my bottles and cans and newspapers were deposited in the appropriately colored barrels, I could press reset on my conscience and trust that someone else would do the rest of the job. Out of sight, out of mind, back inside my gas-guzzling minivan.

Yes, I have a minivan. It gets about 15 miles a gallon, about 7 less than what the sticker said. I love this minivan. It's roomy, has a smooth ride, and sits a foot above the cars in front of me so I can see everything.

I know some people say we Americans are spoiled by our low prices at the gas pump compared with the rest of the world, which pays up to *three times* what we pay. But hey, this ain't Belgium, where you can drive across the entire country in something like thirty-five minutes. We live in a *huge* nation. We need to get around! We've got places to go, things to do. The rest of the world needs to understand that they *benefit* from our ability to get from Point A to Point B. How else are hardworking Americans supposed to get from their first job of the day to their second job at night—which is all part of a greater plan to create a global economy—if they don't have any wheels?

How to Use Less Gas

* *Hitchhike.* It's free; you get to meet new people and have interesting conversations. Bonus feature: strong likelihood of being featured (in a supporting role) on *America's Most Wanted* or in a Lifetime "Woman in Danger" made-for-TV movie.

* *Live in a city with mass transit.* But please don't come to New York City—it's already way too crowded. Try another American city with extensive, dependable mass transit like . . . like . . . well . . . oh, forget it, come to New York. I've got an extra room, you can stay with me.

* *Siphon gas from cars parked at airports.* They're not going anywhere. It's a shame to have all that gas just sitting there going to waste in these waste-conscious times. Plus, it's a safety hazard: just imagine what would happen if a plane were to crash into one of those airport parking lots with

thousands of parked cars filled to the brim with highly explosive petrol. Just don't swallow.

* *Drive behind large semi trucks so your wind drag is reduced.* Highway safety experts may advise against this practice, but it works. You can put the car on cruise and just sit back and enjoy the scenery. Drawback: you may find yourself in a remote truck stop having the crap beaten out of you by a guy with a tattoo on his forehead that says "Itch Me."

* *Live in your office or place of work.* Eliminates both the gas-guzzling commute and annoying monthly rent payments. Bonus: you'll impress the boss by always being the first one in and the last to leave.

See, I come from Flint, Michigan—the Vehicle City, not to be confused with the Motor City. We're an hour north of Detroit, and at one time my hometown built every Buick in the world. They don't build Buicks there any more.

Growing up immersed in a car culture, you come to see your car as an extension of yourself. Your car is your stereo room, your dining room, your bedroom, your home theatre, your office, your reading room, and the first place you do just about anything in your life that means anything.

When I became an adult I decided I didn't want a General Motors car—mainly because they broke down more often than I did. So I bought Volkswagens and Hondas and drove them around town with pride. If anyone asked me why I didn't "buy American," I'd make them open their hood and show them the MADE IN BRAZIL plate on their engine, the MADE IN

MEXICO lettering on their fan belt, and the MADE IN SIN-GAPORE label on their radio. Other than the tag on the dashboard implying the entire car was made in America, what exactly could they point to in their car that actually gave a job to anyone in Flint?

My Honda Civic never broke down. For eight years and 115,000 miles, I never had it in the shop for any reason other than regularly scheduled maintenance. The day it died I was broke and on unemployment and stuck in the middle of Pennsylvania Avenue about four blocks from the White House. I just got out, pushed it over to the curb, removed the plates, and bid it farewell.

I didn't buy another car for nine years. Working most of the time in New York City I didn't need one, thanks to the city's fine mass transportation system and reliable taxi drivers. But because I spend a lot of time back home in Michigan, I got tired of renting from Avis and broke down and bought a Chrysler minivan. This much I'll say—you'll never see me stuff myself like a sausage by driving around one of those little tin cans again!

The internal combustion engine has done more to create global warming than anything else on the planet. Almost half the pollutants in our air come from the stuff that spews out of your car—and that air pollution is the cause of some 200,000 deaths per year. Global warming is jacking up the world's temperature, year after year, which can cause increased risk of drought in some countries and have dangerous effects on agriculture and health. We're perilously close to creating a horrible calamity if we don't figure out how to turn down the heat.

But you should see how this minivan handles! And it's so quiet inside—that is, until I crank up my Korn on the combination CD/tape surround-sound deck, complete with eight bitchin' speakers. I can drive 400 miles straight with the music cranked, the air conditioning cranked, the hands-free satellite phone ready to take that all-important call from Rupert Murdoch thanking me for the fine work on this book and letting me know that my execution has been moved up to Thursday so as not to conflict with *America's Wackiest School Shooting Videos*.

Detroit has proved it has the technology to mass-produce cars that get 45 miles per gallon and trucks and vans that get 35 miles per gallon. The year the auto companies reported their best gas mileage—1987, during the reign of Ronald Reagan—the average car got 26 miles per gallon. Yet after the eight years of eco-friendly Bill Clinton—who promised that cars would be getting 40 miles per gallon by the end of his presidency—the average miles per gallon for vehicles went *down* to 24.7. General Motors threw a lavish party in Washington for Clinton's 1993 inauguration. I guess it's just impolite to upset the host of a party given in your honor.

Clinton's greatest gift to the Big Three automakers was exempting SUVs from the mileage requirements of regular passenger cars. Because of this exemption, these gas gluttons use up an extra 280,000 barrels of fuel *each day*. That fuel demand is one of the reasons the Bush administration is pushing to drill in the Arctic National Preserve in Alaska. Bush says the drilling will give us an extra 580,000 barrels of oil each day, enough to double the number of SUVs on the road.

And yet consider: if SUVs had been forced by Clinton to meet the same gas mileage standards my minivan meets (an improvement of only a few miles per gallon), Bush would have no justification for drilling in Alaska.

With all these SUVs on the road, I can no longer see over the vehicle in front of me. They're so big and intimidating, they're like a midget 18-wheeler on crack. What exactly is the point of an SUV? Initially they were developed to give one the ability to drive in the middle of nowhere where there are no roads. I understand how that might make sense in Montana, but what the hell are all these yuppies doing inside them charging down a crowded street in Manhattan?

In June of 2001, a panel of top American scientists reported that global warming was a real problem, and it was getting worse. In their study, requested by the Bush II White House, the group of eleven leading atmospheric scientists (including several who were previously skeptical about the scope of the problem) concluded that human activity is largely responsible for the warming of the earth's atmosphere—and that we're in serious trouble as a result.

The release of the study put George "I Sleep Just Fine" Bush in a tough spot. He and other members of his administration had pointedly avoided using the phrase "global warming" and had repeatedly expressed doubts about the idea that air pollution was heating the atmosphere in dangerous ways. Bush also outraged international leaders in July of 2001 when he rejected the Kyoto Protocol, a pact originally negotiated by more than 160 nations (including the United States) and designed to reduce global warming.

But now Bush's own scientists were saying the Earth was on its way to a major catastrophe.

Well, I dunno: Maybe Young George has a point on this one. After all, I *like* it warm. Coming from Michigan, land of brutal winters and the three-week summer, I kind of enjoy this more "temperate" climate. Ask people if they'd rather have a nice scorchin' hot day at the beach or a bitter, frigid Alberta Clipper that makes their tongues stick to their teeth, and I'll bet you 9 out of 10 Americans already have their shades on and the portable Weber in the trunk. So what if you need sunscreen that says 125 SPF?

Last summer, though, something happened that I found slightly shocking. The *New York Times* reported that for the first time in recorded history the North Pole had ... *melted*. A shipload of scientists boated right up to the top of the world—and the ice was gone! The news induced such panic that within days the *Times* ran a correction, trying to reassure us: it wasn't *really* melted, just a little squishy. *Right*. I remember the last time they tried to quiet things down—back in the 1990s, when they told us about the big asteroid that was heading for a collision with Earth sometime in the next twenty years. Again they took it back immediately, but they should know we can see right through that kind of withdrawal. The powers that be are never going to tell us when the end is nigh, given the risk of mass pandemonium and subscription cancellations it would cause.

The last Ice Age was the result of a global temperature change of only *9 degrees*. Right now, we're halfway there. Some experts are predicting a rise in temperature of 10.4 degrees just in the next century. In Venezuela, four of the country's six glaciers have melted since 1972. The fabled snows of Kilimanjaro are almost gone. When the lighthouse at Cape Hatteras was built in 1870, it was 1,500 feet from the shore; by now the tide has risen to within 160 feet of it, and the lighthouse has had to be moved farther inland.

A melting of the polar ice caps could cause the oceans to rise by up to 30 feet, in effect wiping out every coastal city there is— and taking out the entire state of Florida (voting booths and all). I realize places like New York and Los Angeles could use a good scrubbing, but three stories of salt water over the whole island of Manhattan wasn't what I had in mind.

Speaking of Florida, that state can also be held responsible for *this* sorry mess. Why? Ask Mr. Freon. Before air conditioning, Florida and the rest of the South were lightly populated. The heat and humidity were unbearable. I mean, you can barely *move* on a 100-degree day in Texas. The air is so thick in New Orleans you can hardly breathe. No wonder people down South spoke with such an unintelligible drawl. It was just too damn hot to form a series of vowels and consonants. I believe this brutal, paralyzing heat is also the reason no great inventions, no new ideas,

How to Survive Global Warming

* Identify common household objects that could serve as flotation devices once the ice caps melt. Give special attention to items made of synthetic materials, which tend to be extremely water-resistant.

* Don't forget to look outside, too—those water-proof chairs with built-in cup holders will float just as well in the ocean as in your backyard pool. Who says catastrophic polar meltdown can't be fun?

* Examine topographical maps of your area to determine highest elevation; map out quickest route there. Hold escape drills.

* Invest in Ziploc bags and those yellow waterproof cameras.

* Contact your local YMCA about swimming lessons. Take lessons. *Now.* Pay special attention to instructions for treading water.

* Change your vacation plans from Florida to Montana. Tell your kids to switch their spring break alcohol binge from Daytona Beach to Boise.

and no contributions toward advancing our civilization ever came out of the South (with a few notable exceptions: Lillian Hellman, William Faulkner, R.J. Reynolds). When it's that hot, who can think, let alone read?

Then the air conditioner was invented—and suddenly you could actually get some work done in the South. Skyscrapers went up all over the region—and northerners, sick of the winter, came down in droves. They found that you could drive to work in your air-conditioned car, work all day in your air-conditioned office, study all day in your air-conditioned college. Then you could go home at night to your air-conditioned house to plan the weekend's cross-burning and block club barbecue.

Before we knew it, the South had risen and was now controlling the country. Today, the conserva-tive ideology that was born in the Confederate South has the nation in its grip. Mandating that the Ten Commandments be posted in pub-lic places; teaching creationism; insisting on prayer in school; ban-ning books; fomenting hatred of the federal (northern) government; calling for reduction of govern-ment and social services; thirsting to go to war at a moment's notice;

Things the South Was Right About

Just to balance my portrait of the South as a land of sweat-stained Klansters and latter-day corporate outposts, I've been asked to come up with a list of things we are thankful to the South for giving us. Here it is:

* Beef jerky
* Lemonade
* Fancy balls
* Good manners
* Country music
* Napping in hammocks
* Beauty queens
* Michael Jordan
* Wal-Mart
* Alligator wrestling
* Walt Disney World

and looking to resolve any problem through violence—these are all trademarks of the elected lawmakers of the "New" South. If you think about it, the Confederacy has finally won the Civil War—a long-awaited victory won by luring stupid Yankees down there with a promise of 5,000 BTUs and a built-in icemaker.

Now the South reigns supreme—and if you still don't believe it, just look at our last four presidential elections. If you wanted to win, you had to have been born in the South or adopted it as your home. In fact, in the last *ten* presidential elections, the winner (or Supreme Court appointee) was the one with his feet planted most firmly in the South or West. No longer can anyone from the North get elected to lead the nation.

Air conditioning made it all possible. And now, having opened the door to southern pols and Dixie climes, it's also promising to export those hot southern winds all over the world—by making the hole in the ozone layer a reality. That hole is now over Antarctica—and is two and a half times the size of *Europe*!

The ozone layer in the earth's atmosphere protects us from ultraviolet (UV) radiation, which can give us cancer and kill us. The hole we've ripped in its fabric is caused by chlorinated fluorocarbons (CFCs), chemicals typically used in air conditioners and refrigerators and as propellants in aerosol cans. When these

How to Make Sure Your Drinking Water Is Safe

* Lobby Congress to make bottled water the nation's Official Beverage.

* Reroute and connect city water pipelines directly to the sources of spring water used by commercial bottlers. If that means running feeder pipelines under the Atlantic to tap into some pure alpine water, so be it. We ran a telephone cable under the ocean—surely we can lay a pipe beside it to quench our thirst.

chemicals are released into the atmosphere and struck by high-energy light waves such as ultraviolet light, they form compounds that destroy ozone. The biggest contributor of ozone-depleting CFCs? Car air-conditioning units—one of America's favorite traveling companions.

Which reminds me of another (literally) indispensable accessory du jour for hip young Americans on the go: bottled water. Why drink water out of a tap or fountain for free when you can pay $1.20 for the same thing—*and* get a plastic bottle you can pretend to recycle later?

I didn't always drink bottled water in New York. In fact, I used to put faith in the folk legend that New York's water supply is among the cleanest in the world. The water itself, I learned, is collected and stored in twenty-two open-air reservoirs in the Catskills and upper Hudson River area and brought down to the city through an elaborate aqueduct system. It all sounded so pristine.

But one night, at a party at a friend's house, an acquaintance remarked that he and his family "try to get up to our cabin on the Croton Reservoir every chance we get."

I asked, "How can you have a cabin on the shores of our drinking water?"

"Oh, it's not right *on* the reservoir. It's across the road."

"You mean, there's a *highway* that surrounds the water we drink? What about all the runoff from the road, all those oil spills and tire shavings and the like?"

"Oh, they sterilize everything once the water gets to New York City," he replied.

"You can't sterilize anything once it gets here!" I protested. "By the time it gets to New York it must already have every known germ-killing agent available to mankind already in full battle mode."

He then went on to rhapsodize about how wonderful it is to boat around the reservoir.

Other Water Additives I'd Like to See

The government currently adds fluoride to the water supply, while many fine companies make products that add caffeine, vitamins, fruit flavors, and microscopic disease-causing organisms to bottled water. But can't they do better? Why stop with something the dentist says is good for you? Besides, there's already fluoride in the toothpaste! Why not make water available in these popular flavors:

* Beef bouillon
* Tex-Mex
* Prozac-enhanced
* Spicy Cajun!
* Soy-based toffee
* Chunky-style tomato
* Cool Ranch (lite)

"BOAT?" I cried. "You're boating in my drinking water?"

"Oh, sure—and fishing, too! The state lets us keep our boat right on the shore."

That was when the cases of Evian began entering my apartment.

Of course, the downside of drinking bottled water (other than the outrageous cost) is that, like the recycling bins, it prevents me from giving a moment's further thought to the state of our water in America. As long as I can sell enough books to afford my "French" spring water, why should I waste any time worrying about the PCBs General Electric has dumped in the Hudson River? After all, hundreds of years ago the Indians dumped their refuse into the Hudson, and the early white settlers used the river as a nonstop sewage drain. And look at the great metropolis they went on to create!

Manhattan is also a great place to get a steak. Until a few years ago, I don't think there was day in my adult life when I didn't eat beef—and often twice a day. Then, for no distinct reason, one

Where's the Beef? Nowhere!
How to Become a Hindu

Entering Hinduism has traditionally required little more than accepting and living according to Hindu beliefs. Among those beliefs is that the cow should be revered as a mother to all because of the nourishing milk it provides. Therefore slaughter of cows is sacrilegious.

Generally, the steps to becoming a Hindu are:

* Join a Hindu worship community (you can find one near you at www.hindu.org/temples-ashrams/).

* Complete a course of study comparing Hinduism to other beliefs.

* Discuss your changed beliefs with representatives of your former faith, and if needed, obtain a letter of release from your former religious organization.

* Adopt a Hindu name at a name-giving ceremony.

* Run an announcement in a local newspaper for three days explaining that you have severed your ties with your former faith and have adopted a new name.

* Obtain a certificate testifying that an authorized Hindu priest has approved your entrance into the faith.

day I just stopped eating it. I went a full four years without a morsel of cow passing my lips. I have to say those were the four healthiest years I've ever had. (Note: Guys like me define *healthy* as "I didn't die.")

Maybe it was hearing Oprah Winfrey say on her show back in 1996 that learning about mad cow disease "just stopped me cold from eating another burger." Of course, Oprah then had to contend with a threat that was equally dangerous: the Texas cattlemen, who sued her (and the former rancher and beef lobbyist who appeared on the show to speak about the dangers of mad cow disease) for $12 million. They claimed that Oprah and Howard Lyman violated a Texas statute that prohibits the false disparagement of perishable food products. (Please note that it was *Oprah* who said she was "stopped cold from eating another burger," not me—because, again, nobody here wants to be sued.) Oprah won the lawsuit in 1998; then, just to mess with their heads in Texas, she declared, "I'm still off hamburgers."

I, on the other hand, have unfortunately fallen off the chuck wagon, nibbling every now and then on poor Elsie. You'd think I would have learned my lesson back in the mid seventies when, instead of eating beef, I ate fire retardant.

Like millions of Michiganders, I spent a year ingesting PBB, the chemical used in kids' pajamas—and didn't even know it. The PBB came in the form of a product called Firemaster, manufactured by a company that also happened to make cattle feed. At one point they accidentally mixed up the bags they poured the stuff into and sent the fire retardant (labeled as "feed") to a big centralized operation in Michigan that distributed the feed to farms all over the state. Soon the cows were eating PBB—and we were eating the cows and drinking their milk, full of PBB.

The problem with PBB is that the body doesn't excrete it or eliminate it in any way. It just stays in your stomach and digestive system. When this fiasco was uncovered—and we learned that the state of Michigan had tried to keep the news from the public—the residents of Michigan flipped out. Heads rolled, politicians were thrown out of office. And we were told that scientists had no idea what the PBB would do to us—and we probably wouldn't find out for another twenty-five years.

> ## Other Things I Have Eaten That Were Meant for Industrial Use
>
> * Pop-Tarts
> * Tab
> * Mom's meatloaf
> * Tang
> * Spam
> * Hostess pink Sno Balls
> * Stuff inside wax "lips"
> * Airplane breakfast sausages

Well, the quarter-century fuse has run out, and I guess the good news is that my stomach has never caught on fire. But I'm still sitting here full of anxiety, waiting for the other hoof to drop. I can't help thinking about Centralia, Pennsylvania—the town where residents continued about their daily business while underground fires raged on nonstop for years. Science does NOT have an answer for everything! Are millions of Michiganders fixing to develop fleece-lined cancers and kick the milk bucket? Or will we just lose our minds and find ourselves working for a candidate who can't win but can do a lot of collateral damage?

I don't have the answers, and neither does anyone else. If you know a native Michigander (and I guarantee there's one within shouting distance of you right now, thanks to the Reagan-sponsored diaspora of our people in the 1980s), ask her about PBB and see the ashen look that crosses her face. It's the dirty little secret we don't like to discuss.

* * *

But there's a much greater bovine threat afoot among us today—one that knows no state or regional boundaries, one that deserves the Poeian moniker it wears like a bell around the neck.

Mad cow.

This is truly the scariest threat the human race has ever faced. Worse than AIDS, worse than the black plague, worse than not flossing.

Mad cow disease has no cure. It has no preventive vaccine. Everyone who gets it dies, without exception, a gruesomely painful death.

And the worst part is that this is a man-made disease—born of a moment of human madness, when we took innocent cows and turned them into cannibals. Here's how it started:

Two researchers went to Papua New Guinea to study the effects of human cannibalism and how it made many Papuans go insane. They discovered that what these people were suffering from was a transmissible spongiform encephalopathic disease (or TSE). The native people called it kuru. What happens in TSE is that rogue proteins—prions—latch onto brain cells and twist into abnormal shapes. Instead of breaking down the way a good protein is supposed to do, these guys hang out and make a mess of your nervous tissue, leaving your brain full of holes like a wheel of well-aged Swiss.

Turns out that in Papua New Guinea, these prions were being spread by cannibalism. No one seems to know where these prions originally come from, but when they get into your system they wreak havoc. Some suggest that a mere speck of prion-infected meat—only the size of a peppercorn—is enough to infect a cow. Once the little buggers are released from the beef you've ingested, they spread like an army of Pac Men, heading straight for your brain and devouring everything in sight.

And here's the unbelievable part—you can't kill them . . . *because they're not alive!*

The disease first entered the food chain in Britain through sheep, then spread to cows, when they were fed ground-up body parts of their fellow sheep and cows. Ultimately the diseased beef was sold to the British public. The disease may lie dormant for up to thirty years before it unleashes its holy hell; only after the deaths of ten young people in 1996 did the British government acknowledge that something was wrong with the meat supply—something they had suspected for ten years.

The British solution for eradicating the source of the disease is to destroy any cow suspected of kuru, or mad cow disease, by cremation. But when you burn them, the threat doesn't disappear; *you can't kill them, as I said*. The smoke and ash just carry them to another new location, setting them free to find their way once again to the British dinner table.

Americans are not immune from this deadly disease. Some experts estimate that some 200,000 U.S. citizens diagnosed with Alzheimer's may, in fact, be carrying the alien protein and that their dementia is actually a form of mad cow.

Britain and many other countries have since banned the cannibalistic feeding of animals to their own kind, and no scraps or leftovers of food intended for humans can be used on cattle farms. The U.S. Food and Drug Administration has followed suit, banning the feeding of animals to other animals of their own kind. But cannibalistic products still get through. And how's this for scary: many drugs and vaccines, including those for polio, diphtheria, and tetanus, may have been made with products that could, in theory, carry mad cow disease.

Both Britain and the United States have been slow to act regarding this growing plague. Make sure, if you have to eat a burger or a steak, to cook that sucker until it's black. The leaner the meat, the better your chances.

Me? I'm going to stop eating all beef unless someone can

prove to me that the PBB I'm hauling around in my innards can vaporize the damn human-brain-eating mad cow parasites.

I've thought about just moving to California and becoming a veg-etarian. *No—wait!* Not California. Talk about a place with eco-logical mayhem afoot everywhere you turn. If the Golden State isn't being hit with earthquakes, it's being burned to the ground by uncontrollable wildfires. Whatever the fires don't destroy, the mudslides finish off. If the state isn't experiencing a major drought, then it's being hit with La Niña, El Niño, or El Loco. The West Coast is a crazy place to drop a bunch of humans: I'm convinced that nature *never* intended for our species to settle there. It just isn't constructed ecologically for our survival. No matter how much sod you lay down over desert sand or how much water you pump from the Colorado River a thousand miles away, you can't fool Mother Nature—and when you try, Mother Nature gets really shit-faced.

The Indians figured this out early. Some scientists say there was more pollution in the Los Angeles basin when tens of thou-sands of Indians and their campfires were there than there is now with eight million cars on its freeways. The Indians couldn't stand the way their smoke just hung in the air, trapped by the moun-tains. And when the earth moved and split apart, they got the message and got the hell out.

But not us. California is our dream. Thirty-four million peo-ple—one-eighth of our population—are crammed along a strip of land between a mountain range and an ocean. This means manna to the energy companies: thirty-four million suckers to take advantage of.

Welcome, Rolling Blackouts!

Back in the good old days, California's electricity was supplied by regional monopolies whose rates were set by the state legisla-ture. Then, in the mid-1990s, deregulation was touted as a way for the companies to escape the high costs they'd incurred by building nuclear power plants—and as a way to make much more money. One of the most vocal advocates for deregulation was Enron—a major contributor to the Republican party, and George W. Bush in particular.

Deregulation went into effect in 1996, thanks to a piece of legislation that took a whopping three weeks to pass and included a $20 billion bailout payment to the California utilities—most of which was used to cover their bad investment decisions of the past. For four years prices were frozen—at above-average levels—but so was competition, which is supposed to increase in a deregulated market. There was a block in effect against new power plant construction, so Californians grew more dependent on out-of-state, independent providers for their power. Thus, on and off for the past year, power has been bought on the daily spot market—at outrageously inflated prices.

Today utility customers not only pay more, they're forced to go through certain parts of the day without electricity. But it's not because there isn't enough power. The Independent System Operator, the California agency that oversees the transmission of electricity, has access to about 45,000 megawatts of power—the amount needed for summertime peak demand. The power companies are holding back as much as 13,000 megawatts of this power by going off-line (for reasons they don't have to divulge). The *Wall Street Journal* reported in August of 2000 that 461 percent more capacity was off-line than in the previous year. And, of course, tighter supply means higher prices.

But this is not the case in those cities served by community-owned utilities. People in Los Angeles and other areas where the *public* still owns the energy have not experienced blackouts. Other states in the Southwest and Pacific Northwest have sufficient supplies of energy to have bailed much of California out of this recent crisis by providing almost 25 percent of its power.

While all of this Hollywood drama has been going on, Junior

and Uncle Dick have been seizing the moment to scare up public support to build more nuclear plants, burn more coal, drill
for more oil. In other words, they want to make bad matters
worse. Meanwhile, Bush has built a new home on his Texas
ranch that is an environmentalist's dream. It is fueled by solar
energy, and its wastewater is recycled. And Cheney's vice-
presidential residence is equipped with state-of-the-art energy

George W.'s Ecologically Correct Texas Ranch

President Bush may not care about the rest of the
environment, but his new Crawford, Texas, ranch is
shockingly ecologically correct. The house features:

* Geothermal heating and cooling systems that use
  25 percent of the electricity of traditional mecha-
  nisms.

* Water at a constant 67 degrees piped up from a
  source 300 feet below ground and through the
  house for cooling in the summer and heating in the
  winter. This same system heats the swimming pool.

* A 25,000-gallon cistern that collects house wastewater and rainwater for reuse in irrigating the gar-
  dens.

* Its own water purification system, which uses recycled household water to help restore native wild-
  flowers and grasses on the property.

conservation devices that were installed by the President-in-Exile, Al Gore.

Clean, renewable energy is okay for them, but the rest of us get the message, loud and clear:

"LET THEM DRIVE MINIVANS!"

"LET THEM EAT BEEF!"

SEVEN

The End of Men

EARLIER THIS YEAR, my wife and I attended the baptism of our new nephew, Anthony. Our teenage daughter had been asked to be his godmother, a job that would require her to be there for little Anthony should he need to be burped, or raised Catholic, or both.

The baptism ceremony, we discovered, has changed a lot in the Catholic Church. Instead of just "hurry up and pour a little water on his forehead before we lose his soul to Satan," the Church now makes it a joyful event during Sunday Mass.

About halfway through the service, Father Andy asked the entire extended family to gather round the big baptismal font while little Anthony Proffer was submerged in the holy water and then wrapped in a pure white garment. The priest then held Anthony up for all the congregation to see, and everyone in the church applauded enthusiastically.

No one was applauding louder than me.

For this was the first time in thirteen years a BOY had been born into our family.

Thirteen babies in thirteen years in our family. That's eleven girls and two boys.

Now I think most of us would agree that having a girl is, well, a little less work. Not that we love boys any less; and with a strong health insurance plan that covers broken arms, teeth, and collar bones, with additional coverage for fingers caught in car doors and personal injury claims from neighbors who allege our dear sweet little boy torched their Celica "just to see how fast Toyota paint burns," they're no more difficult to raise than girls.

I have lived my entire life in households where men were decidedly in the minority. I have no brothers, but two wonderful sisters. Between them and our mother, they made sure I did all the "woman's work" in the house, while my dad was granted occasional leave to watch a Sunday golf tournament. I tried to even things out a bit, claiming I deserved more of a say because I was the oldest, but that only galvanized my sisters' childhood feminist majority. To this day, as testimony to their assertive behavior, those who meet us when we're together are convinced that my sisters are older than I am, and that I'm the baby of the family.

I now live with my wife and my daughter. Outnumbered again. Whatever frightening male habits were not exorcised by my sisters and mother, these two have been merciless in finishing off. The latest was breaking me of spitting toothpaste all over the bathroom mirror while brushing my teeth. That one only took nineteen years. They tell me the list is now down to a single page, with only three or four appalling behaviors left to annihilate (balancing my Big Gulp in the open space on the steering wheel while driving; leaving permanent ink stains on the arm of the chair I fall asleep in; snoring—though I fear this one may ultimately only be corrected by a pillow being "accidentally" slipped over my face and mysteriously held there, tightly, for a good three to five minutes).

Truth be told, I am a better person for having lived my life surrounded by strong, intelligent, and loving women. It just would have been nice to play catch. Once.

My parents have no grandsons. My sisters and I have only daughters. My wife's parents had four daughters and only two boys. They, in turn, produced eight more girls and only two additional boys. My wife's two brothers and I have only girls. Our family hasn't seen a game of tackle football or mumblety-peg since high school. This sacrifice appears to have gone unnoticed by nearly everyone involved.

I offer this little glimpse into the gender makeup of my family to point out a much larger discovery I've made. Pondering this lopsided ratio, I began asking around to find out if other people were experiencing the same thing—more girl babies being born than boy babies. Much to my surprise, I was not alone.

Lately, when I'm asked to speak at a university or community group, I leave the prepared agenda for a moment to ask how many in the room are seeing more girls being born in their families than boys. Scores of hands always shoot up.

Countless people began sharing their secret with me—that the ranks of boys are dwindling. In some families, it seems, they're altogether extinct. I always reassure them that there's no need to feel any shame in their inability to produce male offspring.

Then it hit me . . . *something* is up.

And sure enough, something is. The Census Bureau confirms that the number of male babies being born has been *declining every year in the United States since 1990*! Plus, women are living longer and longer: 80 years, on average, versus only 74.2 for men. When I was a kid, the country seemed pretty much 50–50 male-female, with women maybe holding a slight lead. Then the ratio went to 51–49, with women in the majority. Soon it'll be 52–48.

So I have come to one ugly but irrefutable conclusion:

Guys! *Nature is trying to kill us off!*

Why is Mother Nature doing this? Are we not the carriers of the seed of life? What have we men done to deserve this?

As it turns out, plenty.

In the early years of Man, we served a critical and necessary function in the growth of the species. We hunted and gathered the food, protected the women and children from larger animals conspiring to eat them, and helped the number of *Homo sapiens* multiply rapidly through a lot of random, unrestricted sex. It's been downhill for us ever since.

In the past few centuries, things seem to have taken a fatal turn for our gender. As is our wont, we commenced work on a series of projects that stunk everything up and made a mess of our world. Women? They deserve none of the blame. They continued to bring life into this world; we continued to destroy it whenever we could. How many women have come up with the idea of exterminating a whole race of people? None that I've met at the gym. How many women have spilled oil in the oceans, dumped toxins in our food supply, or insisted that the new SUV designs had to be bigger, bigger, BIGGER? Hmmm. Let me see. . . .

Of the 816 species that have gone extinct since Columbus got lost and landed here (another man who wouldn't ask for directions)—most of which are necessary links in our fragile ecosystem—how many do you think were eradicated by women? Once again, I think we all know the answer.

If you were Nature, how would you respond to such a brutal assault? And what would you do if you noticed that it was one particular gender of humans that was going out of its way to destroy you? Well, Mother Nature has a habit of cutting to the chase. She'd defend herself *by any means necessary*, that's what she'd do. She'd pull out every stop to save her life, to survive at all costs, even if it meant eliminating one half of the very thing that was supposed to keep her most advanced species going.

Yes, Nature had graciously granted our species the highest form of intelligence and entrusted us with her future—but suddenly it looked like one of the genders had decided to throw the kegger of all keggers on Mother Earth's watch. Now, hung over and cranky, Mother is pissed at whoever slipped the mickey in her drink.

The culprit has a receding hairline, a potbelly, and never screws the cap back onto anything.

Yup, guys, we've been fingered; there's no way to hide from Nature's wrath. We can't pin any of this on the women: it wasn't a woman who dropped napalm bombs, or who invented plastic, or who said, "Dammit, what we need is a beer can with a pop-top!" Unfortunately, every bit of plunder and pillage, every attack on the environment, everything that has brought horror and destruction to all that was once pure and good has come from hands that, well, when they aren't busy bringing pleasure to one-self, are working overtime to wipe out this beautiful, wonderful home we were given free of charge—no security deposit required, no background check needed.

No wonder Nature is getting rid of us.

If we men had any sense, we'd try to get Nature to forgive us by cleaning up our act. You know, do the obvious stuff: quit desecrating the Arctic wilderness, pick up after ourselves, stop throwing Whopper remains out the car window.

Nature would probably put up with a lot of our guff if we still served some important purpose. For eons we had two things women didn't have that made us a *necessity*: (1) we provided the sperm to keep the species going, and (2) we were able to reach and get whatever they needed off the top shelf.

Unfortunately for us, some traitor guy invented *in vitro* fertilization, which means that now females only need the sperm from *a few of us* in order to have babies. In fact someone (probably a woman) in Arizona has announced that science has found a means of human reproduction that doesn't even require sperm to fertilize an egg—now they can do it with DNA. No longer do women have to crawl out from underneath some slobbering man with his

How to Trick Nature into Making More Men

＊A company in Virginia has developed a method that allows you to choose the gender of your baby. The Genetic and IVF (In Vitro Fertilization) Institute, an infertility clinic in Fairfax, Virginia, uses a process that separates the male chromosome from the female chromosome sperm, allowing parents to determine the sex of their baby before it is conceived. Be EXTRA nice to your wife before going to this clinic, because ultimately it's her right to decide what is placed inside her body. And give these people in Virginia more federal funds!

＊Keep Your Sperm Strong. Quit violating yourself on a daily basis. It weakens the sperm and lessens their numbers.

＊Before sex, think *manly* thoughts. Go over the instant replay one more time in your head. *You* would never have let that ball roll between *your* legs in game six of the '86 World Series. Hear the crowd at Shea roar as you scoop up the ball and throw Ray Knight out! You did it! You da MAN!

＊Conceive your children earlier in life. A recent epidemiological study concluded that older parents are more likely to have girls than boys.

face buried in the pillow simply because they wish to have babies. All they need now is a test tube.

The other invention that did the male population in was the stepladder. *The portable, easy-to-carry aluminum stepladder*, to be precise. Who was the bastard that came up with that bright idea? Now what possible excuse can we have for sticking around?

Nature has a way of getting rid of its weakest links, those that no longer serve a useful purpose, the dead weight. That, my friends, is *us*. Reproductive science and three little aluminum steps rising above the earth's surface have made us guys about as useful as an eight-track tape.

Well, look at the bright side: We've had one helluva run! Thousands of years of total domination over the social order— and still going strong! Think about it—there has not been a *single day* when we weren't in charge, when we weren't calling the shots and running the world! Not even the Yankees can claim such an unbroken reign of unchallenged power. I mean, here we are, *the minority*, and yet we men have ruled over the female majority since time immemorial. In other countries we call that apartheid; in America we call it normal. Since the birth of this country, for more than 225 years, we have seen to it that not a single woman has held either the number one or number two offices in the

Other Things Already Rendered Useless by Nature

* Typewriters
* The Washington Senators
* Bosco
* Walking
* Skorts
* The busy signal
* Bank tellers
* A college degree
* Malt-O-Meal
* Hair on a man's back
* AYDS weight-loss candies
* The Supreme Court

land. For the better part of that time we've made sure that damn few of them have held any office at all. In fact, for the first 130 years of presidential elections, it was illegal for women even to *vote*.

Then in 1920, just to show women we're good sports, we gave them the right to vote. And guess what? *We remained in power!*

Go figure. Suddenly, women had more votes; they could have thrown our collective male ass into the political trash heap. But what did they do? They voted for *us!* How cool is that? Have you ever heard of any group of oppressed people that suddenly, by their sheer numbers, takes charge—and then votes in overwhelming numbers to keep their oppressors in power? The blacks of South Africa, once free, did not continue apartheid by voting for whites. I know no Jews in America who voted for George Wallace or David Duke or Pat Buchanan (Florida debacle included).

No, the usual thing a sane society does is give the boot to the boot that's been on its neck for umpteen years.

Yet more than eighty years after they gained the right to vote—and despite the growth of a massive women's movement—here's where we stand:

* Not a single woman has been on the ballot of the major parties for President or Vice President in twenty of the twenty-one national elections since 1920.

* Currently there are only five women governors in fifty states.

* Women hold only 13 percent of the seats in Congress.

* 496 of the top 500 companies in America are run by men.

* Just four of the top twenty-one universities in the United States are run by women.

* 40 percent of all women who are divorced between the ages of twenty-five and thirty-four end up in poverty, compared with only 8 percent of married women who live below the poverty line.

* Women's earnings average 76 cents for every $1 earned by men—resulting in a lifetime loss of over $650,133.

* To make the same annual salary as her male counterpart, a woman would have to work the entire year PLUS an additional four months.

Sooner or later, women are going to figure out how to seize power—and when that happens, let's pray for mercy. After all, they *are* the stronger gender. Contrary to popular myth, it is men who are the weaker sex. Consider the evidence:

* We don't live as long as women.

* Our brains are less well formed and shrink at a faster rate than women's as we age.

* Proportionately, we are more likely than women to suffer from catastrophic illnesses such as heart disease, strokes, ulcers, and liver failure.

* Men are more likely to carry sexually transmitted diseases (which they pass on to their unsuspecting wives and girlfriends).

* Men's major body systems—our circulatory, respiratory, digestive, and excretory functions—are all likely to break down long before women's (though I guess the breakdown of the excretory system was no surprise, considering the case of air freshener you've got under the bathroom sink).

Mike's Fantasy List of Women Presidents

✳ President Cynthia McKinney (the best person in Congress today)

✳ President Hillary Clinton (only if I could get invited for sleepovers)

✳ President Oprah (the fireside chats with Dr. Phil would save us all)

✳ President Katrina vanden Heuvel (editor of *The Nation*, a perfect candidate for president of the nation!)

✳ President Sherry Lansing (she runs Paramount Pictures; she put me in a picture; 'nuff said)

✳ President Karen Duffy (correspondent for *TV Nation*; would run circles around any foreign leader who dared to challenge her)

✳ President Caroline Kennedy (just because it would be right)

✳ President Bella Abzug (even dead she'd do better than Junior)

✳ President Leigh Taylor-Young (the first naked woman I ever saw, in the movie *The Big Bounce*, also starring Ryan O'Neal. You see, there were like six of us guys, all sixteen years old, and we had snuck into the South Dort Drive-In, and . . . oh, never mind.)

* Only our reproductive system—the ability to produce sperm—lasts longer than a woman's ability to produce eggs, but our delivery system peters out years before a woman discovers the benefits of enjoying a warm bath and a good novel.

* Men are unable to give birth, to keep the species going.

* Men lose their hair.

* Men lose their minds (we're four times more likely to attempt suicide than women).

* Men are three times more likely to die in an accident than women.

* Men are just not as smart as women: girls generally score higher than boys on the elementary school tests—and face it, we don't get any smarter with age.

Perhaps there's no logical explanation for this disparity. Maybe, as the nuns taught us, it's just all part of God's plan. But if that's the case, why did God make women so much better? The nuns must have had the inside dope on this—after all, they were all women themselves. They knew God's secret, and they certainly weren't going to share it with the likes of me.

It is my belief—and this is purely from my personal observation of the woman I live with—that when God was creating the world, he spent the better part of Day Six creating what women would look like. I mean, you can't help but notice the skillful craft of an artisan at the top of His field. The shapes, the curves, the symmetry, all constitute extraordinary art. Their skin is soft and smooth and perfect; their hair is rich and thick and vibrant. I am not speaking from a prurient perspective here—these are simply the conclusions of the art critic in me. Women—I think we all agree—are stunningly beautiful.

How to Survive Your Bed Being Set on Fire

* Get on the floor and crawl. Stay low.

* If you can, put a wet washcloth or towel over your face.

* Head in the direction where you believe the door is. Always feel the door before opening it. If it's hot, DON'T open it. Find another way out.

* If she's locked all the doors, break a window and climb out.

* Always keep a fire extinguisher handy. Place it by the gun under your pillow if necessary. A fresh bucket of water nearby is also recommended.

* If you've been abusing your wife, it's probably best to wear only fire-retardant pajamas to bed. They might just save your life.

* Call the local fire department and get your name placed on the special "bastard" list—the roster of local men who believe they stand the best chance of being eliminated by a "loved one." The fire department will then know exactly where you live and where your bedroom is.

So what happened to God when it came to us? It's like he used up all his best tricks inventing women. By the time he got to us, he was obviously ready to get it over with, move on to something more important, like that seventh day of rest.

So men ended up like Chevys, rushed off the assembly line and guaranteed to break down after limited use. That's why we try to stay in our Naugahyde recliners as long as we can—the exertion required to pick up after ourselves can lead to an early coronary. Our bodies were built to lift, carry, haul, and throw, but for a limited time only. And, I have to say it, what's with this extra *thing* we were given? Well, let me put this as delicately as possible: In God's rush to finish up, it looks like he just grabbed a stray part he had lying around in the shop and stuck it on us—'cause it sure as hell don't look right. If you took an item like this and glued it on to a lamppost or a tree, you'd say, "Naww, I don't think so." But nobody questions its presence on a guy. Like a creature from *Alien* reupholstered by Frank Purdue, the male organ is testimony to the fact that every now and again, as with the floods in Bangladesh or the teeth of the British, God just fails to get it right.

Saddled with the odds against us, some men have simply gone insane and taken to fighting back any way they can. If Nature is going to favor women, they figure, then they must take matters into their own hands. Their attitude: If we can't beat 'em, let's beat 'em.

These days, the tendency of men to injure, maim, or murder women is seen by most as "politically incorrect," and laws have been strengthened to protect women from us. But as we know, laws are only made to exact punishment *after* a crime has been committed. Few laws have stopped those men who are intent on wreaking their vengeance on women. Women know all too well that 911 is only there to notify the police that they'd better bring a body bag and some strong cleanser to mop up the mess, because by the time they get there that restraining order the court issued to keep him away will be stuffed in her mouth and rigor mortis will be setting in nicely, thank you.

Men gifted with more subtlety often resort to means other than outright murder to even the score between men and women. For instance, the tobacco companies (all run by men) have been extremely successful in convincing women to smoke—at a time when the number of *male* smokers is declining. Thanks to all this new female smoking, lung cancer has now surpassed breast cancer as the leading cancer killer of women. Total number of women eliminated each year by smoking: 165,000!

Denial of treatment is another trick men employ in paring down the female population. If you need an organ transplant to stay alive, you're 86 percent more likely to get it if you are a man. Men suffering from heart disease are 115 percent more likely to undergo a heart bypass than women with the same condition. And if you're a woman, you're more likely to pay higher insurance premiums than men for this shoddy care.

Of course, when all else fails, you can also go back to murder. It usually works. A woman is five times more likely to be killed by a husband or boyfriend than a man is likely to be murdered by his wife or girlfriend.

Keep that up, and we might just make it after all.

HOW MEN CAN AVOID EXTINCTION

As bad as the future looks for us, there is some hope that we, as men, can delay our demise—if we learn to adopt some very important new behaviors. There are many things we can learn from women and how they function sanely. Here are a few:

1. Remember That Your Car Is Not a Weapon of Mass Destruction.
Stop getting pissed off at that car that just cut you off. Why do

you really care? You're going to get home in the same amount of time anyway. So some jerk cost you four seconds on the road. Big deal! Get a grip. Women couldn't care less about stuff like this, and they live longer for it. When they see an asshole on the road, they just shake their heads and laugh—and it works! Guys, we have *got* to relax. We're damaging our hearts with every minute of uptight, tense, and angry behavior. Quit walking around like you've got a pineapple up your ass. Nothing matters THAT much. (Except a real pineapple. *That* would matter something awful.)

2. Lighten Up on the Food and Drink. We need to think more about what we put in our mouths. If you and I would eat less and drink less, we'd live a lot longer. When's the last time you saw a woman pig out like it was her last meal? Sure, we've all seen women pound back the liquor, but how many females have you seen just drop their pants and start peeing on the curb? Why do you think so many of us men get colon and stomach cancer and liver disease? Because we can't say no to Jack (Daniels) or Jim (Beam) or a pound and a half of half-cooked beef topped with fried onion rings, year-old jalapeños, and Tabasco sauce. There's a reason you've never seen a woman take a newspaper into a bathroom. Get a clue!

3. Step Aside, You'll Live Longer. Listen, why don't we retire and let women run the world? Okay, so you don't want women having power, because you're a conservative redneck. But what would you say if I told you that letting them worry about building that nuclear plant in Bahrain, or declaring war against China, or finding a solution to the continuing abuse of the infield fly rule, would give us men eight more years of life? Let's step aside and shut up! Is it that big a cheap thrill just to be "the boss" and have to deal with hundreds of employees and all their crap? Who needs it? Let's back off, take a break, and let the women have this crazy unmanageable world for the next ten thousand years. Think of all the reading you'll catch up on.

4. Wash Your Hands Across America. It's time to wise up: our personal habits are so revolting it's a wonder women are willing even to breathe the same air we do. If we men could only get our act together and change a few simple things, we'd immediately score more empathy and companionship. For starters, we should keep our hands where they belong. They weren't intended to be used in nostrils, anuses, ears, or navels. They were not designed to tear out articles from the newspaper before she has a chance to read it, or to pick a loose piece of kielbasa skin from between your teeth, or to sandpaper that patch of dandruff on your head. Stop checking (and adjusting) your crotch in public—nothing has disappeared since your last inventory, roughly a minute ago. Keep your legs together, so you don't take up three seats on buses and trains. Wear underwear—preferably underwear that's been washed *this year*, in a *washing machine*, with actual *laundry soap*.

5. Learn How a Toilet Seat Works. All right, boys, I thought for sure we'd be over this by now, but the foul evidence in airports and train stations and fast-food emporia all over this great land tells me this: despite the constant carping of TV comics everywhere, *we just haven't gotten the message*. So here's a quick refresher course:

* First, lift the movable oval cover into an upright position. Then lift the movable oval seat beneath it into an upright position. They will both automatically lock into place. That's so you can use both hands. It's just like steering a car. You wouldn't want the car to go off the road, would you? Fine, and the women in your house feel the same way about your piss all over the wallpaper.

* Aim, hold, release, return to pants.

* Take one hand and gently return oval seat and its top to their lowered positions. No audible sound of the seat hitting the ceramic bowl should be heard.

* Grasp the little silver handle at left and FLUSH. (This is not optional, even in a public restroom.) If the first flush doesn't take, you may not leave the scene: stay there till you're looking at a clean bowl.

* Wash hands. Dry them on the towels provided, not the shirt you're wearing. Throw the paper towel into the trash receptacle—or, if the towel is made of cloth, place it back on towel rack (usually a metal or plastic rod protruding from the wall near the sink). If you're in your own home, put the cloth towel into the laundry at least once a week. Wash. Return to bathroom.

6. Bathe Daily. Throwing some water in your face to wake up in the morning does not constitute bathing. Neither does being doused with a Heineken at a party the night before. Step into the tub. Turn handle halfway between HOT and COLD. Lift stem on faucet to create shower effect. Take bar of soap and washcloth and scrub all areas of the body. Do NOT place the bar of soap in body cavities to "get them extra clean." Someone else has to use that bar of soap on her face. Rinse. When finished, leave shower area and dry off, creating as little a water trail as possible.

7. Tone It Down. Lower your voice. Try listening. Here's how it works: When someone else is talking, pay close attention to what they are saying. Maintain eye contact. Do not interrupt. When he or she is finished, pause and reflect on what was said. Try saying nothing at all. Notice how what you have heard is stimulating thoughts, concepts, feelings, and ideas in your head. This may lead to something brilliant. You will then be able to take those ideas, claim them as yours, and become famous!

8. Get Your Hearing Checked. If the above doesn't work, there may be something physically wrong with you. May is National Better Health and Speech Month; many hospitals and community groups offer free screening for hearing loss. Check your local newspaper for announcements of free hearing tests in your area. In addition, most hospitals offer periodic free hearing tests throughout the year. You can also find on-line quizzes to help you determine if you should seek a professional hearing evaluation. One such test can be found at: health.aol.thriveonline.oxygen.com/medical/wgames/gen/health.hearing.html.

9. Know That Women Are onto Us. Cut out the sensitive-man crap. They know the drill. Don't try convincing anyone you're a "feminist." You don't qualify: you play for the other team. It's like a Klansman chanting, "KEEP HOPE ALIVE!" You are a specimen of the gender that will always make more money, that will always have the door swing open wide and far to wherever you want to go in life.

This does not mean you can't help make things better. The best way to help women is to work on your fellow men. That's where the real struggle is—getting enlightenment through the concrete block known as a man's head.

Help end the wage gap by looking at your own paycheck. Make sure women doing the same job at work are getting paid the same as you. Participate in Equal Pay Day, usually held in early April on the day that marks the point in the new year when a woman has finally earned the wages paid to a man in a comparable job during the previous year. Contact fairplay@aol.com for more info.

And you can join in the effort to push Congress to pass two pieces of national legislation affecting equal pay. The Fair Pay Act would allow women to bring suit based on the principle of equal pay for equal work and would allow employees within a single company to sue if they believe they are being paid less than someone with an equivalent job and equivalent training. The Paycheck Fairness Act provides for higher damages in these types of lawsuits and protects employees who share salary information. The Center for Policy Alternatives has been working for pay equity for the past twenty-five years. To find out more, go to www.cfpa.org, or contact them at 202-387-6030.

Finally, join a union—or try to start one. According to the AFL-CIO, a thirty-year-old female union member making $30,000 a year stands to lose about $650,133 over a lifetime because of unequal pay. If she's not a union member, on the other hand, she'll lose about $870,327. If you convince the other men on the job to unionize the establishment, then you'll have greatly improved your female coworkers' lives, and your own.

HOW WOMEN CAN SURVIVE WITHOUT MEN

1. Visit a Sperm Bank or an Adoption Agency. Most communities have adoption agencies or sperm banks available for women who would love to have children but, for whatever reason, want to do it without a man. It's good for kids to have two parents (and easier for the parents, too!), but everything you've heard about how damaged children turn out to be if they were raised by a single mother—well, that's one of the Big Lies of our culture. In his book *The Culture of Fear*, Barry Glassner points out that "those raised by single mothers had income and education levels roughly equal to those raised by two parents. Research shows that as a group, children of single moms tend to fare better emotionally and socially than do offspring from high-conflict marriages, or from those in which the father is emotionally absent or abusive."

2. Learn Where to Buy a Stepladder. There are many fine brands, sizes, and styles available at affordable prices. Try Home Depot at www.homedepot.com. And for further information about this revolutionary invention, go to the American Ladder Institute Web site at www.americanladderinstitute.org.

3. When All Else Fails, Love Yourself. Some folks who can lend a hand (so to speak):

By phone or online:

Good Vibrations
800-289-8423 or 415-974-8990
www.goodvibes.com

The Pleasure Chest
800-753-4536
fax: 323-650-1176
www.thepleasurechest.com

Xandria
800-242-2823 or 415-468-3805
fax: 415-468-3912
www.xandria.com

Retail stores:

Good Vibrations
2504 San Pablo Avenue
Berkeley, CA 94702
510-841-8987

The Pleasure Chest
7733 Santa Monica Blvd.
Santa Monica, CA 90046
323-650-1022

Xandria
1210 Valencia Street
San Francisco, CA 94110
415-974-8980

EIGHT

We're Number One!

THE HEADLINE COULD not have been clearer: "All Nations on Earth Sign Global Warming Agreement, U.S. Refuses."

Yes, once again, the whole world hates our guts.

Boo hoo hoo. So what's new?

We're the country everyone loves to hate. And who can blame them? We obviously hate ourselves—how else can you explain "President" W? In olden times, his head would already be adorning one of the bridges over the Potomac. Instead he prances around the world telling people he's our "elected leader," and we just look like ignoramuses and fools. The world is laughing at us, not with us.

How sad—after all, not too long ago things were looking up

for us internationally for the first time in a long while. We successfully midwifed the first peace treaty in Northern Ireland. We got the warring factions in Israel and the Occupied Territories to sit down and chill out (and for the first time the Palestinians got some land of their own). We finally recognized the existence of Vietnam (though we still haven't brought ourselves to apologize for killing three million of their people. I guess the Germans set the bar pretty high; we were just few million short). American pressure on South Africa had helped free Nelson Mandela, pushed the country toward democracy, resulting in Mandela's election as president.

And finally, we returned a little boy to his father in Cuba—marking the first time a bunch of crazy Miamians didn't call the shots regarding our foreign policy in this hemisphere.

Yes, I have to say, things were looking pretty good for Uncle Sam in the eyes of the world—until this dolt, who we are told had never crossed an ocean in his life, took over the controls at 1600 Pennsylvania Avenue.

In his first four months in office, here's how George W. Bush dealt with the rest of the world:

* He reneged on our agreement with the European Community to cut our carbon dioxide emissions.

* He started a new Cold War, this time with China, over an American spy plane that knocked one of their planes out of the sky, killing the pilot.

* He allowed the peace process in the Middle East to crumble, resulting in some of the worst slaughter we've ever seen between Israelis and Palestinians.

* He started a new Cold War with Russia by actively preparing to violate the anti–ballistic missile (ABM) treaties of the 1970s.

* He threatened to unilaterally reduce our presence in the former Yugoslavia, resulting in renewed violence between the ethnic groups in the region.

* He defied UN human rights agreements, resulting in the United Nations removing the United States from its Human Rights Commission.

* He bombed civilians in Iraq, just like Daddy did.

* He stepped up the drug war in South America, resulting in the United States helping the Peruvians to shoot down a plane full of American missionaries, killing a Michigan mother and her child.

* He cut off any hope of reducing tensions with North Korea, guaranteeing not only that mass starvation there will continue but that its leader, film-nut Kim Jong Il, will never return his overdue videos to Blockbuster.

* He turned basically every country in the world against us by stating he was going to go ahead and build the nutty "Star Wars" missile defense system.

All this was accomplished in less than 120 short days—and that's just in between bouts of knocking the wind out of our domestic policy, as we've already seen. Those of us who thought Junior was an underachiever have certainly been impressed by his get up and goad.

So now the world is back to hating us. At least we're back on familiar ground.

But on the other hand, it's a damn shame we've reverted to the role of the pariah. It was nice having foreigners think we were the good guys for once. Clinton's charm allowed us to get away with a lot: quietly increasing the use of sweatshops and child labor in the Third World by American companies, dumping unsafe products in poor countries, and exporting even *worse* Hollywood movies abroad.

Typical Day in the Life of "President" George W. Bush

8:00 A.M.—The President of the United States (POTUS) rises, checks to see if he is still in White House.

8:30 A.M.—Breakfast in bed. Rumsfeld reads him horoscope and comic strips.

9:00 A.M.—"Co-President" Cheney stops by to help George get dressed, goes over situation in Yemen, reminds George to brush his teeth.

9:30 A.M.—POTUS arrives at Oval Office, greets secretary.

9:35 A.M.—POTUS leaves Oval Office to go work out in White House gym.

11:00 A.M.—Massage and pedicure.

Noon—Lunch with Baseball Commissioner Bud Selig. Selig confirms still no jobs open in front office.

1:00 P.M.—Nap.

2:30 P.M.—Photo op with Little League "team of the day."

3:00 P.M.—POTUS back in Oval Office to discuss legislation with members of Congress.

3:05 P.M.—Meeting adjourns; Congressmen tell press, "Meeting was very fruitful. The president told us to 'get some laws passed,' and then he had us shag balls on the South Lawn."

3:10 P.M.—Cheney briefs POTUS on energy policy, tells Junior Bush to "send thank-you notes" to heads of oil companies.

3:12 P.M.—POTUS asks to see map of the world; seems surprised by "how big the world has gotten."

3:40 P.M.—POTUS has memorized all 191 capitals in less than half an hour.

3:44 P.M.—Bush calls prime minister of Romania "just because I can"; challenges Romanian prime minister to name capital of Burma; prime minister cannot understand a word he is saying, as POTUS is speaking in Spanish.

3:58 P.M.—POTUS accepts collect call from Austin jail. POTUS offspring being held for desecrating portrait of POTUS as governor that hangs in state capitol building. POTUS pretends he has a bad connection, impersonates voice of a Mexican woman who has "cut in" on the call, then hangs up. Is heard to say, "She's a chip off the ol' block."

4:00 P.M.—Work day ends; POTUS retires to living quarters for brief "catnap."

6:00 P.M.—State dinner with African heads of state. Tells Cheney he "can't think about Africa right now—it's the 'Dark Continent,' you know!" POTUS asks Co-President to sit in for him.

6:05 P.M.—POTUS goes for swim in White House pool.

7:00 P.M.—Phone call to Laura at Texas ranch ("just checking in").

7:02 P.M.—POTUS goes to White House screening room; watches *Dave* (again); falls asleep.

8:30 P.M.—Cheney awakens POTUS, takes him to his room, tucks him in, says good night. Co-POTUS goes downstairs and resumes plotting destruction of Planet Earth.

In fact, Clinton did many of the same things Bush is now doing—he just didn't rub people's faces in it. You see, Clinton was cool—so cool that most of the time few even knew what he was up to. Clinton gave us such good cover that for a few years Americans could travel safely in most countries without the threat of a mob chasing us down and beating the Ho-Ho's out of us.

But now, thanks to Bush's "Bite Me" foreign policy, it's a lot harder to justify why we in the most arrogant 4 percent of the world's population should own more than a quarter of its wealth. If we don't watch our backs, all those uppity emaciated foreigners are going to start thinking they deserve their own digital pagers and recessed lighting. And the doubters and naysayers who abound in oppressed countries may catch on that just the three richest men in America own more personal assets than the combined assets owned by the entire populations of the sixty poorest countries.

What if the teeming billions of Asia, Africa, and Latin America get to thinking that the one billion of them without clean drinking water should actually *have* it? Do you know what that would cost? At least 25 percent of our "Star Wars" program!

And what if the 30 percent of the world still not wired—to *electricity*—suddenly wants to screw in a light bulb and read a book? *Whoa!* Look out!

My greatest fear comes from the 50 percent of our fellow Earthlings who have *never made a phone call!* What if all of sudden they get the idea to phone home on Mother's Day, or start tying up the lines with calls for sushi take-out? Haven't they heard there aren't any more phone numbers to go around?

There's no reason to heap more anger onto these people; they're already mad enough at us, thanks to Bush's sorry performance. Plus, we got bigger fish to nuke.

Whose dumb idea was it to ignore the Russians' offer *fifteen years ago* to get rid of *all* nuclear weapons? Has everyone forgotten they were willing to disarm *unilaterally* after the old Soviet Union dissolved? Way back in 1986 (before the breakup of the USSR), at the summit in Iceland, Mikhail Gorbachev put on the table a goal of "final elimination of the nuclear weapons by the year 2000." (He couldn't make a deal with Reagan because of Reagan's refusal to give up developing—you guessed it—"Star Wars.") In case Reagan didn't hear him the first time, Gorbachev reiterated the offer to Bush the Elected in 1989: "To keep the peace in Europe we need nuclear arms control, not nuclear deterrence. Best of all would be the abolition of nuclear weapons."

At that time, we had lived for nearly forty years under the constant and imminent threat of nuclear annihilation. And then suddenly one day the Commies were gone and the Cold War was over. We were left holding more than twenty thousand nuclear warheads—and the ex-Soviets had thirty-nine thousand for themselves. That was enough firepower to blow up the entire world forty times over.

I think most of us born in the Baby Boom grew up thinking there was probably no way we were going to get to the end of our natural lives without at least an "accidental" launching of one of those missiles. How could it be avoided? With that many weapons just waiting to be fired at a moment's notice, it seemed inevitable that either some nut case with a trigger finger would hit The Button, or some misunderstanding would lead to an all-out attack, or some terrorist would get his hands on the materials and set one off by himself. We cowered under a cloud of fear, which affected everything we did as a nation. And we spent trillions trying to alleviate that fear—by building even *more* weapons of mass destruction.

Spending all this tax money on a bunch of useless warheads we

hoped never to use, we let our schools go to hell, we failed to provide health care for our citizens, and more than half of our scientists ended up working on projects for the military instead of
discovering the cure for cancer or the next great invention to
improve our quality of life.

The $250 billion the Pentagon plans to spend to build 2,800
new Joint Strike Fighter planes is more than enough to pay the
tuition of every college student in America.

The proposed combined budgets for the Pentagon over the
next five years is $1.6 *trillion*. The amount the General Account-
ing Office says is needed to renovate and upgrade every school in
America is $112 *billion*.

If we decided not to build the rest of the F-22 fighter jets the
Air Force asked for back during the Cold War (which Clinton,
and now Bush the Selected, still insist on funding), that money—
$45 billion—would fully fund Head Start preschool for every
child in America who needed it, *for the next six years*.

In the mid-1980s, another remarkable thing happened. Challenging Reagan to follow his lead, Gorbachev also announced
that the Soviet Union would no longer test any new nuclear
weapons. Gorbachev said he was taking this action whether the
United States joined him or not. It was a stunning moment—forgotten now, I'm sure, by most Americans. It was the first time any
of us were given a stitch of hope that maybe we wouldn't blow
ourselves to smithereens after all.

The insane arms race that *we* started and the Soviets felt compelled to keep up with eventually contributed to the bankruptcy
of the USSR. By the time the Soviets built their first A-bomb in
1949, the United States already had 235 of them. Ten years later
we had 15,468 nuclear weapons; the Russians were way behind,
with "only" 1,060. But over the next twenty years the Soviet
Union spent billions more on bombs—while its people shivered
in the cold—and sure enough they finally caught up with us. By

If you're finding yourself in a massive fit of rage, and start itching to put this damn book down and contact your congressman/woman, then folks, do it. Call 202-224-3121 (the U.S. Capitol switchboard). You can find your representative's E-mail address at www.senate.gov or www.house.gov. Or send snail mail to: Office of Senator (NAME), U.S. Senate, Washington, DC 20510—or— Office of Representative (NAME), U.S. House of Representatives, Washington, DC 20515. And for those of you trying to figure out who represents you, check out www.vote-smart.org and they'll figure it out for you.

1978 they had a whopping 25,393 nuclear warheads—while we had running water, Stevie Nicks, and a comfortable 24,424 nukes.

Gorbachev inherited a nation that was broke, its people hungry and yearning for the occasional roll of toilet paper.

But even as the USSR was on the brink of dissolving in 1989, it was maintaining an unbelievable 39,000 nuclear warheads. The Pentagon just sat back and laughed—our boys were fine with their measly 22,827. Was Washington's real mission to drive the Communists into such poverty that their people would eventually revolt? Gorbachev, who had this figured out, threw in the towel—but it was too late. By the end of 1991 the Soviet Union was no more.

In the euphoria of that moment, the new Russian and Ukrainian leaders, eager to distance themselves from the days of old, came out of the gate offering doves and olive branches to the United States. The Ukrainians said they were out of the arms race business, and immediately decommissioned their warheads. The

Russians turned off all the computer coordinates that had pointed their missiles at various U.S. cities. Then they offered to join the Americans in a permanent elimination of atomic weapons.

And what was our response to this incredible, unprecedented offer?

Zip.

That did not deter the Russians. They waited patiently for an answer. They continued to wait. And they waited some more, trusting that we'd eventually take them up on their generous offer.

They also hoped we might show a little compassion and send them some food, a little modern machinery, a couple of light bulbs—anything that would lift them out of their misery. They assumed we would do for them what we did for Western Europe after World War II—a relief and rebuilding effort that has resulted in a continuous and unbroken peace in Western Europe for more than fifty-five years, the longest in centuries.

Yes, the Russians figured life was about to get a lot better—and the world a whole lot safer.

Well, you know what happened. Nada. We just let them sit there and rot while the Russian mob took over. Discontent and despair grew among the people. The knight in shining armor never came as promised. Food shortages continued, the infrastructure collapsed, and the proletariat still had to run outside to take a crap. Their new president, Boris Yeltsin, turned out to be a drunk and a buffoon, and because they were unwilling to turn their country into a sweatshop for American corporations (as China had), there was no gushing pipeline of dollars flowing into the former USSR. Hardline politicians from the dark side of Russian politics seized office, and the opportunity to eliminate their twenty-five thousand still-operational nuclear warheads just faded away.

Now the new Russian leaders talk of building *more* weapons—and of selling arms to Iran and North Korea.

Boris Yeltsin vs. the Bush Twins

We believe our Bush girls can outdrink and outsmart any of these Ruskies. Just compare their records:

BUSH TWINS: Caught drinking at Austin nightclub
YELTSIN: Caught drinking at G-7 meeting

BUSH TWINS: Got Secret Service to spring boyfriend from jail
YELTSIN: Got KGB to drive him to liquor store

BUSH TWINS: Arrested for using fake ID in order to drink
YELTSIN: Never arrested; uses fake excuses to drink

We had missed the chance of a lifetime—to end an insane arms race and create a new ally in the new world order. The window of opportunity wasn't open long—and it went as fast as Rasputin rummaging through Monica Lewinsky's handbag.

Monica Lewinsky. That's how we spent the latter half of the nineties, fixated on a friggin' stain on a blue dress. Our Congress put aside insignificant matters like sparing the world from nuclear annihilation to focus on how exactly a Commander-in-Chief inserts a cigar into an intern. THAT is what captured our undivided attention—along with slow-moving Broncos, six-year-old strangled beauty queens, and Hugh Grant's dating habits. We had a chance to make the world safe for generations to come, but we were too greedy enjoying the orgy being thrown on Wall Street. That's what happens in a nation of slackers and crooks. Joyfully and willingly keeping ourselves as stupid as possible about what is happening beyond the ChemLawn in the front yard. After all, that's our job as leaders of the free world.

But, hey, don't despair! Among the top twenty industrialized nations, WE'RE number one!!

We're number one in millionaires.

We're number one in billionaires.

We're number one in military spending.

We're number one in firearm deaths.

We're number one in beef production.

We're number one in per capita energy use.

We're number one in carbon dioxide emissions (more than Australia, Brazil, Canada, France, India, Indonesia, Germany, Italy, Mexico, and the United Kingdom combined).

We're number one in total and per capita municipal waste (720 kilograms per person per year).

We're number one in hazardous waste produced (by a factor of more than twenty times our nearest competitor, Germany).

We're number one in oil consumption.

We're number one in natural gas consumption.

We're number one in the least amount of tax revenue generated (as a percentage of gross domestic product).

We're number one in the least amount of federal and state government expenditure (as a percentage of GDP).

We're number one in daily per capita consumption of calories.

We're number one in lowest voter turnout.

We're number one in fewest number of political parties represented in the lower or single house.

We're number one in recorded rapes (by a factor of almost three times our nearest competitor—Canada).

We're number one in injuries and deaths from road accidents (almost twice as many as runner-up Canada).

We're number one in births to mothers under the age of twenty (again, more than twice as many as Canada, and nearly twice as many as number two New Zealand).

We're number one in the number of international human rights treaties not signed.

We're number one among countries in the United Nations with a legally constituted government to not ratify the UN Convention on the Rights of the Child.

We're number one in number of known executions of child offenders.

We're number one in likelihood of children under the age of fifteen to die from gunfire.

We're number one in likelihood of children under the age of fifteen to commit suicide with a gun.

We're number one in lowest eighth-grade math scores.

We're number one in becoming the first society in history in which the poorest group in the population are children.

Pause for a moment and reflect on that list. Doesn't it make the heart swell with a sense of pride, knowing that we as Americans—*and no one else*—can get to the top in so many categories? Sorta makes you nostalgic for the days when East Germany won all the medals at the Olympics. This is no easy feat to pull off, folks. Give yourselves a pat on the back, and the rich another tax cut.

In the interest of trying to be more empathetic toward those in the other 191 nations on earth, I'd like to offer a few suggestions to help bring about world peace. I modestly call this "Mike's

Comprehensive Peace Plan." The way I look at it, we're all stuck on this island, no one gets to claim immunity—and no one's getting voted off any time soon. So whether it's simply the right thing to do, or it's because we don't want to end up with a Bin Laden lurking in every airport in America, we need to help set some things right in the world.

I would begin in the Middle East, Northern Ireland, the former Yugoslavia, and North Korea.

THE HOLY LAND

Such a nice name—the Holy Land—for a place with more evil acts per square mile than the VIP room at Satan's annual marshmallow roast.

In January of 1988, just one month after the beginning of the First Palestinian Intifada, a few friends and I traveled to Israel, the West Bank, and Gaza to see for ourselves what all the commotion was about.

Although in my life I had already traveled through Central America, China, Southeast Asia, and other parts of the Middle East, I wasn't ready for what I saw in the refugee camps in the Occupied Territories. I had never encountered such squalor, debasement, and utter misery. To force human beings to live in these conditions—and do so at the barrel of a gun, for more than forty years—just made no sense.

I am deeply saddened and angered by the horror and misery the Jewish citizens of this earth have had to endure. No group has consistently seen more death and torture come their way than the Jews, at the hands of a bigotry that has lasted not just centuries but *millennia*.

What amazes me is not the nature of this hatred—after all, ethnic war seems a fact of life—but the consistency with which it has been passed down, for thousands of years. Hate isn't like a

Tourist Guide to Holy Land Hot Spots

LOCATION	HISTORICAL SIGNIFICANCE	BLOODSHED
Tel Aviv	On the outskirts of modern Tel Aviv is the ancient port of Jaffa, believed to be founded in the wake of the great flood by Noah's son, Japheth, and site of the House of Simon the Tanner, traditionally believed to be where the Apostle Peter once stayed.	2001: 21 young Israelis killed and more than 100 injured by a Palestinian suicide bomber outside a beachfront disco.
Joseph's Tomb, Nabulus/ Shechem	Christians believe the tomb is where Joseph of Arimathea placed Jesus' body after the Crucifixion and where his resurrection occurred. Many Jews believe the tomb is that of Jacob's son Joseph (with his Technicolor dreamcoat).	2000: Border Police Cpl. Yosef Madhat and Rabbi Binyamin Herling killed by Palestinians. 2000: A two-year-old Palestinian girl riding in the backseat of her parents' car killed by bullets fired from the direction of a nearby Jewish settlement.
Temple Mount, Jerusalem	Main site of Islamic worship in Jerusalem. King David's tomb, the site of the Last Supper, etc., nearby.	1990: 17 Palestinians killed by Israeli soldiers.

continued

LOCATION	HISTORICAL SIGNIFICANCE	BLOODSHED
Tomb of the Patriarchs, Hebron (also known as the Mosque of Machpelah)	Sacred site for Christians, Muslims, and Jews. Believed to be where Abraham, his wife, Sarah, and their descendants Isaac and Jacob are buried.	1929: Arab massacre of the Jewish community. 1994: Jewish settler Baruch Goldstein murdered 29 Muslims worshiping in the mosque.

grandfather clock or a gold watch; you can't leave it behind for your next of kin. If my great-great-great-grandfather hated Canadians or Presbyterians, I would have absolutely no way of knowing about it. And yet somehow hatred of Jews has been passed down, like a language or a song or an oral tradition, among so many people. Usually we humans are able to shake our bad ideas. Remember "The earth is flat"? We stopped pushing that nonsense six hundred years ago! We've gotten over the one about Creation taking only until Saturday night, and the one about eggs being bad for your cholesterol. So why haven't people wised up and sent their bigotry against Jews to the same dustbin that holds our Seals and Croft records?

Well, here's one complicating factor in the case of the Palestinians: the unfortunate thing about us humans is that once abused, some of us seek to abuse others. It's no surprise that abused kids grow up to abuse their own kids. After the Americans bombed the peaceful, neutral Cambodians over and over and over, slaughtering hundreds of thousands of them during the *Vietnam* War, it shouldn't have been a shock when the Killing Fields followed and Cambodians turned the slaughter on each other. After the Soviet Union lost over twenty million citizens in

World War II, it's no surprise that they sought insurance against future invasion by seizing and dominating nearly every country that bordered them.

Sometimes people just go crazy from too much abuse and violence and take drastic, irrational measures to protect themselves.

I don't want to involve myself in the various arguments about why Israel was created, or what the historical or biblical claims are to the land. Rather, I want to deal with the situation at hand—which is the ongoing killing on both sides of the question: the continued hatred toward the Jews by the Palestinians, and the appalling oppression of the Palestinians by the Israelis.

It's true that there's also much oppression of Palestinians in Arab countries, where Palestinians aren't allowed to vote or own property and are treated as second-class citizens and pawns in the fight against Israel. But I'm not going to spend my time on this, since there isn't a whole lot I can do about it. You and I don't give $3 billion a year to Syria, as we do to Israel. And since that's *our money*, we must consider ourselves responsible for the oppression, killing, and apartheid conditions that have been created in Israel's Occupied Territories.

The fighting in the Middle East has got to stop—and now. Israel has nuclear weapons, some Arab countries soon will, and we'd better stop this madness quickly before we ALL pay a huge price for it.

I, for one, don't want apartheid being funded in my name—anywhere. I believe (stop me if you've heard this before) that all human beings deserve the right to self-determination, the right to the ballot, the right to have life, liberty, and the pursuit of happiness. Arabs who live in the West Bank and Gaza have *none* of this. They are not free to travel. They are under constant curfew. They are taxed with no representation. They are arrested and jailed without trial. Their homes are bulldozed without warning. Their land is stolen and given to "settlers." Their children are murdered for throwing stones—or for just walking down the street.

Of course they throw stones! Of course they kill Israeli set-tlers! That's what abused people do—they fight back, and abuse others. Who should know this better than the Israelis? The world butchers them to near-extinction in the last century, and they'll be damned if they're going to be annihilated in this mil-lennium.

At times like this, those of us who have been fortunate enough to avoid this kind of suffering in our own lives must step in and stop the killing. That is what I want my country to do. And here's how: *Quit sending over a blank check, and start getting in there with both parties to stop the barbarism.* My plan:

1. Congress should inform Israel that it has thirty days to end the bloodshed perpetrated in its/our name—or we cut off the entire $3 billion. Individual terrorism is bad enough, but state-sponsored terrorism is truly evil. I understand that the world will always have the occasional lone crazy with grievances he feels compelled to avenge with violence. But for the Israelis, a group of otherwise good and intelligent people, to collectively enforce a system of terror against another group simply because of their race or religion is unconscionable. And you and I and millions of other taxpaying Americans put up the money for Israel's unconscionable actions—actions that could not exist if each of us wasn't having 4 cents taken from our paychecks today and every day to buy the bullets that go into the Israeli guns that kill the Palestinian children.

2. If it wants to keep receiving our tax dollars, Israel should be given a year to work out a plan with the Palestinians to create a nation called Palestine (formed from the West Bank, Gaza, and some strip of land that connects them). This new nation of Palestine must then present a Constitution that not only prohibits any form of aggression against Israel but also guarantees full democratic rights to every Palestinian man, woman, and child.

3. The United States will then give Palestine *double* what it has given Israel in funding (for a permanent peace, I'd gladly give up my portion of this—pennies a week). This is not free cash for corrupt public officials like the ones we have in our country. This is Marshall Plan–style direct aid that builds roads, schools, and industries that provide decent-paying jobs.

4. The United Nations should then commit to defending Israel against anyone who still wants it destroyed—*and* vow to defend a democratic Palestine from its neighboring Arab regimes (who are going to go bonkers if their own oppressed peoples see how good these Palestinian Arabs have it living in freedom and prosperity).

Of course, who's going to listen to me? Apparently it's too much fun continuing this stupid soap opera over a wedge of land you can cross in the time it takes to get from Oakland to San Francisco in rush hour.

Well, maybe there is one person who will listen.

Dear President Arafat:

We've never met. That's not an attempt to cop an invite over for dinner or a game of horseshoes. You're a busy man, I'm a busy man (though I can't get anyone in the office here to call me President, or respond to my directives with, "Ya, Sir!").

Sorry. That's the kind of humor that has kept me relegated to appearing only on basic cable in America (Channel 64, right after the Italian language station in New York City).

I have the key to your success. I know how you can unilaterally end the killing on both sides—and, as a bonus, *wind up with a Palestinian state!*

I know, you're thinking, "Hey, who *is* this guy?" And you're right.

But hear me out. I want to propose something so revolutionary that it will flip out every Israeli right-winger and send every Israeli peacenik running to your side.

My proposal is not a new idea. It involves no armies, no money, and no UN resolutions. It's dirt cheap. It has been tried many times, in many countries—AND IT HAS NEVER FAILED. It demands no hatred and requires no weapons. In fact, it is all about *no weapons*.

It's called mass nonviolent civil disobedience. It worked for Martin Luther King Jr.—his nonviolent movement brought an abrupt end to legal segregation in America. It worked for Gandhi—he and his fellow Indians brought the British Empire to its knees without firing a shot. It worked for Nelson Mandela—he and the African National Congress brought about an end to apartheid with no violent revolution.

If it worked for them, trust me, it can work for you.

Sure, you can still win through violence. The Vietnamese proved that they could whip the mightiest country on earth. And look at us—we spent eight years picking off Redcoats, and got ourselves a big country out of all the shooting!

So killing *does* work, I guess. The only problem is, after the killing stops you're a little messed in the head, and it takes a while before you learn to put down your guns (225 years later and *we* still haven't learned).

But if you'd like to try the *nonviolent* approach, you not only get to see fewer people die—you get your own country in the end!

Here's how it works:

1. Just sit your ass down. That's it. It's simple. You just lay your bodies down—often just a few thousand in the middle of the road will do—and don't move and don't fight back when they try to drag you away. Instead of Israel always shutting down the borders to Gaza and the West Bank, *you* shut *them* down. Just march peacefully up to the checkpoint and then sit down. No Israelis will be able to get to their settlements. No Israelis will be able to transport goods and natural resources from your land into Israel. There is no Israeli vehicle I know of that can drive over mounds of thousands of people (not even a pair of snow tires will do the job!). Of course, they may try, and a number of your people may be injured or killed. Still, don't move. Just sit. The world will be watching—especially if you embrace the wonderful world of public relations, and alert the media to your plans. (Trust me, CNN will take your call.) And you'll end up with far fewer dead Palestinians than you yield under your current plan.

2. Call a general strike. Refuse to work for the Israelis. Their economy is based on the near-slave labor you provide them. Don't do it anymore. Who will do all their shitwork for them if Palestinians won't? Other Israelis? I don't think so! They need you and your willingness to break your backs for them for substandard wages. Watch how quickly a deal is struck once every single Arab refuses to go to work. Of course, they'll try to break you. They will cut off your water, your roads, your food—but you must stand firm. Stockpile, then strike nonviolently, and never give in. They will.

A few years back, over a million Israelis attended a Peace Now rally in Tel Aviv. That was an amazing sight. It also means that you, the Palestinians, have a million Jewish allies— a third of the country—in the nation you know as your enemy. A million of your "enemies" will come to your aid if you protest in a nonviolent way. Try it! Between your people and theirs, you will outnumber those in Israel who want to drive you into the sea.

Unfortunately, I know your inclination is to keep drawing

blood. You think this will bring you liberation. It will not. It will turn you into those who are now killing you. And if you haven't figured out one thing about the Israelis by now, you'd better get a clue—they ain't goin' *anywhere*. For God's sake, man—they had six million of their people massacred by the most advanced civilization on earth. Do you think they're going to let a few stones and car bombs get in the way of their own survival? They live in a world where they're isolated and all alone. They won't quit until you or the rest of the earth annihilates every last one of them. Is that what you want? Every last Jew wiped from the planet? If it is, then you need serious help—and you're gonna have to get past me before you touch another one of their children.

But if, as I suspect, you would prefer peace and quiet to constant war and displacement, then you must lay down all arms, lay down your bodies in the middle of the road and then . . . just wait. Yes, the Israelis will beat many of your people. They will drag your women by the hair, they will sic dogs on you, they may even get out the firehoses (and other tricks they've learned from us Americans). YOU MUST NOT FIGHT BACK! Trust me, when the pictures of your suffering at the hands of these brutes go out across the world, there will be such an outcry that the Israeli government will be unable to continue its oppression.

Well, there you go. If you want, I will come and join you in your nonviolent protest. It's the least I can do after helping finance the bullets and bombs that have killed your people.

Yours,

Michael Moore

THE UNITED KINGDOM OF GREAT BRITAIN AND NORTHERN IRELAND

Once again, the name itself gives it away: the people in charge of this one *knew* they were running a scam. If the United Kingdom felt it had any real moral authority to claim jurisdiction over Northern Ireland, it would simply declare it part of Great Britain and leave it at that, without drawing attention to a six-county area across a sea that it has no business claiming.

Now don't get me wrong—I've come to like the British people. British networks and studios fund my work when the Americans won't. The Brits—if you'll allow me a sweeping generalization that can be disproved at any British soccer riot—are an intelligent people with a great sense of humor and a rabid appreciation of political satire. Unlike us, they have numerous media outlets (London alone has eleven daily papers, and their four national networks have more to offer on any given night than our two hundred plus channels combined). The British media offer a wide spectrum of editorial viewpoints. No one is left out of the political discourse in the United Kingdom.

Except the Catholics of Northern Ireland.

As with the Palestinian "situation," I'm not going to spend time rehashing eight hundred years of history, so let me get right to the present conundrum. Catholics in Northern Ireland are second-class citizens whose rights are continually violated, who are kept on the lowest tier economically, and who live under the thumb of an occupational force of British soldiers. This has led to a lot of random killing in the past thirty-three years. Bill Clinton was able to bring the two sides together during his presidency, and helped work out a peace settlement that would have included Catholics in the power structure of Northern Ireland. Everyone was relieved and hopeful.

But that hope didn't last long, as the Protestants soon insisted they wouldn't share power until every IRA gun was turned in. Most saw this as an excuse to try and back out of the agreement, and new bloodshed ensued. Since then, prospects have grown bleak.

This nonsense has gone on long enough. I have a solution that will bring permanent peace to the area:

Convert the Protestants of Northern Ireland to Catholicism.

That's right. No more bickering and battling over religion when everyone belongs to the same religion! Naturally, most of the Protestants won't want to convert—but since when has that stopped the Catholic Church? From the Crusades of the Middle Ages to the Spanish conquistadors of Latin America, the Church has always known how to "convince" the natives to see the light.

Because Catholics already make up 43 percent of Northern Ireland, we need to convert only 8 percent of the Protestants to create a Catholic majority. That ought to be a cinch. Especially once the Protestants consider the following benefits of being a Roman Catholic:

* **One guy in charge**—the Pope. There are several thousand Protestant sects. Some are run by committee, some by an elected chair, others simply run like a food co-op, with no one calling the shots. Going Catholic means having a leader for *life*, someone unafraid of making a decision, giving the faithful a fixed set of rules and boundaries that give one's life order and clarity. And after the Pope dies, no messy elections—a couple hundred guys wearing red gather in a room, vote, and a puff of white smoke out of the chimney tells everyone the decision has been made. No campaign speeches, no pandering to the electorate, no recounts.

✻ **More sex.** Catholics, as we all know, have more babies, and so, you know, that means only one thing— more sex! Sorry, but in the Catholic Church you can't get the babies without the sex. And who couldn't use a little extra sex these days? I'm telling you, let those Protestant Orangemen know they're going to be getting some, and watch how fast they end those silly parades.

✻ **More days off.** The Catholic Church has six official Holy Days. In countries where the majority of citizens practice Catholicism, these are fully paid days off from work and schooldays off for the kids. Can you name one Protestant Holy Day—not counting the day the Eddie Bauer Christmas catalog comes out? I didn't think so.

✻ **Free alcohol.** You go to Mass every day, you get a free drink of wine. True, you must accept that you're drinking the Blood of Christ, but hey, you can do that! How many times have you told people that the gin and tonic you are nursing is "just water"? Have a little faith!

✻ **Catholic girls** (see above).

✻ **A guaranteed spot in heaven** at the right hand of God himself! It's all there in the Bible—Jesus made Peter the head of the Church, and then he made it clear that only members of the "one true Catholic church" get past the velvet rope at the pearly gates. So you can continue your allegiance to the Queen and then burn in hell for eternity—or you can get on the "A list" and enjoy Forever with a first-class seat.

Once a list like the one above is made available to the Protestant population of Northern Ireland, it will only be a matter of hours before we see a mad rush toward the gates of the Falls Road. And here's the easy part: any Catholic may perform the sacrament of Baptism if one believes that the non-Catholic may die without ever being saved. I think it's safe to say that includes all of the Protestants of the United Kingdom.

All you need is a little water to pour over any Protestant's forehead, and then repeat the following words: "I baptize thee in the name of the Father, the Son, and the Holy Ghost, Amen."

That's it! It takes longer to join Weight Watchers! (And if the Protestants seem reluctant, then Catholics can just run through Protestant neighborhoods—not with guns, but with garden hoses blessed by the parish priest. Spray the baptismal waters at them, shout the words—and then start running like hell.)

THE FORMER YUGOSLAVIA

This godforsaken corner of the world has been the source of much of our collective misery for the last century. Its residents' inability to get along—with Serbs fighting Croats fighting Muslims fighting Macedonians fighting Albanians fighting Kosovars fighting Serbs—can be traced to the following single event: in 1914 a Serb anarchist by the name of Gavrilo Princip assassinated the Archduke Ferdinand. This incident kicked off World War I. Which led to World War II. Over fifty million people died from both wars.

I don't know what it is about these people. I mean, I don't go around killing Texans. I don't go burn down whole villages in Florida. I've learned to live with it. Why can't they?

It hasn't always been this violent in Yugoslavia. After World War II, those few Yugoslavians who had fought against Hitler (mostly the Serbs; the Croats and others welcomed the Nazis and their Final Solution with open arms) took over and formed a Communist government under the leadership of Marshall Tito.

Tito refused to answer to Moscow, and set off on his own mission of uniting the ethnic factions of his country.

For nearly forty years the people of Yugoslavia stopped killing each other. They became a civilized country. They made Yugos. Basketball became the national sport. Life was good.

Then Tito died, and all hell broke loose. Croats started killing Serbs. Serbs killed Muslims in Bosnia. Serbs killed Albanians in Kosovo. Then the United States bombed Kosovo, to show them

---

Twelve Steps for Recovery from Addiction to Violence in Yugoslavia

Frankly, you people haven't got time for all twelve steps—you're *dying* out there. Try these three steps—and make it quick!

* Admit that you are powerless over your addiction to violence, and that your lives have become unmanageable.

* Make a decision to turn your will and your lives over to the care of the United Nations, NATO, and any other organizations that stand between you and your Hatfield and McCoy–like compulsion for tribal warfare.

* Make direct amends to all persons you have harmed, wherever possible, except when to do so would injure them or others (or when they, like thousands of other Yugoslavians, are already dead).

killing was wrong. In the past few years there has been peace, then war, then peace again, and now war again. It never stops. These people are addicts.

And that means it's time for an intervention.

Not a military one, but a twelve-step intervention, the kind you do with an alcoholic.

I am suggesting to the people of the former Yugoslavia that you take a pledge to wean yourselves off the violence. Set up weekly meetings in church basements all across the country (what's left of it), sit in a circle, and get it—whatever "it" is—off your chest. Yes, you can smoke there, and there's plenty of coffee.

If you don't do this, we are going to drop thousands of those shitty little Yugo cars from cargo planes high above your country. It will never be safe to go out of the house because you'll never know when one of those 2,000-pound lemons is heading for your head.

Then again, maybe science has a better solution: perhaps this is that occasion we've been looking for, to invent a way to bring someone back from the dead. Nobody in America liked Tito much when he was alive, but now he looks like Lady Bird Johnson. If we can clone humans, shouldn't we be able to bring one back who's already been alive? I wouldn't mind seeing the U.S. Government commit a few billion dollars to this Lazarus Project. That big lug in his silly hat taking charge of his unruly citizens once more would be a sight for sore eyes. In the name of the millions who didn't need to die in the twentieth century thanks to Yugoslavian misbehavior, we may have no other hope to restore Yugoslavian domestic peace and tranquility. Arise, Tito!

NORTH KOREA

Here's the thing about North Korea's ruler, Kim Jong Il: he's a *huge* movie buff, with a home collection of more than fifteen thousand videos. Maybe he's been looking to all those movies for guidance on how to save the oppressed and starving people of his country. But since his favorite films (in addition to pornography) apparently include American westerns, Elizabeth Taylor movies, and the *Friday the 13th* series, it just may be that he's looking at the wrong movies.

The dictator/film fan has also written a book on the art of the cinema, and even founded a film school. "Kim Jong Il watches every single film made in North Korea," said Kim Hae Young, a North Korean actress who defected to the South. "He gives comments on acting, directing, and everything else. If he compliments some actor, he or she suddenly becomes a star."

He shares an appreciation of the whimsical world of entertainment with his eldest son, Kim John-nam, who recently flew to Japan, desperate to visit the new Japanese Disney World. He used a fake Dominican Republic passport (sure, *he* looks Dominican!) to try to gain entry to the country. When immigration realized who he was, they called his daddy and had him sent back to his room in North Korea.

Kim Jong Il reportedly receives blood transfusions from young virgins on a regular basis "to slow the aging process." He is also an avid sports fan, and fully understands the difference between zone and man-to-man defense in American basketball. He wears platform shoes to increase his height, and is rumored to be the largest individual purchaser of Hennessy Cognac in the world.

The problem is, millions of people are starving to death in North Korea, mostly because Kim Jong Il is also a dictator who spends 25 percent of his country's GNP on the military. Now you can get away with that if you're an American—I mean, we've got a lot of amber waves of grain, so we won't (all) starve giving the majority of our money to the Pentagon. But in North Korea, a rocky peninsula with lots of snails, you just can't operate from that scenario.

Since 1948, when the Korean peninsula was divided into the
Communist North and capitalist/fascist South, the citizens of
both Koreas have endured harsh conditions. They've lived
through the Korean War, which never officially ended (we're still
in "ceasefire" mode), decades of repression and isolation (which
for South Korea ended with the pro-democracy movement of the
1980s, but for North Korea continues today), economic depriva-
tion, floods, and famine. North Koreans have only been allowed
reunions with family members from South Korea twice in more
than fifty years: in 1985, just fifty people from each side were
allowed to meet with their relatives, and in August of 2000, one
hundred more were permitted reunions.

Kim Jong Il, referred to in North Korea as "Dear Leader," has
a reputation for being an eccentric, irresponsible playboy. "The
assessment a couple of years ago was of a drunken kook who
didn't understand the world around him," a former senior Clinton official has said. After he succeeded his father—who ruled the
country from 1948 to 1994—as the country's official leader, Kim
was accused of being responsible for the bombing deaths of several members of the South Korean cabinet, and for the explosion
of a South Korean civilian airliner. He has a huge army, and is
even suspected of having the atomic bomb.

In the past two years, though, Kim Jong Il has begun showing
signs of a change of heart, signs that he's emerging from the shad-
ows. When the famine began in 1995, Kim refused to allow foreign aid workers free access to the countryside, and had some
food aid diverted to the army. But last year he allowed almost 150
representatives of international governmental organizations to
set up camp in North Korea. He recently hosted a summit with
the president of South Korea, who has been encouraging North
Korea to end its dangerous isolation. Then Kim even allowed a
visit from U.S. Secretary of State Madeleine Albright, who found
him capable of having serious diplomatic discussions. (They actu-

ally hit it off quite well; he dragged her to a bunch of events—shows, dinners . . . and movies.)

Now that Kim is getting in the groove—and realizing, like me, that sitting in a dark theater watching all kinds of movies can be the road to peace and tranquillity (he allegedly had two film producers kidnapped from South Korea to make documentaries in North Korea)—I have a number of ideas that may help the wacky dictator save his country from total destruction:

* **Watch better movies**. Kim Jong Il has got to broaden himself past the porn and John Wayne. He once remarked that he was so moved by the performance of Leonardo DiCaprio that he "probably could not bear to watch *Titanic* a second time." We understand. Here is the list of tapes I plan to send to him instead for his viewing pleasure:

  Easy Rider—The first thing Dear Leader needs to do is loosen up. This movie ought to help.

  200 Motels—If Dennis Hopper can't do the trick, Frank Zappa will.

  Dude, Where's My Car?—All you need to know about America is contained in this movie.

  My Dinner with André—Sure, it's just two guys eating and talking for two hours, but at least he'll get to see what a real meal looks like. The dinner conversation will help him refine his communication skills.

* **Bring him to Hollywood** for his own pitch meeting. He must have *thousands* of ideas for movies. One of

them will surely be right for Rob Schneider. Tell the dictator we'll get Tom Cruise to play him in his life story, *Long Jong Gone*. Give him a first-look deal and a bungalow on the studio lot. Fill up his day with needless meetings with development executives and talent agents. That should keep him busy for a couple of years. By that time, North Korea should benefit from his absence and pull itself out of its slump.

* **If all else fails, finance a theme park** in Pyongyang. Theme parks *always* work. Even if they don't restore an economy, at least they make people feel good. Especially Dear Leader's "Dominican" son. And isn't that what really matters? Make him assistant manager.

NINE

One Big Happy Prison

IT WAS A few minutes after 10:00 P.M. on October 4, 2000, one month before the presidential election. The previous night, the first of three debates between Al Gore and George W. Bush had taken place.

On this balmy October evening in Lebanon, Tennessee, John Adams, sixty-four, had just sat down in his favorite tan recliner to watch the evening news. His cane, the result of a stroke a few years earlier, rested beside him. A well-respected member of Lebanon's African-American community, Adams was now on disability after working for years at the Precision Rubber plant.

The anchors on TV were dishing out their postmortems on the debate. Adams and his wife, Lorine, were discussing their intention to vote for Al Gore when there was a knock at the door.

Mrs. Adams left the room, came to the door, and asked who was there. Two men demanded that she open the door and let them in. She asked again who they were, but they refused to identify themselves. She again refused to open the door.

At that moment, two unidentified officers from the Lebanon Police Department's drug task force broke down the door, grabbed Mrs. Adams, and immediately handcuffed her. Seven other officers burst into the house. Two of them ran around the corner into the back room, guns drawn, and pumped several bullets into John Adams. Three hours later, he was pronounced dead at Vanderbilt University Medical Center.

The raid on the Adams house had been ordered after an undercover informant purchased drugs in the house at 1120 Joseph Street. Lebanon's narcotics unit, funded along with thousands of others around the country as part of the Clinton administration's "War on Drugs," obtained warrants from a local judge to arrest the occupants of the house.

The only problem: the Adamses live at 70 Joseph Street. The drug-war police had the wrong house.

A few miles down the road in Nashville, as John Adams was being accidentally executed, scores of paid and volunteer staff bustled about inside Al Gore's national campaign headquarters. Their main concern that night was damage control, as they tried to distract voters from the spectacle of their candidate sighing through Bush's responses the previous night. Phones were lighting up, shipments of bumper stickers and yard signs were being rerouted, strategists were huddling to plan the next day's campaign stops. On the table sat copies of Gore's anticrime proposals, including more funding for additional police and more money to fight the Drug War. None of them knew that their out-of-control efforts to eradicate drugs had just cost them a potential vote— that of an elderly black man across town.

Killing off your voters is no way to win an election.

This was just one of too many incidents in recent years where innocent people have been shot by local or federal drug police who thought they "had their man."

Worse still is the way so many citizens have been locked up in the past decade thanks to Clinton/Gore policies. At the beginning of the nineties, there were about a million people in prison in the United States. By the end of the Clinton/Gore years, that number had grown to TWO MILLION. The bulk of this increase was the result of new laws being enforced against drug *users*, not pushers. Eighty percent of those who go to prison for drugs are in there for possession, not dealing. The penalties for crack use are three times as high as those for cocaine use.

It doesn't take much to figure out why the drug of choice in the white community is treated with so much more leniency than the drug that constitutes the only affordable high in the poor black and Hispanic community. For eight years there was an intense, aggressive move to lock up as many of these minority citizens as possible. Instead of providing the treatment their condition demands, we dealt with the problem by sending them to rot inside a prison cell.

But forget for a moment about helping the less fortunate. Who was the genius in the Clinton/Gore administration who said, "Hey, I've got an idea—why don't we go after the black and Hispanic community—plenty of drug users there! Lock 'em up in record numbers, decimating the voting power of a group that votes for our side nine to one!"

It doesn't make sense, does it? What kind of campaign would purposely destroy its own voting base? You don't see Republicans sitting around trying to plot ways to incarcerate corporate executives and NRA members. Trust me, you won't see Karl Rove convening a White House meeting to figure out a way to lock up and strip the voting rights from a million members of the Christian Coalition.

In fact, just the opposite. The Bush people are committed to seeing that none of their supporters ever enjoys the hospitality of a prison shower room. Much was made after Clinton left office of the pardons he granted to dubious fat cats like Marc Rich. The entire country was up in arms over the absolution given to a fugitive who got away without paying his taxes. A rich person who got away without paying taxes! We were shocked— SHOCKED!

And yet no attention at all was paid to the "pardons" of David Lamp, Vincent Mietlicki, John Wadsworth, or James Weathers Jr. And no one called for a congressional investigation of why criminal charges were dropped against Koch Industries, the largest privately held oil company in America, whose CEO and vice president are the brothers Charles and David Koch. Why was this?

Because *those* "pardons" came during the reign of George W. Bush.

In September 2000, the federal government brought a 97-count indictment against Koch Industries and its four employees—Lamp, Mietlicki, Wadsworth, and Weathers, who were Koch's environmental and plant managers—for *knowingly* releasing 91 metric tons of benzene, a cancer-causing agent, into the air and water, and for covering up the deadly release from federal regulators.

This wasn't Koch's first run-in with the law; it wasn't even their first *that year*. Earlier in 2000, Koch had been fined $35 million for illegal pollution in six states.

But with the George W. Bush's election "decided," Koch's fortunes suddenly changed. Koch executives had just contributed some $800,000 to Bush's presidential campaign and other Republican candidates and causes. In January, as John Ashcroft waited in the wings, the government dropped the charges first from 97 to 11 and then to a mere nine.

Koch Industries, however, still faced fines totaling $352 million. Bush's new administration, now firmly in place, quickly fixed that. In March, they dropped two more charges. Then, two days before the case was to go to court, Ashcroft's Justice Department settled the case.

Koch Industries pled guilty to a new charge of falsifying documents, and the government dropped all environmental charges against the company, including all felony counts against their four employees.

Following hard on the heels of their generosity, the Koch executives facing possible prison terms were freed from any prosecution. The company itself had all 90 of the serious counts against it dismissed and in the end paid a fine that wiped out the 7 remaining counts. According to the *Houston Chronicle*, "Koch executives celebrated the conclusion of the case," company spokesman Jay Rosser crowing about how the dropping of charges was proof of Koch's "vindication."

I won't defend the actions of Marc Rich, but correct me if I'm wrong: I believe the willful spewing into the air and water of a deadly chemical that causes cancer (and will surely contribute to who knows how many people's deaths) is a little more serious than skipping out on Rudy Giuliani to go on an eighteen-year ski trip to Switzerland. Yet I'm sure none of you have heard of the pardons granted to Charles and David Koch and their oil company and its executives. Why should you? It was just business as usual, under a national press that's thoroughly asleep at the wheel.

It's too bad that Anthony Lemar Taylor forgot to send in his contribution to the Bush campaign. Taylor was another repeat offender—a petty thief who decided one day in 1999 to pretend he was golf superstar Tiger Woods.

Though Taylor looked nothing at all like Woods (but, hey, they all look alike, don't they?), he was able to use a fake driver's license and credit cards identifying him as Tiger Woods to purchase a 70-inch TV, a few stereos, and a used luxury car.

Then somebody finally figured out he wasn't Tiger Woods, and he was arrested and tried for theft and perjury.

His sentence? TWO HUNDRED YEARS TO LIFE!

You read it right. Two hundred years to life, thanks to California's "three-strikes" law, which says that upon a third criminal conviction, you're put away for life. To date, no corporate executive has been sent away for life after being caught three times polluting a river or ripping off its customers. In America, we reserve that special treatment for those who happen to be poor or African-American or fail to contribute to one of our fine political parties.

Of course, sometimes the justice system, ever the steamroller, is so hell-bent on punishing the have-nots it doesn't care who it locks up, guilty or not.

Kerry Sanders, the youngest child of nine, suffered from paranoid schizophrenia. By the age of twenty-seven he had fought the demons in his mind for over seven years and had been in and out of mental institutions for much of that time. Sometimes, when he went off his medication, he would end up on the streets of Los Angeles, as he did one day in October 1993.

While sleeping on a bench outside the USC Medical Center, Kerry was arrested for trespassing. But Kerry's luck turned worse when a routine warrant check showed that one Robert Sanders, a career criminal, had escaped five weeks earlier from a New York State prison, where he was serving time for attempting to kill a man over cocaine in 1990.

Of course, Kerry Sanders of California wasn't Robert Sanders of New York. But I guess "Kerry" and "Robert" are close enough, and California and New York . . . well, um, they're both BIG STATES, after all. . . .

Unfortunately for Kerry, what he *did* share with Robert was a birthday.

That was enough for the L.A. cop, even though the same computerized warrant search showed that *Kerry* Sanders had been stopped for jaywalking on a Los Angeles street in July 1993—while *Robert* Sanders was still in his New York prison.

No matter: Kerry Sanders was sent to New York to serve out

Robert Sanders's sentence. He remained in the New York penitentiary for *two years*, while his mother searched all over Los Angeles for him. Somehow the L.A. cops failed to compare the two records—which would have revealed that their guy had the wrong fingerprints.

Kerry had only one person in the whole process who was supposed to help him—the public defender appointed to protect his interests. But this thirty-year veteran PD encouraged him *not* to fight extradition. The PD explained to Kerry that fighting back would only prolong his stay in the L.A. county jail before being returned to New York anyway. Apparently the PD didn't even notice that Kerry was "slow," much less suffering from severe mental illness. Or would it have even mattered?

The PD failed to ask basic questions. He failed to spend more than a brief few minutes with a helpless client. He never looked into whether Kerry had any family who might be contacted to assist in his defense.

The PD also failed to check the system for any pending cases, or a prior record, or his client's financial status. He didn't even take the time to match the description on the warrant with Kerry, much less demand a fingerprint or booking photo comparison. *So what*, you say? After all, both men were black; they were both the same age—they even shared a birthdate! Isn't that good enough?

It gets worse. During the hearing to waive Kerry Sanders's right to fight the New York extradition, he was asked to sign a form. The form read: "I, *Robert* Sanders, do hereby freely and voluntarily state that I am the identical Robert Sanders"—and then Kerry signed it "Kerry Sanders."

He also drew doodles all over one copy of the waiver.

No bells? No red flags? Not for this public defender!

Finally given his chance to appear before a judge, Kerry was asked if he had read the document he had signed. He said he had not. The judge stopped the extradition proceeding.

"Did *you* sign it?" asked the judge.

"Yeah," Kerry replied.

"Why did you sign it?"

"Because they told me to sign it," Kerry Sanders answered.

Kerry's public defender was ordered by the judge to review the form again with his client. Within minutes the judge was satisfied, and both the court and the public defender moved on to the next case.

After Kerry Sanders was sold down the river by his L.A. public defender, he was shipped across the country to spend the next two years in Green Haven maximum-security prison, sixty miles north of New York City, where he was sexually assaulted by other inmates.

In October 1995, after federal agents in Cleveland arrested the *real* Robert Sanders, Kerry Sanders was reunited with his mother, Mary Sanders Lee. Had it not been for the chance arrest of Robert Sanders, Kerry Sanders would still be in prison today.

Kerry was sent home from Green Haven with $48.13, a plastic bag with some medicine, a soda, and a pack of cigarettes. He told his sister, Roberta: "They took me to New York. It was so cold there. They put me in this little room."

This is not a rare case of the system making a horrible mistake. In a sense, it is not even a mistake. It is the natural result of a society that recklessly locks up anyone who *may* be a criminal, even if they *aren't* a criminal, because it's better to be safe than right. Our courts are nothing but a haphazard assembly line for the poor to be routed *away* from us, out of sight—out of my damn way!

Well, this is America, and I guess if it's good enough to remove thousands of innocent black men from the voting rolls in Florida, it should be good enough to railroad an innocent black man in Los Angeles.

In this assembly-line system of justice, the one thing that mucks up the wholesale delivery of the accused to jail is the jury trial. Why? Because jury trials are shit-disturbers. They force everyone to do their job. The judges, prosecutors, and public defenders do everything in their power to coerce the defendant into accepting a guilty plea to AVOID THE BRUTAL PRISON SENTENCE WE WILL GIVE YOU IF YOU DEMAND A JURY TRIAL. If they can get the defendant not only to plead guilty but also to sign a waiver of his right to appeal, then they've hit a home run—and everyone can laugh about it later at the country club.

My sister, Anne, was a public defender in California. She insisted on defending her clients, and getting them a jury trial if that's what they wanted. For that, she was subjected to incredible harassment from the other PDs in the office. In 1998 the public defender's office in her county allowed only one felony client *out of almost nine hundred defendants* to have a jury trial.

Obviously, that didn't mean every single one of the other 899 accused were guilty. They were just coerced into pleading that way, with many of them ending up in prison, perhaps for crimes they didn't commit. But we'll never know, because their Sixth Amendment right to a trial by a jury of their peers was taken from them.

With this standardized railroading of the poor going on daily in every city in America, our justice system has nothing to do with justice. Our judges and lawyers are more like glorified garbage men, rounding up and disposing of society's refuse—ethnic cleansing, American style.

What happens when this fast-track chute sends innocent people to their death? It took only one college class full of kids at Northwestern University in Evanston, Illinois, to uncover and prove that five individuals on Illinois's death row were, in fact, innocent. Those students and their professor saved the lives of five people.

If one college class could do that, how many other hundreds of innocent people on death rows across the country are also sitting there awaiting their permanent disposal?

Thirty-eight states have the death penalty. So does the federal government and the U.S. military. Twelve states, plus the District of Columbia (that little piece of swampland with a majority of African-Americans and those offensive license plates), do not.

Since 1976, there have been over seven hundred executions in the United States.

The top execution-happy states are:

Texas (248 executions—nearly one-third of all U.S. executions since 1976)
Virginia (82)
Florida (51)
Missouri (50)
Oklahoma (43)
Louisiana (26)
South Carolina (25)
Arkansas (24)
Alabama (23)
Arizona (22)
North Carolina (17)
Delaware (13)
Illinois (12)
California (9)
Nevada (9)
Indiana (8)
Utah (6)

Since 1973, some ninety-five death row inmates have been *fully exonerated* by the courts—that is, found innocent of the crimes for which they were sentenced to die.

A shocking recent death penalty study of 4,578 cases in a twenty-three-year period (1973–1995) concluded that the courts found serious, reversible error in nearly 7 of every 10 capital sentence cases that were fully reviewed during the period. In 85 percent of the death penalty states, the error rates were 60 percent or higher. Three-fifths of these states have error rates of at least 70 percent.

And what were the most common errors?

1. Egregiously incompetent defense lawyers who didn't even look for, or missed important evidence that would have proved innocence or demonstrated that their client didn't deserve to die.

2. Police or prosecutors who *did* discover that kind of evidence but *suppressed* it, actively derailing the judicial process.

Catching these errors takes time—a national average of nine years from death sentence to execution. In most cases, death row inmates wait years for the lengthy review procedures needed to uncover all these errors—whereupon their death sentences are very often reversed. This imposes a terrible cost on taxpayers, victims' families, the judicial system, and the wrongly condemned.

Among the inmates involved in the study who had their death verdicts overturned, nearly all were given a sentence less than death (82 percent), and many were found innocent on retrial (7 percent).

The number of errors has risen since 1996, when President Clinton made it tougher for death row inmates to prove their innocence by signing into law a one-year limit on the time inmates have to appeal to federal courts after exhausting their appeals in state courts. In light of the study that proved how many of these inmates are either innocent or not legally deserving of the death penalty, this attempt to curb their appeals was simply outrageous.

We are one of the few countries in the world that puts to death *both* the mentally retarded and juvenile offenders. The United

States is among only six countries that impose the death penalty on juveniles. The others are Iran, Nigeria, Pakistan, Saudi Arabia, and Yemen.

The United States is also the only country besides Somalia that has not signed the United Nations Convention on the Rights of the Child. Why? Because it contains a provision prohibiting the execution of children under eighteen, and we want to remain free to execute our children.

No other industrialized nation executes its children.

Even China prohibits the death penalty for those under eighteen—this from a country that has shown an intolerable lack of respect for human rights.

Currently the total number of death row inmates in the United States tops 3,700. Seventy of those death row inmates are minors (or were when they committed their crime).

But our Supreme Court doesn't find it cruel and unusual punishment (in the terms of the Eighth Amendment to the U.S. Constitution) to execute those who were sixteen years old when they committed a capital crime. This despite the fact that same court has ruled that sixteen-year-olds do not have "the maturity or judgment" to sign *contracts*.

Odd, isn't it, that a child's diminished capacity for signing contracts is viewed as a legal barrier to enforcing a contract, but when it comes to the right to be executed, a child's capacity is equal to that of an adult?

Eighteen states allow juvenile offenders as young as sixteen to be executed. Five others allow the execution of those who were seventeen or older when they committed their crime. In 1999 Oklahoma executed Sean Sellers, who was sixteen at the time of the murders he was found guilty of committing. Sellers's multiple personality disorder wasn't revealed to the jury that convicted him. A federal appeals court found that Sellers might have been "factually innocent" because of his mental disorder, but that "innocence alone is not sufficient to grant federal relief." Unbelievable.

The American public is not stupid, and now that the truth has been coming out about the innocent people who have been sent to death row, they are at least responding with a sense of shame. Just a few years ago public opinion polls showed that upwards of 80 percent of the American people supported the death penalty. But now, with the truth out, a recent *Washington Post*/ABC News poll found that public approval of capital punishment has declined, while the proportion of Americans who favor replacing the death penalty with life in prison has increased. Fifty-one percent favored halting all executions until a commission is established to determine whether the death penalty is being administered fairly.

Sixty-eight percent said the death penalty is unfair because innocent people are sometimes executed. Recent Gallup Polls have shown that support for the death penalty is at a nineteen-year low. Sixty-five percent agreed that a poor person is more likely than a person of average or above-average income to receive the death penalty for the same crime. Fifty percent agreed that a black person is more likely than a white person to receive the death penalty for the same crime. Even in the killing machine known as the state of Texas, the *Houston Chronicle* reported that 59 percent of Texans surveyed believed that their state *has executed an innocent person!*, while 72 percent favor changing state law to include the sentencing option of life without parole, and 60 percent are now opposed to the state executing an inmate who is mentally retarded.

What we have done, in this great country, is to wage a war *not* on crime *but on the poor we feel comfortable blaming for it*. Somewhere along the way we forgot about people's rights, because we didn't want to spend the money.

We live in a society that rewards and honors corporate

gangsters—corporate leaders who directly and indirectly plunder the earth's resources and look out for the shareholders' profits above all else—while subjecting the poor to a random and brutal system of "justice."

But the public is starting to realize this is wrong.

We need to reorder society so that every person within it is seen as precious, sacred, and valuable, and that NO man is above the law, no matter how many candidates he buys off. Until this changes, we can utter the words "with liberty and justice for all" only with shame.

TEN

Democrats, DOA

HE HAS SIGNED a bill providing for federal funds to be distributed to "faith-based" charitable organizations.

He has expanded the number of federal crimes for which the death penalty can be given to a total of sixty.

He has signed a bill outlawing gay marriages and has taken out ads on Christian radio stations touting his opposition to any form of legal same-sex couplings.

In a short span of time, he has been able to kick ten million people off welfare—that's ten million out of fourteen million total recipients.

He has promised states "bonus funds" if they can reduce their welfare numbers further, and made it easier to get these funds by not requiring the states to help the ex-welfare recipients find jobs.

He has introduced a plan that would bar any assistance to teenage parents if they drop out of school or leave their parents' home.

Though he is careful not to draw attention to it, he supports many of the old provisions of Newt Gingrich's "Contract With America," including lowering the capital gains tax.

In spite of calls from Republican governors like George Ryan of Illinois to support a moratorium on capital punishment, he rejected all efforts to slow down the number of executions even after it was revealed that there are dozens of people on death row who are innocent.

He has released funds for local communities to hire over a hundred thousand new police officers and supports laws that put people behind bars for life after committing three crimes—even if those crimes were shoplifting or not paying for a pizza.

There are now more people in America without health insurance than when he took office.

He has signed orders prohibiting any form of health care to poor people who are in the United States illegally.

He supports a ban on late-term abortions and promised to sign the first bill to cross his desk that includes an exemption only if the life of the mother is in jeopardy.

He has signed an order prohibiting any U.S. funds going to any country to be used in helping women secure an abortion.

He signed a one-year gag order that prohibits using any federal funds in foreign countries where birth control agencies mention abortion as an option to pregnant women.

He has refused to sign the international Land Mine Ban Treaty already signed by 137 nations—but not by Iraq, Libya, North Korea, or the United States.

He has scuttled the Kyoto Protocol by insisting that "sinks" (e.g., farmlands and forests) be counted toward the U.S. percentage of emissions reductions, thus making a mockery of the whole treaty (which was written primarily to reduce the carbon dioxide pollution from cars and factories).

He has accelerated drilling for gas and oil on federal lands at a pace that matches, and in some areas exceeds, the production level during the Reagan administration.

He has approved the sale of one California oil field in the largest privatization deal in American history, and he opened the National Petroleum Reserve in Alaska (something even Reagan wasn't able to do).

And he became the first President since Richard Nixon not to force the auto manufacturers to improve their mileage per gallon—which would have saved millions of barrels of oil each day.

Yes, you'd have to agree, considering all of his above accomplishments, that Bill Clinton was one of the best Republican Presidents we've ever had.

There has been much hand-wringing since George W. Bush was given the office, with good people and liberals everywhere freaked out that the son-of-a-Bush would wreak havoc with the environment, turn back the clock on women's rights, and have us all reciting prayers in schools and at traffic lights. They are right to be concerned.

But Bush is only the uglier and somewhat meaner version of what we already had throughout the nineties—except that back then it came dressed in a charming smile from a guy who played soul tunes on a sax and told us what kind of underwear he (and his interns) wore. We liked that. It felt good, normal. He could sing the Black National Anthem. He partied with Gloria Steinem. He watched my show! I liked the guy!

We were all relieved that the Reagan/Bush years were over, and it was kind of cool that we had a President who had smoked pot and called himself "the first Black President of the United States." But we had a tendency to turn our heads the other way and block out things like his undermining key provisions of the Kyoto Agreement just weeks before the November 2000 election.

We didn't want to know about stuff like that; after all, what was our alternative? Baby Bush? Pat Buchanan? *Ralph Nader?*

Oh, God, no—not Ralph Nader. Why on earth would we want to support someone who agreed with us on all the issues? That's no fun!

The anger now leveled at Nader seems so personal, so intense, from Baby Boomers who blame him for Gore losing the election (he didn't lose). I look at these individuals in the their forties and fifties and I wonder why Nader seems so personally threatening to them.

It's taken a while, but I think I've got it figured out: Nader represents who they used to be but no longer are. He never changed. He never lost the faith, never compromised, never gave up. That's why they hate him. He didn't change his tune, didn't move to the suburbs, didn't start structuring his life around "Let's see how I can make the most money for me, me, ME!" He didn't conform to the new Baby Boom Code of Sell-Out Ethics in order to advance his power. No wonder millions of high school and college kids love him. He's the opposite of their parents, the people who "raised" them by handing them a latchkey, a Ritalin, and a remote for the TV set in the bedroom. Nader didn't make the trek down the dial from Sgt. Pepper to AOR to Kenny G. He stayed in the same rumpled clothes. Those who beat up on him now are like the bullies in high school who will not cease their harassment until you conform and start to look, think, and smell like them.

Well, guess what, fellow Boomers—this Nader dude ain't ever going to change. So why don't you save your breath, increase your Prozac dosage, and get some suburban therapist to see you once a week? Or just chill out and be thankful there are people like Ralph Nader out there. He'll do all the work; you just relax and order up another margarita.

I know it's a bitter pill to swallow, having to get up each morning to feed the corporate beast, to take your check from the bastards and try to look the other way despite all the crap they're shoving down your throat.

But somewhere in the deep recesses of your mind there's a little nerve ending going off, like the faint and blinking light of your cell phone a few minutes before it goes dead. It's your brain's memory bank reminding you about a time when you were younger and you passionately believed that *you and you alone* could make a difference, before the forces of adulthood surrounded you and told you to get with the program—or spend your lonely life barely scraping by.

And so you did. You learned to compromise your values while believing you still maintained them ("Yes, I drive an SUV—but I give to the Sierra Club!"). You learned to mollify your conscience at your lousy job, out of fear of the only imaginable alternative—homelessness and starvation! You put up with the oppressive nature of your church because, well, Jesus *did* say a lot of good things ("Love your enemy"), and so what if the money you just put in the collection plate is going to a woman-hating organization? You learned to say nothing when friends or coworkers spoke in coded racist terms because you knew *you* didn't hate black people and you were sure *they* didn't either . . . but why don't we cross over to the other side of the street just to be safe?

Best of all, you got to keep voting for the Democrats, the way you always had. After all, they say they have your best interests at heart—and just for saying that, you believe them! What kind of nut would vote for a third-party candidate, anyway? Why even think of going there—of revisiting the younger version of you, who was ready to get his head busted open while standing up for what was right? Out here in Adult World, you better forget about what's "right"—you gotta *win*. Winning is what it's all about, whether it's your company's market share, your own stock portfolio, or your kid's ability to beat all the other kids in kindergarten French class.

"Do the right thing?" HA! Go with the winner! Even if the

winner (Clinton) supports executing people, won't ban land mines, signs gag orders, prevents abortion funding, throws the poor out on the street, doubles the prison population, bombs four different countries, killing innocent civilians (Sudan, Afghanistan, Iraq, and Yugoslavia), allows a few conglomerates to own most of the media (which once were split up among nearly a thousand companies), and continually calls for increases in the Pentagon budget, it still feels better than . . . better than . . . well, better than something really, *really* bad.

Friends, when are we going to stop kidding ourselves? Clinton, and most other contemporary Democrats, *did not* and *will not* do what is best for us or the world we live in. We don't pay their bill—the top 10 percent do, and it is their will that will always be done. I know you already know this; it's just hard to say it because the alternative looks so much like . . . Dick Cheney.

Listen, before any of you good Democrats start considering at what temperature books burn, let me get this out of the way: George W. Bush is *worse* than Al Gore or Bill Clinton. No question about it.

But what exactly does that mean? If you put any two humans side by side and force someone to choose which one is "worse," they'll usually choose the one who's the bigger jerk. Hitler was "worse" than Mussolini, a Chevy is "worse" than a Ford, I am definitely "worse" than my wife. So what? This is a child's game. The truth is, the choice between Bush's "compassionate conservatism" and Clintonism is no more meaningful than the choice between castor oil and cherry-flavored Robitussin.

The Bush II administration began with Junior overturning a number of executive orders issued by President Clinton. Immediately he was made out to be some sort of monster. This was an important moment—*symbolically*—for the Democrats. They *needed* the public to believe that Bush was putting arsenic into the water and trying to poison us all. They wanted the people of America to think Bush was going to tear up the national forests, cut off abortion funding, and rape Alaska because he was only concerned with undoing all the good that President Clinton had done.

What's never mentioned is that Clinton spent eight years doing little or nothing with any of these problems, and then, with hours left in his administration, decided to try to leave office looking good (he was always *looking good*)—or set up Bush to look like the heavy. Either way, it worked.

Because the truth is, George W. Bush did little more than CONTINUE the policies of the last eight years of the Clinton/Gore administration. For eight long years, Clinton/Gore resisted all efforts and recommendations to reduce carbon dioxide in our air and arsenic in our water. Just one month before the 2000 election, Senate Democratic leader Tom Daschle and sixteen other Democrats successfully led the way to STOP any reduction of arsenic in the water. Why? Because Clinton and the Democrats were beholden to the rich bastards who had financed their campaigns—and who didn't want the levels of arsenic in the water changed.

Take the fact that Clinton/Gore was the first administration in twenty-five years NOT to demand higher fuel efficiency standards from Detroit. Under their watch, in other words, millions of barrels of oil were unnecessarily refined and spewed out into our air. Ronald Reagan, that icon of conservatism, had a better environmental record on this front: his administration ordered that cars get more miles per gallon. Under his successor, Bush I, the standards were made even stricter. But under Clinton? Nothing. How many more people will die from cancer, how much faster will global warming proceed, thanks to Bill and Al's camaraderie with one of their chief patrons, the top lobbyist for the Big Three auto companies—none other than Andrew Card, who, not surprisingly, is currently chief of staff for Clinton's logical extension, George W. Bush.

So is there a difference between Democrats and Republicans? Sure. The Democrats say one thing ("Save the planet!") and then do another—quietly holding hands behind the scenes with the bastards who make this world a dirtier, meaner place. The Republicans just come right out and give the bastards a corner office in the West Wing. That's the difference.

There's an argument, of course, that it's *more* evil to tell someone you're going to protect them and then rob them than to just go ahead and stick them up. Evil that's out in the open, not hiding in a liberal sheep's clothing, can be much easier to confront and eradicate. Which would you rather have, that roach you see running across the floor, or a house full of invisible termites buried in the wall? The roach may carry disease, but at least you know it's there and can take the appropriate action. The termites let you go on thinking you have the most beautiful living room—until the whole foundation collapses and you wake up in a pile of termite-harvested sawdust.

Bill Clinton waited until the final days of his presidency to sign a raft of presidential decrees and regulations, many of which promised to improve our environment and create safer working conditions. It was the ultimate cynical move. Wait till the last 48 hours of your term to do the right thing, so that everyone will look back and think, *now he was a good president*. But Clinton knew these last-minute orders would all fall under the hand of the new administration coming to power. He knew none of these orders would stand.

It was all about image.

Do you still believe Clinton removed arsenic from our water? Not only had he done nothing to protect us from drinking arsenic-laced water for the last eight years—but the order he signed stipulated that the arsenic was not to be removed from the water "until 2004." That's right. Look it up. Clinton's big environmental gesture in the last minutes of his term guaranteed that we'd be drinking the same levels of arsenic we've been drinking since 1942—the last time a REAL Democrat had the guts to stand up to the mining interests and reduce the levels of this poison. The Canadians and Europeans did it long ago. But Clinton ignored the law that required the EPA to reduce arsenic levels. That resulted in a lawsuit against the

Clinton Attempts a Legacy: Last-Minute Executive Orders and Regulations

Clinton waited eight years before he finally got around to doing some good—the last days of his presidency. On the way out the door, he issued directives that . . .

* Protected sixty million acres of national forests from logging and road-building

* Instituted rules to prevent workplace injuries, including ergonomic and "repetitive stress" regulations

* Raised standards concerning lead in paint, soil and dust, and truck diesel fuel

* Issued new EPA clean air regulations on diesel fuel for large trucks that would force sulfur levels in the fuel be reduced by 95 percent

* Required makers of hot dogs and other ready-to-eat meats to test periodically for *Listeria* bacteria

* Required energy conservation in central air conditioners

* Issued new regulations on washing machine energy efficiency

* Instituted stricter standards for energy-efficient water heaters

* Added protections for sea otters along the West Coast

continued

* Increased requirements for storing imported food

* Proposed revoking approval for the antibiotic enroflaxacin in poultry feed, which has resulted in germs and bacteria resistant to the drug

* Safeguarded Alaskan sea lions

* Required iron, lead, and steel smelting facilities to inform the public of all lead emissions over 100 pounds a year—a dramatic drop from the previous level of 25,000 pounds a year

* Created an eighty-four-million-acre Northwestern Hawaiian Islands Coral Reef Ecosystem Reserve, banning drilling and capping commercial fishing at their current levels

* Issued stricter rules on nutritional labeling for meat

* Outlawed snowmobiles in national parks

* Set child-safety standards for vehicles taking children to Head Start programs

* Limited the information health care providers can give out without permission of the patient

* Protected federal land from hard-rock mining in cases when mining would do irreparable harm to the land

* Allowed federal officers to deny contracts to companies that violate environmental, labor, consumer, and employment laws

* Set standards for using bodily restraint and confinement for those under the age of twenty-one in residential psychiatric facilities

* Proposed to regulate bioengineered pesticides

* Awarded $320 million to Chicago's mass-transit system

* Awarded $7.5 million to states for child-passenger safety education

* Set aside $18 million to buy environmentally sensitive cropland from California farmers

* Revised the regulatory definition of "Discharge of Dredged Material," protecting the nation's wetlands

Clinton administration by the Natural Resources Defense Council. In his last week Clinton finally caved in—but only after inserting language that would put off the change for four years. Thus Clinton made it official that we would all be drinking this poison during the entire Bush administration. Maybe he was doing us a favor.

And how about those carbon dioxide emission regulations Bush II overturned? Did I say "overturned"? Overturned *what*? All Bush did was maintain the Clinton status quo. He said, in essence, "I'm going to pollute the air at the very same levels Clinton did during his entire eight years, just as you're going to drink the same arsenic in the water under my watch as you did under Clinton's."

And, like the built-in four-year delay in his arsenic reductions, Clinton's orders on the toxic emissions in his last days specified that they were not to be reduced immediately either. In mid-November, sensing the fate of the election, he called for strict regulations on four greenhouse gases, including carbon dioxide. Again, his words sounded nice, but if you looked past them you found the new levels wouldn't be in place until 2010. And then, as if that wasn't bad enough, no new regulation could be implemented for another ten to 15 years.

The list goes on and on. For eight years Clinton did NOTH-ING about carpal tunnel syndrome as it relates to OSHA regulations. Then, in the middle of pardoning some rich guys during his all-night Agonistes on January 19, he finally decided to do some good for all those women who sit at keyboards all day and who, with their crippled hands, went to the polls TWICE to make him their President.

Friends, you are being misled and hoodwinked by a bunch of professional "liberals" who did NOTHING themselves for eight years to clean up these messes—and who now can't stop themselves from attacking people like Ralph Nader, who has devoted his entire life to every single one of these causes. What unmitigated gall! They blame Nader for giving us Bush? I blame THEM for *being* Bush! They suck off the same corporate teat, supporting things like NAFTA—which according to the Sierra Club has DOUBLED the pollution along the Mexican border where the American factories have moved.

Had Clinton done the job those of us who voted for him in 1992 expected him to do, we wouldn't be in the trouble we're in. Imagine if, on his first day in office over eight years ago, Clinton had ordered a reduction of arsenic in the drinking water—and all Americans had been drinking cleaner, safer water for the last eight years. Do you think there's any way in hell Junior Bush would have been able to say, "OK, America, you've been drinking water without poison in it long enough. Time to go back to the good old days of sucking down that ol' arsenic!"? Hell no! No one would have stood for it. And he would have known that. He wouldn't even have tried to reverse things. But because Clinton waited until the last minute and never removed any of this crud from the water or the air, there was no political or popular support for the decision. So it was easy for Bush to do what he did. He figured, you're not going to miss what you never had in the first place.

But, of course, Bush forgot one thing—most of us didn't even know we were drinking 1942-level arsenic under Clinton. Thanks to W. wanting to make a big deal of "reversing" Clinton on his first day in office, we, the public, suddenly learned that our water wasn't safe. Now ask yourself this painful question: Since you never knew or made any noise about the high arsenic levels under Clinton, do you think Gore would have removed the arsenic from the water? Why would he do that? You, the people, never knew about it, never complained to the White House that you hate drinking all this arsenic—and the industries that are responsible for much of that arsenic are some of the same people who funded Gore's campaign. I have looked through all of Gore's campaign literature and position statements, and I have yet to find a single word about arsenic in the water.

Let's be honest here: It's only because of Bush and his idiot actions that we're now going to get the arsenic reduced. The whole clamor put the issue in the public's mind—and it hasn't left. So now nineteen Republicans in Congress, feeling the political heat or sensing the PR opportunity, have joined the Democrats in fighting the arsenic—and we, the American people, will end up drinking cleaner water as a result. These nineteen Republicans, with the Democrats, passed a bill not only prohibiting Bush from reversing Clinton's last-minute order but going *beyond* what Clinton had ordered and reducing the arsenic levels even further. That didn't happen under Clinton, and—trust me—President Gore wouldn't have raised the question. Sad to say, but it was having a prick, not a slick, in the White House that made this happen.

Another bad rap Bush got in his first months was his efforts to give our tax money to churches to do "charity work." Oh, the hue and cry over that one! So here's my question: Where were People for the American Way and other liberal groups in 1996, when *that very language* was included in Clinton's welfare reform bill? Faith-based organizations have been receiving federal funds now for more than five years. Why all the sudden screaming about "separation of church and state," when Clinton did what Bush only wants to do more of? Is it because we liked Clinton's "faith" better? (Hey, who wouldn't want to join a belief system that redefined words like *is*?)

And about that order Bush issued to ban money for abortions overseas: wrong again. Pro-choice Clinton, like the two presidents before him, had already signed an order prohibiting any American funds from paying for abortions in foreign countries. What Bush did was expand the order to cut off any monies to foreign birth control groups that offer abortion as an alternative. Worse, yes—but he only got away with it because our Democratic President had laid the groundwork in continuing the abortion-funds cutoff, placing his "liberal" approval on a piece of the right-wing agenda. If you give the devil a bone, he doesn't just go away—he wants the whole damn leg.

So spare me all the moaning about Bush the Lesser. Those who want to turn Bush into some-sort of cartoon monster have an agenda—to keep most of us from seeing the beast they themselves have become. *Of course* they hate Ralph Nader. He's a disquieting reminder of what could happen if we ever elect someone who will represent the bottom 90 percent in this country. Blame Nader, blame Bush, it's all part of the same distraction—to keep you from focusing on one very important fact: Republican arsenic or Democratic arsenic, it really is the same damn crap being forced down your throat.

But Bush will never figure out how to get away with this stuff the way Clinton did. He needs to take a page out of Clinton's Big Book of Charm. Now, *there* was a guy who knew how to win people over. Whatever you thought of him, he was likable, smart, funny, and down-to-earth. He knew that the American people *want* to believe in their President. He discovered that *saying something* was the same as doing it. If you said you were for a clean environment, that was good enough—you didn't have to do anything to *make* it a clean environment. Hell, you could get away with polluting it *more*, and most people would never know the difference. You could say you were pro-choice and then preside over the largest wholesale closing of abortion clinics since the procedure became legal. (What's the point of being pro-choice if, in 86 percent of the counties in America, there is not a single doctor who will perform an abortion and not a single woman who can get one?) Clinton learned that by talking a good feminist line, he could arrange it so that not one feminist leader would decry the order he signed in 1999 to deny federal funds to any foreign group that discussed abortion during consultations. Everyone thinks that was Bush's idea! That's how smart Clinton was. And that's why he got all the women's groups on his side—because he *said* he was with them.

So that's how you do it. Say one (plausible) thing; then do another. Or do nothing.

The point of all this is that our real problem, ultimately, isn't Bush—it's the Democrats. Bush would be paralyzed if the Democrats started behaving like a true opposition party. Bush wouldn't even be there had just one Democrat in the Senate backed the representatives of the Congressional Black Caucus when they tried to challenge the votes of the electoral college. But no senator would.

And for the better part of Bush's first year, it's Democrats who have been Bush's willing and necessary partners to madness.

Start with the Bankruptcy Reform Act, which would have made life much harder for working people who need to file for bankruptcy. Instead of having their debts expunged, this proposal, which passed the House and Senate but died in conference, would have forced those who lost everything to remain indebted to banks and credit card companies—and find ways to pay them off. In other words, millions would never have crawled out from under the rock of crushing debt.

This bill passed the Senate with the support of thirty-seven Democratic senators—including every single female Democratic senator—all of whom sided with the banking industry instead of with America's working families. In an ironic twist, it was the millionaire Democrats in the Senate—Kennedy, Rockefeller, Corzine, Dayton—who voted against this repressive piece of legislation.

Bill after bill that came from the Bush-occupied White House to the Congress found scores of Democrats with open arms. The Bush tax cut bill passed overwhelmingly with Democratic support, even though the bill was designed to benefit the richest 10 percent in the country.

Democrats have also backed Bush on his bombing of Iraq and his aggressive actions toward China. In August 2001, the crowning moment of this collaboration came when the Senate voted to approve drilling for oil in the Alaskan wilderness. Thirty-four Republicans had already jumped ship and said they would vote against their own party on this issue. That was stunning news to those who were concerned about our environment. But the joy soon subsided once the vote was taken—and *thirty-six* Democrats voted in favor of the Bush plan.

The saddest spectacle in this orgy of Democrats sleeping with the enemy was the way they approved *every single one* of Bush's cabinet nominations. Some appointees had the unanimous support of the Democrats in the Senate; even controversial ones, like John Ashcroft, picked up a number of crucial Democratic votes. And not a single Democratic senator was willing to filibuster the way a rabid Republican would have if a Democratic President had selected such a fringe radical as Ashcroft to be attorney general. If I recall, Janet Reno was choice number three for Clinton: the first two nominees were rejected after Republicans went nuts over their views on nannies.

But that's the difference—Democrats have no spine. They *always* back down. There is no one on their side of the aisle willing to go to battle for us the way a Tom Delay or Trent Lott will for his side. Those guys will not rest until they win, no matter how many bodies the road is littered with.

Democrats have become nothing more than Republican wannabes. And so I propose a course of action: the Democrats must merge with the Republican Party. That way, they can keep doing what they both do very well—representing the rich—and save a lot of money by consolidating staff and headquarters into one tight, fit fighting machine for the top 10 percent.

The good news about such a merger? The working people of this country will finally get to have their own party! What's so terribly wrong with that? It'll be the second party of the two-party system. Except it'll represent the other 90 percent of us.

To speed things along, I now make this offer to the Democrats and Republicans: I will personally pay, out of my own pocket, for the legal charges and other fees to file the papers with the Federal Elections Commission making the merger official: the all-new Democratic-Republican Party! As a gift, I'll even let you keep the ass, the Democrats' mascot, which you can breed with the Republican elephant. Now that oughta be fun!

Therefore, I'm asking that by midnight on December 31, 2001, the leaders of the Democratic Party turn over the keys to the Party's headquarters at 430 South Capital Street in Washington, D.C., to me (or anybody else who wants to be responsible for the keys, 'cause I'll probably lose them). There are about 200-plus million of us who would like to see a real two-party system (or three-party, or four-party—hey, it's a big country!), with one party fighting for the right to write off one's backyard tennis court as a business expense and the other fighting for the right to see a doctor if one gets sick. It really is that simple.

If the current Democratic leadership is unwilling to give me the keys, then I plan to file a class-action suit on behalf of any of us who ever voted for a Democrat, charging fraud and trademark infringement. After all, these so-called "Democrats" are actually impersonating Republicans, and therefore committing a deception against the citizens who gave them their money, time, and votes. I will seek an injunction to prohibit them from continuing to use the word "Democrat" without "Republican" attached to it.

The rest of us, then, can move on. We can call our party the New Democrats or the Green Democrats or the Free Beer Democrats. We'll work that out later in committee.

(Readers who wish to save me the cost of this lawsuit can promise to vote out all the phony Democrats and vote for honest, progressive candidates fighting for the opposite of what the Republicans stand for.)

Meanwhile, to those Democratic officials who want to survive the political carnage ahead, I have one piece of advice for you: Quit moonlighting for the competition. That's my last bit of free advice to the party that sent nine boys from my high school to their graves in Vietnam. If you can't clean up your act, fuck you and the donkey you rode in on.

Time to Remove These "Democrats"

This list shows just how far off your Democratic representatives to Congress are from a progressive agenda. The percentages represent how often they voted *against* liberal legislation and *in favor of* the Republicans. (Source: Americans for Democratic Action; based on voting records in the year 2000).

U.S. HOUSE OF REPRESENTATIVES

Ralph M. Hall, TX (voted with GOP 80% of the time)
Ken Lucas, KY (75%)
Christopher John, LA (70%)
Jim Traficant, OH (70%)
Marion Berry, AR (65%)
Bud Cramer, AL (65%)
Ronnie Shows, MS (65%)
Jim Barcia, MI (60%)
Ike Skelton, MO (60%)
William O. Lipinski, IL (55%)
Tim Roemer, IN (55%)
Adam Smith, WA (55%)
Charlie Stenholm, TX (55%)

John Tanner, TN (55%)
Gene Taylor, MS (55%)
Sanford D. Bishop Jr., GA (50%)
Allen Boyd, FL (50%)
Gary Condit, CA (50%)
David Phelps, IL (50%)
Leonard Boswell, IA (45%)
Jerry Costello, IL (45%)
Tim Holden, PA (45%)
Paul E. Kanjorski, PA (45%)
James H. Maloney, CT (45%)
Michael R. McNulty, NY (45%)
Bob Clement, TN (40%)
Bob Etheridge, NC (40%)
Harold Ford, TN (40%)
Bart Gordon, TN (40%)
Collin C. Peterson, MN (40%)
Max Sandlin, TX (40%)
Shelley Berkley, NV (35%)
Peter Deutsch, FL (35%)

Mike Doyle, PA (35%)
John J. LaFalce, NY (35%)
Frank Mascara, PA (35%)
Carolyn McCarthy, NY (35%)
Dennis Moore, KS (35%)
Solomon P. Ortiz, TX (35%)
Loretta Sanchez, CA (35%)
Bart Stupak, MI (35%)
Brian Baird, WA (30%)
Lois Capps, CA (30%)
Eva Clayton, NC (30%)
Cal Dooley, CA (30%)
Barry Hill, IN (30%)
Darlene Hooley, OR (30%)
Jay Inslee, WA (30%)
William J. Jefferson, LA (30%)
Jim Moran, VA (30%)
Nick Rahall, WV (30%)
Vic Snyder, AR (30%)
John Spratt, SC (30%)
Ellen Tauscher, CA (30%)

SENATE

Zell Miller, GA (Voted with the GOP 100% of the time)

John Breaux, LA (50%)
Daniel Inouye, HI (40%)
Max Cleland, GA (30%)
Blanche Lincoln, AR (30%)

Vulnerable Republicans Who Can Be Beaten

The following Republican members of Congress are the most likely to be defeated if a strong and *real* Democrat runs against them:

SENATE

Wayne Allard, CO
Susan Collins, ME
Pete Domenici, NM
Tim Hutchinson, AR
Mitch McConnell, KY

Bob Smith, NH
Gordon Smith, OR
Ted Stevens, AK
Strom Thurmond, SC

HOUSE

Shelley Moore Capito, WV
Mike Ferguson, NJ
Melissa Hart, PA
Steve Horn, CA
Mark Kennedy, MN
Doug Ose, CA

Charles (Chip) Pickering, MS
Mike Rogers, MI
Rob Simmons, CT
Heather Wilson, NM

ELEVEN

The People's Prayer

I THINK IT was Thomas Aquinas who once observed, "There's nothing like your own shit to make you realize how much you stink."

In July 2001, Nancy Reagan, then keeping a round-the-clock watch at her husband's deathbed, dispatched former Reagan henchmen Michael Deaver and Kenneth Duberstein to Washington, D.C., with a private message to George W. Bush and the Republican leadership. The party had been divided over the issue of stem cell research, the ongoing science of taking stem cells from discarded human embryos and using those cells to treat people with debilitating conditions like Alzheimer's (the affliction that had visited former President Reagan), or find cures for other life-threatening diseases. The antiabortion zealots (among

whom are included the Reagans and the Bushes) who have controlled the party for decades demanded that there be no embryonic research, regardless of the suffering of the living.

W. had been leaning toward banning the research, telling the
public, in essence, that he saw those dead embryos as living
babies. I guess he feared that women would run out and fertilize
their eggs just so they could get an embryo, have an abortion, and
then sell the embryos for research. Such is the active fantasy life
of the conservative nutcases who run this country.

But now the nuts were coming unscrewed, as a number of
conservatives, from Tommy Thompson to Connie Mack, were
giving their approval to stem cell research, declaring that it had
nothing to do with the taking of a "human life." Suddenly the
media were full of stories of a conservative mutiny on the issue.
Right to Life went to war to stop the flood toward reason.

W., though, seemed unfazed and unmoved, more concerned
with the brand of toothpaste the British prime minister was using
than with changing his antiabortion position.

But then the word came from Nancy. The soon-to-be-widow
asked Bush to change his mind and approve, support, fund, and
champion stem cell research. The research, she relayed to him
through her errand boys, might save Ronnie or future Ronnies
suffering from Alzheimer's, Parkinson's, Lou Gehrig's, and other
catastrophic illnesses. Nancy had already been modifying her
abortion stance over the past few years, and now she was coming
out for the first time and saying, no, an embryo is NOT a human
being.

In that one moment, the entire playing field shifted. The call
from the front office had been made: SCREW THE UNBORN!
SAVE THE GIPPER!

And sure enough, within days, Baby Bush's principles were
disappearing faster than a Condit intern. Word came from the
White House that now there was nothing wrong with "certain"
stem cell research. Bush went on TV and would not say that a

human embryo was a *human being*. After decades of cramming it down our throats that "human life begins at conception," we were now being told by the same individuals who trashed a woman's right to an abortion that these "unborn babies" were actually nothing more that some dead embryonic tissue—which might just keep some sick rich people alive a few more years!

All over the country, Republican honchos joined in the call for more stem cell research. Orrin Hatch led the charge, saying, "This is not a question of the destruction of human life, it's a question of facilitation of human life." Even Strom "only-in-cases-of-rape-or-incest" Thurmond agreed. "Stem cell research could potentially treat and cure such maladies as multiple sclerosis, Alzheimer's, Parkinson's, heart disease, various types of cancer, and diabetes. . . . I am encouraged by this pioneering science and support federal funding for its research," said the old man, whose daughter, not so coincidentally, suffers from juvenile diabetes.

There's nothing more lovable than an unembarrassed hypocrite from the Right. They spend their entire lives making everyone else's life miserable, but as soon as a little misery enters their lives, then it's "Belief system be damned—I want results!" They devote all their energies for years to making it hard for blacks, chicks, or guys who like guys to get ahead or be treated with an ounce of dignity, but the minute someone in *their* family is being held back—whoa, you better get outta my kid's way, buster—he's special!

Reagan, Bush, Cheney, and the whole Lott of them are responsible for decades of cruel legislation designed to punish the poor, imprison those with health problems (drug addictions), or strip rights from desperate people here in America "illegally." But when they find *themselves* in a desperate situation, suddenly they have the compassion of St. Francis and the mercy of Mother Teresa.

The rich and powerful make it their mission in life to destroy our air, poison our water, rip us off, and make it impossible for us to get any sort of help at the customer service window, but when their actions come back to haunt *them* they aren't spooked—they're looking for a handout.

Well, I say that's a good thing! Let's hope they get all they're looking for. If it takes a personal tragedy for them to come to their senses, so be it. After all, in spite of their seven-bathroom houses and garages full of Bentleys, they're just like us. They are H-U-M-A-N. And when a loved one of theirs is lying in bed constantly soiling their adult diapers, pissing all over the new designer sheets, and blabbering on like the crippled souls whose care and funding they just cut from the federal budget—well, in times like these, rich or poor, pus from facial sores all starts looking the same. Equality achieved—one nation, incapacitated, justice for all.

So now, thanks to Ronald Reagan's misfortune, we're going to get a little federally funded stem cell research—maybe even find a cure for Alzheimer's and God knows what else. Just think about that for a minute. This is what it takes today to get a little responsible scientific research funded. Our beloved former leader, who helped ruin the lives of millions of women because he thought these embryos were little tykes, now finds himself in a debilitating pickle—and just because hordes of conservatives consider him a saint, millions of average Americans will finally be relieved of their suffering?

This phenomenon—the well-heeled changing their tune as soon as they become the victims—is happening everywhere. In New York City, Republican mayor Rudolph Giuliani, who for years opposed the city paying for health care for uninsured children, did an abrupt about-face—after he came down with cancer. "I have to admit," a humbled Giuliani explained to the press, "Once I got cancer, I began to see a lot of things in a new light."

Or take Big Dick Cheney. Cheney quietly halts any antigay initiatives that may come from the White House. Why? Because his daughter is a lesbian. Where would Dick Cheney stand on this issue if a loved one of his weren't gay? Probably not too far down that road in Wyoming where Matthew Shepard was left to die on a cross of fence posts. These faggots and fairies take on a whole new dimension when one of them sprang from your loins. The day his daughter came out of the closet was at least one day Dick Cheney stopped being a fat-cat Republican and responded like a human being and a father. When it hits home, it's very hard to keep acting like an asshole.

So I've decided that the only hope we have in this country to bring aid to the sick, protection to the victims of discrimination, and a better life to those who suffer is to pray like crazy that those in power are afflicted with the worst possible diseases, tragedies, and circumstances in life. Because I can guarantee you, as soon as it's their ass on the line, we're all on the way to being saved.

With that in mind, I've written a prayer to speed the recovery of all those in need, by asking God to smite every political leader and corporate executive with some form of deadly disease. I know it isn't nice to ask God to bring harm to others, but I'd like to think that God is not only merciful and just, he also has a highly developed sense of irony. I think he'd like to see a little grief come to those who have abused his planet and his children.

So I have written "A Prayer to Afflict the Comfortable with As Many Afflictions As Possible." After all, history tells us that God enjoys a good old-fashioned smiting every now and then—and who better to smite than the Stupid White types who got us into this mess?

Please pray this prayer with me each morning, preferably before the opening bell of the NYSE. It matters not what religion you claim, or if you claim none at all. This prayer is nondiscriminatory, portable, and requires no collection plate.

Half of Africa will soon be dying of AIDS. Twelve million kids in America today do not get to eat the food they need. Texas is still executing innocent citizens. Time's a-wasting. Bow your heads and join with me now. . . .

A Prayer to Afflict the Comfortable

Dear Lord (God/Yahweh/Buddha/Bob/Nobody):

We beseech You, O merciful One, to bring comfort to those who suffer today for whatever reason You, Nature, or the World Bank has deemed appropriate. We realize, O heavenly Father, that You cannot cure all the sick at once—that would surely empty out the hospitals the good nuns have established in Your name. And we accept that You, the Omniscient One, cannot eliminate all the evil in the world, for that would surely put Thee out of a job.

Rather, dear Lord, we ask that You inflict every member of the House of Representatives with horrible, incurable cancers of the brain, penis, and hand (though not necessarily in that order). We ask, Our Loving Father, that every senator from the South be rendered addicted to drugs and find himself locked away for life. We beseech You to make the children of every senator in the Mountain Time Zone gay—*really* gay. Put the children of senators from the East in a wheelchair and the children of senators from the West in a public school. We implore, Most Merciful One, just as You turned Lot's wife into a pillar of salt, that You turn the rich—*all* the rich—into paupers and homeless, wiping out their entire savings, assets, and mutual funds. Remove from them their positions of power, and yea, may they walk through the valley and into the darkness of a welfare office. Condemn them to a life of flipping burgers and dodging bill collectors. Let them hear the wailing of the innocents as they sit in the middle seat of row 43 in coach and let them feel the gnashing of teeth that are abscessed and rotted like the 108 million who have no dental coverage.

Heavenly Father, we pray that all white leaders (especially the alumni of Bob Jones University) who believe black people have it good these days be risen from their sleep tomorrow morning with their skin as black as a stretch limo so that they may enjoy the riches and reap the bountiful fruits of being black in America. We humbly request that Your anointed ones, the bishops of the Holy Roman Catholic Church, be smitten with ovaries and unplanned pregnancies and a pamphlet about the rhythm method.

Finally, dear Lord, we call upon You to have Jack Welch swim the Hudson he has polluted, to force Hollywood's executives to sit and watch their own movies over and over and over, to have Jesse Helms kissed on the lips by a man of his own gender, to make Chris Matthews go mute, to let the air—quickly—out of Bill O'Reilly, and turn to ash all who are responsible for those who smoke in my office. Oh, yes, and unleash with a fury a plague of locusts to nest in the toupee of the Senate Minority Leader from the great state of Mississippi.

May You hear our prayers and grant them, O King of Kings, Who sits on high and watches over us as best You can, considering what screwups we are. Grant us some relief from our misery and suffering, as we know that the men You shall smite will be swift in their efforts to rid themselves of their misfortune, which in turn may rid us of ours.

With this we pray, in the name of the Father, and of the Son, and of the Holy-Spirit-Who-Used-to-Be-a-Ghost, Amen.

TWELVE

Tallahassee Hi-Ho

I HAVE A confession to make:

I am the person responsible for the "presidency" of George W. Bush. Me. Michael Moore. I could have prevented it all.

Now I have made a lot of people angry, and the country is in the crapper.

That's why I'm in hiding.

I am writing this epilogue from my bunker in the woods of northern Michigan, somewhere along the forty-fifth parallel. The locals say that I am sitting exactly halfway between the Equator and the North Pole, but to me it feels like a million miles from nowhere.

I am no longer thinking about how we can save the country or the planet—my only concern now is how to save my own sorry ass.

It all started in Tallahassee. Tallahassee, Florida. Yes, *that* Tallahassee.

My presence in the state capital of Florida had nothing to do with the thirty-six-day media circus that followed the 2000 election. That little piece of slo-mo roadkill was for those who hadn't had their OJ/Monica fix for a while and desperately needed to watch one more ugly seam of the nation unravel like a Newt Gingrich marriage. That was not what brought me to Tallahassee, and I was there for *none* of those thirty-seven days.

I landed in Tallahassee 15 days *before* the election. What I *didn't* count on was a pre-dawn meeting with the Governor of Florida, Jeb Bush. Just him and me on a dark street in downtown Tallahassee, his bodyguards lurking nearby, ready at a moment's notice to eat me for breakfast.

I had gone to Florida to try and stop his brother from winning the election, to ward off a disaster that loomed on the horizon, to defeat the enemy. *Twenty Seconds over Tallahassee!*

It was a mission destined to fail.

As a result of my actions, I don't know whom I should fear more—the oilmen who now run the corporation known as "The United States of America" from inside the Oval Office, or the deranged liberals who want my head because they think I was somehow the mastermind behind the Nader campaign, and that I . . . I . . . I . . .

OKAY! ALL RIGHT! IT'S TRUE!! IT *WAS* ME—YES ME! ME! ME! IT'S *ALL* MY FAULT!! WHAT WAS I THINKING??? DID I REALLY WANT TO MEET SUSAN SARANDON *THAT* BADLY? Oh God, forgive me, I have wrecked the country—this wonderful psycho nation of idealists and accountants who only want the right to drive their Chevy Blazers across the fruited plain, whose only request is to someday be told the difference between "partly sunny" and "partly cloudy," who seek nothing more than a cellular plan with enough peak-time free minutes so they'll always be ready if one of their kids should call from inside a school shooting because they need Mommy or Daddy to phone CNN immediately and start negotiating the rights to the really cool footage they're shooting *right now* of the carnage in the cafeteria.

Somehow I think I can outwit the thugs from Halliburton and Enron (now referred to as "Special Assistants to the Vice President"). They will be contained, quarantined, and put out of their misery soon enough.

But no amount of contrition will satisfy the Gorestapo who are rightfully upset that their man has been barred from the office he won. They're brimming with anger. I have to tell you, I have not seen liberals this angry since . . . since . . . well, I don't think I've really *ever* seen liberals get too worked up about anything! After all, it's not like they're the Christian Right, who have managed—with God and insanity on their side—to always get their way.

Except now all these liberals agree finally on one thing: Blaming Ralph Nader—*and blaming me!* Why blame me? They don't know the whole story! Ralph Nader *fired me* in 1988—kicked me out on the street, penniless!

Now, in order to survive, to protect the ones I love, and to get this book I've written out to those of you lucky enough to find it amid the latest literature from our national wrestling heroes, I have retreated deep into the forest with my laptop and my compass, living off the land the way Nature intended, jotting down my final thoughts in the hopes that some lessons can be learned.

Last week, while I was changing planes in Detroit, a guy with a big smile on his face comes up to me, puts out his hand, and offers this greeting: "Everyone says you're an asshole, so I just wanted to meet you!" He turned and ran, missing my response: "Everybody is right!"

The whole state of Michigan is full of people like this. Honest and polite. Like the letter I got today, a letter similar to many I've received of late:

"Dear Jerk," it read. "I hope you are satisfied with what you have done. You and that egomaniac Ralph Nader will have us all drinking arsenic in our water before we know it. Do us a favor: drop dead."

I could write back and tell him that Ralph Nader is responsible for nothing other than inspiring over a million new voters to come to the polls, because he was the only candidate to tell the *truth* about what is happening to this country. The rich made out like bandits during the Democratic Years of the 1990s. Absolutely nothing has been done to alleviate the hardships faced by forty-five million Americans who have no health coverage. The minimum wage remains unchanged at a slave wage of $5.15 an hour.

I could tell him that because Ralph Nader was on the ballot in the state of Washington, the majority of those 101,906 citizens who voted for Nader also voted for the Democrat for U.S. Senate. Thanks to these Nader voters, Maria Cantwell became Washington's new senator by only 2,229 votes. If you're going to blame Nader for taking votes from Gore in Florida, then you must also give credit to Nader for bringing thousands of new voters to the polls who made the difference for Cantwell—thus allowing the Democrats to force a 50–50 tie in the Senate. Then, once there was a tie, one senator from Vermont realized he suddenly had a lot of power—and used it to turn the Senate over to the Democrats by leaving the Republican Party. None of that could have happened without Nader.

I could remind my correspondent that the only people who cost Gore the election he rightfully won were the five justices of the Supreme Court who would not let all the votes be counted. And I could point out that Gore never would have found himself in the jam he was in had he won his own state, or won Clinton's home state, or won, decisively, at least one of the three debates. Gore did none of that, and that's what put him in the jam he found himself in. And to Gore's credit, *he* has not blamed Ralph Nader. He blames the zipper on Clinton's pants!

I could write back and tell my friendly correspondent all of this, but I won't. Instead I would like to tell him (and you) a story that until now I have only told a few close friends—a story about my fourteen hours in hell, in a place called Tallahassee.

I avoid Florida. It's so sticky and humid that you have to carry around a roll of the Quicker Picker-Upper just to stay dry. The state is full of bugs and mosquitoes. They kidnap little Cuban boys and won't return them to their fathers. It's like every day is hunting season for German tourists in rental cars. Then there's Walt Disney World. And Gloria Estefan. The Kennedys running around in their freshly changed underwear in West Palm Beach. Not to mention hurricanes, Bebe Rebozo, Ted Bundy, Anita Bryant, swamps, cheap guns, and the *National Enquirer*. I hate Florida.

Yet something deep inside was compelling me to go down there as the November election drew near. Maybe it was just something I ate, maybe not.

I had been asked to come and speak to the student body at Florida State University. At first I had said yes, but later had to cancel due to the shooting schedule on my film.

Then Al Gore failed to win the third and final debate with George W. Bush. Now where I come from, the smart guy wins in a debate; the dumb guy loses. It really is that simple. But not this time. I couldn't believe my eyes. It was clear that Al Gore was doing everything he could to lose the election.

I called the people back at Florida State in Tallahassee to see if I was still welcome, and they were more than happy to accommodate me. A date was set for me to address the student body, the following week, now just two weeks before Election Day. I would also hold a press conference for the statewide media and make an announcement.

I had something I wanted to say about Ralph Nader.

My relationship with Ralph is a complicated one. I had once worked in his office back in the late eighties. He had given me a job when I was unemployed, and this generous act was something I resolved to never forget.

From my cubicle next to Ralph's office on the second floor of a building built by Andrew Carnegie, I published a media-watch newsletter, modestly called *Moore's Weekly*. I also started shooting what would become *Roger & Me*.

Everything was fine until the day I signed a deal with a publisher to write a book about General Motors. When Ralph heard the news of my good fortune, he wasn't breaking out the $50 cigars.

"What makes you qualified to write a book about General Motors?" he demanded. He also wanted to know by what right I was making this film, why I was spending more time in Flint than in D.C., and why wasn't that newsletter being published more regularly?

Finally he peered down at me and just shook his head in pity. "Well, you can take Mike out of Flint," he offered derisively, "but you can't take the Flint out of Mike." He asked that I pack up and leave.

I was crushed. I found a place to edit my film and moved on. When the movie came out, as a show of support and no hard feelings, I called Ralph and offered to give his projects the proceeds from my Washington premiere. He refused the offer. Instead, he and an associate trashed me in the *New York Times*. I was crushed again. Two crushes and I get the message. I didn't speak to him for the next eight years.

By the late nineties, I figured it was time to give him a call. (I must have been not getting enough rejection in my life.) I invited him and his staff to attend the opening of my latest film, *The Big One*. They did. I stood in the back of the theatre and watched Ralph having a good time and a hearty laugh. Afterward I had him stand and take a bow, which was received by loud and enthusiastic applause. On the way out I gave him a hug. Ralph is not a hugger—actually, neither am I. I guess I saw it a movie some-where and it looked cool.

Two years later, I'm sitting on the porch in Michigan minding my own business when Ralph calls and asks that I endorse him for President of the United States. I try not to endorse politicians because—well, for the same reason *you* don't—they're all so slick, they have bad hair, they can't get through two sentences without telling a lie. Ralph was none of these things, just a cranky genius. In other words, not presidential material. In 1996 he put his name on the ballot and then did virtually no campaigning. It was a big letdown to those who supported him. Was he serious this time? Yes, he told me, this time it was the "real thing." He was going to raise a good chunk of money, and he was committed to visiting all fifty states. He would have a full-time staff. Lucky them!

I wanted to get off the phone and go back to doing nothing. I didn't want to get mixed up in all the hoo-ha I knew would come from such a run. But what was my choice? Pretend the country was in great shape? Put my faith in one of the major party candidates who were being funded by the same big shots I spend my time fighting and filming? Sit in Michigan and feed the squirrels?

I couldn't let Ralph down. He had not let me down a long time ago, and he had never let the country down. If his voice wasn't heard during this election, then none of the issues we care deeply about would ever get mentioned, let alone debated.

Before saying yes, I decided to send a personal letter to Al Gore, giving him a chance to explain himself and tell me why I should even think of voting for him, considering the Clinton/Gore record.

He sent me back a four-page letter, the kind where the first paragraph and the last sentence are personalized and the rest is spit out at you from a computer. He thanked me for my "provocative letter," and then went on to repeat his positions, which I already knew. Although I had kept an open mind, nothing he said convinced me that we were going to see anything different out of him if he made it to the Oval Office. I called Ralph and told him I was on board, as long as I didn't have to wear a gray suit, eat hummus, or gut a whale.

Ralph's campaign was distributing a column by Molly Ivins that offered advice to those who would like to vote for Nader but didn't want to put George W. Bush in the White House. If they lived in a state where either Gore or Bush was expected to win by a wide margin, she suggested, then they should use their vote to send a message, and give it to Ralph Nader. But if they lived in one of the states where the election was close, then they must vote for Gore to block Bush. Me, I normally vote for whoever I think is the best candidate, just like I was taught in seventh grade civics—but what do I know?

Privately, I think most people in the Nader camp thought what I thought—that once Gore had a chance to wipe the floor with Bush in a debate, the election would be over. So we figured, let's get out millions of votes for Nader to show the next President—Al Gore—that there's a large number of Americans who don't want him pushing the Democratic Party further to the right. A strong vote for Nader might be a way to check Gore and his promise to do things like spend more on the military and less on jobs.

Yeah, we were real geniuses.

Then came the debates. Ralph was shut out of them, which left America with three ninety-minute shows in which Gore and Bush agreed with each other more than they disagreed. In the second debate, the two of them said they agreed with each other on *thirty-seven different issues.* It was stunning to watch.

Gore had blown it. He had failed to unmask Bush's ignorance and stupidity. He had failed to set himself apart and show the nation there was a real difference on the ballot. He had *three* chances to nuke that smirking son of a Bush, and he couldn't do it! Message to the country: If this is how he caves with Junior, what will happen when he gets in a room with the Russians? *Or the Canadians!*

I was shocked by the implications. It was starting to look as if Gore would lose. He was going to lose his home state. He was going to lose Clinton's home state. He couldn't convince the Democratic dean of the Senate, Robert Byrd of West Virginia, to endorse him until *five days* before the election (thus sacrificing West Virginia, a traditional Democratic stronghold, to Bush). Any *one* of these states would have given Gore all the electoral votes he would need to win the White House.

Gore was imploding—and Nader voters everywhere were like rats jumping off a sinking ship (nice rats, though—the lovable fluffy kind). Ralph saw his poll numbers cut in half. It appeared that he would not get the 5 percent necessary to receive federal matching funds in the next election.

Things at Nader Central went crazy. A decision was made to disavow the Ivins plan and go out on a second tour—of states where Gore might win or lose by a percentage point, and Ralph's presence would make all the difference. (In some of these states Nader's poll numbers were as high as 12 percent.) It was a bold, in-your-face strategy that said to the Democrats, "You have deserted your base. You are no longer Democrats. It is now time you were taught a lesson." Nothing like a good switch to the buttocks from Headmaster Nader!

Look, we all know the only thing a politician fears is being removed from that nice cozy office with the interns and the expense account. (That, and the prospect of having to get a real job.) If you don't hold that over their heads, they will never behave, never listen to us, never get out of bed in the morning and show up for work. Ralph Nader represented the country's only hope of pushing Gore toward doing the right thing.

Everyone knew this effort to barnstorm in the swing states could cost Gore the election and put Bush in the White House. But when you've seen the administration you voted for side more often with the Republicans than the traditional Democrats; when you've watched as these Democrats make life harder for the poor, paving the way for the rich to have their biggest orgy in history; when my hometown ends up losing *more* GM jobs during the eight years of *Clinton/Gore* than during those twelve years of Reagan/Bush—well, here's your choice: Do you want to get fucked by someone who tells you they're going to fuck you, or do you want to get fucked by someone who lies to you, and then fucks you?

I am sorry for the language, but that's probably the *nicest* way to explain how I and millions of other Americans saw this election. You don't have to agree, you don't have to like it, you just have to read that sentence one more time if you want to even come close to comprehending the level of our anger.

I know a lot of good people could see no other way but to vote for the Democrat. They would rather be told "I love you" while getting screwed than have to look at the face of the Beast on top of them for the next four years. I know that feeling. Tell me that you love me and you can do just about anything to me—including trashing me in the *New York Times*!

But these Reluctant Democrats for Gore were really our allies. They wanted many of the same things we did, they just took a different path. My attitude was, if Bush won, we were going to have to work with these well-meaning liberals to save the world from the Lesser Bush. It was not right to just tell them to go to hell.

So I told the Nader staff: Hey, there's no reason to purposely piss these people—our friends, or potential friends—off. Our fight is with those who have stolen the name Democrat—the party hacks, the lobbyists, the weasels who somehow couldn't cut it in the Republican Party because they didn't have what it takes to destroy a national forest, or close a thousand libraries, or take free breakfasts away from the malnourished little ones in the inner city. You have to have *real* guts to do stuff like that, and you have to enjoy it. Those who don't, get jobs over at the Democratic Party.

Our fight wasn't with the core voters who still feel some desperate connection to what is called the "Democratic Party." The fact that millions of Americans still hold out hope that the Democrats are going to represent their interests better than the Republicans is more a comment on *our* failure to show the country just how similar these two parties are—and how the Democrats will sell them out nearly every time.

The Nader campaign asked me to go with them on this tour of the swing states in the final weeks before the election. I declined. I told them I would rather work hard in those states where Ralph could get a lot of votes *without* being responsible for Bush winning the election. Why not spend our energies in New York and Texas where the outcome is clearly known? Tell people in those states not to waste their votes on Gore, they will have zero impact. But they could send a strong message if Nader were to pull down 10 percent of the vote.

That was not the strategy that had been decided. They respected my decision and wished me well.

I landed in Tallahassee on the afternoon of October 23, 2000. A student from Florida State, his brother, and his sister-in-law picked me up at the airport, and as we walked toward the car, they started asking about "the invite" they heard I had extended Jeb Bush.

"Everyone's talking about it!" they told me.

"What 'invite' are you talking about?" I asked.

"The one you made in the paper yesterday."

They handed me a copy of Sunday's *Tallahassee Democrat*, the city's daily paper, and there on the front page of a section was an interview I had done with a reporter the week before on the phone from New York. A big picture of me and a quote challenging the Governor to show up and face me on the stage that night. Ooh, Mr. Tough Guy! Real easy to throw down the gauntlet when you're a thousand miles away, isn't it? Of course, it's a whole other thing when you're suddenly all alone in a state full of people who don't take kindly to smart-ass northerners. But I wasn't thinking that far ahead.

I arrived at the university and began the press conference. I was nervous. I didn't want any misunderstandings over what I was about to say.

I told the media present that Bush had to be stopped. I appealed to the people in Florida that if Gore was their man, then by all means, they should get out and vote for him. But if you were voting for Nader, I wanted you to think long and hard about your vote. The stakes, I felt, would be different in Florida. If it's more important to you to stop Bush, then you might have to vote for Gore. I would understand and respect your decision.

The reporters were a bit surprised. Was I switching my vote to Gore? No, I said, I'm voting for Ralph. Of course, that's easy for me to say—I live in a state where Gore is already going to win by a landslide. But if you live in Florida, things are different.

The story went out across the state that one of Ralph Nader's "celebrity backers" had given the green light to vote for Gore in Florida if that's what voters thought was the right thing to do.

When the press conference finished, I ran into the bathroom and got sick. It was time for me to go on stage. An overflow crowd of two thousand people packed the auditorium. The organizer banged on the door. "We need to start," she shouted.

"Just give me a few minutes," I replied. I got sicker. Another bang on the door. "Show them a segment from my TV show," I said. "I'll be okay in a minute."

I didn't know if I was sick because of this horrible pressure I felt or because I'd been treated to a "Whataburger" burger (a Tallahassee favorite) on the way into town. Maybe I just knew that the whole election—the whole country—was in the shitcan with me, and there was no escape for any of us.

Twenty minutes late, I walked onto the stage. The Greens were all sitting down front, Nader signs in hand. I told them, and the rest of the audience, that there was a bitter pill I knew some of them wanted to swallow. I told the crowd, *You have to use your best judgment—follow your conscience*. Please know that I will think no less of you if you feel you have to vote for Gore. I will still be voting for Nader, I said, and went over the litany of reasons why it was a matter of conscience for me (I cannot ever vote for someone who believes in the execution of other human beings, who believes that we should continue the weekly bombing of civilians in other countries, who thinks that the minimum wage should go up by only a dollar an hour, who wants to sign additional trade agreements like NAFTA so that even more Americans can lose their jobs).

I told the crowd that I couldn't pull the lever (or punch the hole) for Gore, a man who wanted to spend more on the military than Bush did, who wouldn't seek guaranteed health care for all our citizens immediately, who thought that Janet Reno was wrong to return little Elián Gonzales to Cuba. That's who Al Gore was.

But, I said, I understand your unique dilemma here in Florida. So don't listen to me, do what you think is best, we'll sort it all out later. And God bless these Nader kids down front here for their courage and dedication, something that many of their sixties-era parents had long ago snuffed.

The Q & A that followed the speech, plus another discussion in the student union afterward with a couple hundred students and community activists (some of whom had driven three hours to be there), was a powerful back-and-forth about how to handle the coming deluge. By the time it was over, it was 1:30 A.M., five and a half hours after I had resolved my issues with the Whataburger. I left with a sense that a storm was brewing here in Florida, and it might be wise to take cover.

I was driven to my hotel, a quaint little place that sat on the pedestrian mall leading up the block to the state capitol building. I turned on the TV and watched a replay of the eleven o'clock news. "A chief Nader backer says Bush must be stopped, no matter what," the anchor said. I turned out the lights and went to sleep.

I awoke at 6:30 A.M. to catch my plane home. A student was waiting downstairs to drive me to the airport. As I was checking out at the counter, the kid yelled, "Governor Bush just walked by!"

"Stop him!" I shouted—without thinking, really. (Perhaps it was a reflex—whether I'm in Texas or Florida, when I hear the words *Governor Bush*, I instinctively respond with a "STOP HIM!") The kid opened the door and called out, "Governor Bush, there's someone who would like to meet you!" By that time I was already out the door. There, on this deserted pedestrian mall, which looked like a dark alley in the final minutes before dawn, were Governor Jeb Bush and his bodyguard, walking to work. A black SUV carrying more security was creeping along the car-free street, about 40 feet behind the Governor.

Bush turned to see who was asking for him, and then saw me standing there. He gave that Bush smirk, and began walking back toward me. I moved toward him, and the bodyguard went into stand-by-to-beat-the-punk-to-a-pulp mode.

"Mr. Moore," Bush said, shaking his head like he'd just been fed the same plate of Sloppy Joes for the third day in a row. I held out my hand and Bush took it.

"Just wanted to shake your hand and say hi, Governor," I said politely. He squeezed tightly, not wanting to let go until he had said what he had to say. His eyes were like needles that locked right on mine. The bodyguard moved closer.

"So—did they pay you *enough* to come down here?" he snapped at me pointedly, and the translation was clear: "You suck, Moore." My mouth went dry; my heart was beating so hard I was worried he could hear it.

"It's *never* enough, Governor, you know that," I replied with the first words I could muster. Why did he care who paid me or how much? Then it dawned on me—HE paid for it! *Florida* State

University! No wonder he was pissed: he'd picked up the tab for my visit to tell thousands of Floridians—especially Nader voters—that beating Bush was the important thing. This was NOT what the Bush camp wanted Naderites to be thinking.

Had he seen the news from the night before? Bush glared at me and withdrew his hand.

"Kevin with you?" he asked me suddenly. Huh? Kevin? Was this some secret codeword to alert the bodyguard that it was time to Linda Blair my neck? Then it hit me—he was asking about his cousin, Kevin Rafferty, the filmmaker who'd helped me out with *Roger & Me.* I hadn't worked with Kevin in twelve years—why was he asking me this? I didn't know what to say.

"Uh, no, he's not here," I mumbled.

"Well, give him my best," he said.

"Sure," I responded.

"Leaving, are you?" he asked.

"Yes," I replied. "Right now."

"Good."

He gave me that famous Bush smirk again, nodded his head as if to say good riddance, and then turned and left. As he walked down the deserted alley I tried to think of some witty comeback, but he was already twenty paces ahead of me. The black SUV rolled down its window; the state trooper inside sized me up, then slowly drove past my feet. The first light of day was making its way over the capitol dome. I would not see this place again until I saw it on nonstop television two weeks later.

Every time I've run into one of the Bush kids it's been a defeating, debilitating experience. For some reason they always seem to get the upper hand. When I came across George W. in Iowa and tried to ask him a question for my TV show, he shouted at me to "go find real work." The entire crowd in the place roared with laughter. I didn't know what to say—he was right, this isn't real work! I had no comeback.

The day I ran into Neil Bush, the unindicted co-conspirator in the Silverado Savings & Loan scandal, I was in the lobby of General Motors in Detroit doing a radio interview. He walked through the door with these four Asian guys—"bankers from Taiwan," he later told me. When he spotted me, he freaked out. I was the last person he expected to see at General Motors.

"Where's your camera?" he demanded, his eyes darting all over the place.

"Oh, uh, I don't have a camera with me today," I said sheepishly and regretfully. A big smile beamed across his face.

"Aw, Mikey didn't bring his camera?" He reached out and pinched my cheek. "Toooo baaaaad!" He walked away laughing and explaining to the Chinese guys who I was and how he just put one over on me.

The only Bush I've been able to reduce to a pulp, I say with shame, is the only girl—their sister, Dorothy. She's sweet; she's a mom. And she had no idea what to say when I asked her which of her brothers she thought would win the "Let's See Who Can Kill More Inmates on Death Row" race, George or Jeb.

She was visibly offended; in truth, she looked genuinely hurt by the implication that her brothers are cold-blooded killers. She looked as if she was going to cry. I felt like a jerk. *Way to go, Mike, you finally took a Bush down!*

Of course, there is one other Bush brother, Marvin—though you wouldn't know it from the media. I have never met Marvin. You have never met Marvin. No one has ever met Marvin. God knows where he is or what he's up to—other than planning how to get one over on me.

After the chilling encounter with Jeb, I boarded my plane to L.A., unable to get the episode out of my head. Then, as I was trying to open the bag of honey roasted peanuts, a bolt of something struck me—and it wasn't the guy's seat three inches in front of me. I got on one of those expensive air phones and called Ralph. I spoke to the three people who were running his campaign, aware there was a chance the man himself was also listening in.

"Guys," I said. "Has it crossed your mind that the most powerful man in America today is . . . *Ralph Nader*?"

Silence on the other end of the phone.

"I'm serious. His five percent is going to make the difference.
Bush, more than anything else this week, needs Ralph to do well
in order for *him* to win. And Gore needs Nader out of the way in
order for *him* to win. If Ralph wasn't in the race, Gore would win.
Only one man can call the shots here, only one candidate has any
real say today. And that's Ralph Nader."

I continued. "But after November seventh, that power is
gone. The power is only good for the next week or so, as Gore
and Bush see all their plans hanging on the actions of one man—
Ralph Nader. Why not use this position of power for some
good?"

"What did you have in mind?" asked one of them.

"Ralph holds Gore's future in his hands. What if he were to
call Gore and say, 'Hey, you wanna be president, this is what you
have to do by noon tomorrow . . . ,' and then give Gore a laundry
list to pick from—universal health care, an end to the phony drug
war, no tax cuts for the rich—whatever. Ralph asks nothing for
himself—no cabinet position, no funding for his projects. He just
wants Gore to do the right thing, and if Gore publicly commits to
doing so, then Ralph goes on TV and says, "We've made our
point. We have helped Al Gore see the need for x, y, or z. He's
told the nation he is committed to doing that. So next Tuesday, if
you live in one of the swing states and you're supporting me, I
want you to vote for Gore. The rest of you, in the other forty
states, I still need your vote so that we can build a viable third
party to keep Gore's feet to the fire.'

"In other words, declare victory! After all, the reason Ralph's
running in the first place—to push the political agenda more our
way—will have been accomplished.

"What do you think?"

"We can't count on getting our five percent unless we get every vote we can in *every* state," the campaign manager responded. "We can't give up a single vote at this point."

"But, the day after you get that five percent," I replied, "that's *all* you'll have—five percent of the vote, and *zero percent of the power!* Today though, you—we—hold all the power. One candidate needs Nader in, the other needs Nader out. This election is going to be decided by a percentage point or two. Ralph holds anywhere from two to five percent. Today, right now, you and Ralph get to say who the next President is going to be! You will never have this kind of power in your hands again, the rest of your lives."

A longtime Nader colleague who was on the call understood what I was trying to say. "But you're never going to get Ralph to back down now," he said. "It will look like he gave in when things got too hot. Plus, the Democrats have treated him with such disrespect, you'll never convince him that he should help them with anything.

"Plus," he continued, "What makes you think Gore would keep his promise? These people keep *no* promises."

"What about all these thousands of kids on the campuses who have worked so hard?" the campaign manager chimed in. "What about the tens of thousands who came to the rallies you and Ralph spoke at? What about them? Here's their first experience with electoral politics—and the candidate they gave everything for just throws in the towel near the end. You can't do that to them. It will only turn them into cynical adults who won't want to get involved in an election again."

That certainly made a lot of sense. The last thing I wanted to do was to add to the cynical hordes who've given up any interest in voting at all.

"But," I offered, "isn't there a way we can do this so it is accepted for what it is—a victory for the Greens, for Ralph, for everyone who has worked for him, because by getting Gore to change his positions, we've succeeded in a way we never thought possible? You know, it's like that ultraconservative party in Israel that only has, like, five seats in the Knesset, but their five votes are always needed to form a majority government. Whichever party gives them the most of what they want on their agenda gets their votes. If they join with the liberals to form the government, their ultraconservative supporters don't get mad at them and accuse them of selling out. Just the opposite—they're hailed as heroes because, although they're only five votes, they get their way every time."

Wow, that was profound, I said to myself. Teaching political science at 30,000 feet!

"Mike," a voice on the phone replied. "Are you okay? This is not the Israeli Knesset. You're in the United States. That's not how it works here. Ralph will be crucified if he backs Gore, and Gore will be crucified if he changes his positions at such a late date. It's not going to happen."

I told them I understood. I reminded them that Ralph didn't have to drop out, just throw the vote to Gore in a few swing states, that's all. Gore would owe him BIG TIME once he was in the White House. We could have our cake and eat it, too.

No one seemed interested in any cake.

I thanked them for listening and hung up from the $140 call. Then I sank down in my seat and ordered my first drink ever on a plane. Somewhere over Texas, I fell asleep.

What happened on November 7, 2000, will now always have its own page in the history books. Nader was polling 6 percent in Florida the day before I arrived. The day after I left, it was down to 4 percent. And by Election Day, it had dropped to 1.6 percent of the vote. But that represented 97,488 Nader votes in Florida. Would at least 538 of these voters changed their vote if they had known on November 7 that *their* specific votes were the ones that would make the difference? Of course they would.

I'm curious, though, why those upset at Nader have directed none of their anger toward the other candidates from the left who also appeared on the Florida presidential ballot—David McReynolds of the Socialist Party, who got 622 votes; James Harris of the Socialist Worker Party, who got 562 votes; or Monica Moorehead of the Workers World Party, who got 1,804 votes. Surely there were 538 voters among *that* group who would have held their nose and voted for Gore had they known Bush and his cronies were going to swipe the election.

Personally, that's who I blame—Monica Moorehead. That's the one thing we learned from the nineties. It's always Monica, and (forgive me), it's always more head.

So blame Monica! Don't blame Ralph! And DON'T BLAME ME!

Or do blame me. Yes, in fact, if the Democrats are insisting on giving that much power to the Naderites, then maybe we should take it. Yes, it was us! *We did it!* We are the mighty Thor, all-powerful and all-knowing. We will destroy all in our path! Change your ways or we will turn you into ash! It was not we who abandoned the Democratic Party—it was YOU! *You* deserted *us* and all those who once believed Democrats stood for something, like fighting for the rights of working people. But you hopped in bed with the Republicans, and we had no choice but to follow our conscience and vote for Ralph Nader. THAT IS THE WAY OF THOR!

So yes, WE denied you the White House. WE tossed your ass out of Washington. And WE will do it again. We have over nine hundred campus Green organizations. We have a mailing list of over 200,000 aggressive, active volunteers. We won twenty-two races around the country in the 2000 election and they joined the fifty-three other elected Greens who held various offices across the country. Since last November, the Greens have won another sixteen seats, making a total of ninety-one Greens currently holding elective office in America. Five cities in California are now

run by Green Party mayors. And, most significantly, the number
of Americans who voted for Nader in 2000 increased by a whopping 500 percent over those who voted for him in 1996.

This is a growing movement. And it's not just about the Green
Party. Heck, I'm not even a member! There are millions of people who have had it with the Democrats and Republicans and
who want a real choice. That's why a professional wrestler won as
governor of Minnesota. That's why Vermont's only congressman
is an Independent (and now so is one of its senators). There will
be more Independents in the coming years; it can't be helped.
Actually, that's not true. It has been helped—greatly—by the
actions/inaction of the Democratic-Republican Party.

So run for your lives—I'm coming out of my bunker! I'm sick
of just "surviving," of taking crap from the whiners who will
never be there on the front lines for the have-nots, risking arrest,
taking a billyclub to the head, giving a few hours of their time
each week to be *citizens*, the highest honor to hold in a democracy.

I want us all to face our fears and stop behaving like our goal in
life is to merely survive. "Surviving" is for wimps and game show
contestants stranded in the jungle or on a desert island. You are
not stranded. You own the store. The bad guys are just a bunch of
silly, stupid white men. And there's a helluva lot more of us than
there are of them. Use your power.

You deserve better.

EPILOGUE

PERHAPS THE WORST thing about having a president nobody elected is that, in a time of national crisis, we have to wonder whose interests he is serving. As he rules not by the will of the people but by electoral theft, is it not safe to assume that "the people" are not necessarily found at the top of "President" George W. Bush's agenda?

Beginning at 8:45 A.M. New York Time on September 11, 2001, the United States suffered the worst single-day attack on its own soil from foreign enemies in the history of the country. As the details of what happened that day are as well known now as the events of December 7, 1941, or September 1, 1939, I will not bother to rehash the number of planes used, the number of bodies strewn, the number of cellular calls of "good-bye" to loved ones that came from those planes in the suicide missions against the World Trade Center and the Pentagon.

What I would like to do, as this book ends, is to ask a number of pointed questions to our Commander-in-Chief who, because he was anointed by his daddy's friends on the Supreme Court, believes that he is not answerable to anyone. Well, 3,000 people died that day, and something about the whole tragic event just doesn't sit right with me and a lot of other people.

So, Mr. Bush, can you explain to me the following:

1. Is it true that the bin Laden family has been funding the Bush family for over twenty years? According to the *New York Times*, your very first oil venture in 1979, a company called Arbusto, was financed, in part, by the bin Ladens. The bin Ladens have been investors in your father's company, the Carlyle Group, one of the largest military contractors in the U.S. Such odd coincidences deserve an explanation.

2. You say that Osama bin Laden was the mastermind behind the September 11 attacks. But numerous news reports have pointed out that this "evildoer" was on dialysis at the time as he had failing kidneys. Are you saying that one man hooked up to a kidney machine somewhere in a cave in Afghanistan controlled this whole operation?

3. In 1997, the BBC ran a story about the Taliban leaders of Afghanistan flying to Houston, Texas, while you were governor and meeting with oil company executives from Unocal to discuss the building of a pipeline across Afghanistan. One of the feasibility studies done for this pipeline was conducted by Enron, the largest contributor to your campaigns, both for governor and president. Haliburton was one of the companies slated to build the pipeline. The chairman of Haliburton at that time was Dick Cheney, your vice-president. Why was your state of Texas hosting these meetings with representatives of a terrorist government? What happened to that pipeline deal?

4. In the days and the weeks following September 11, according to the London *Times*, you allowed a private Saudi-chartered jet to fly around the U.S. to pick up nearly two dozen members and associates of the bin Laden family and take them out of the country. No serious interrogations were conducted by the police or the FBI nor was a grand jury convened to see what any of these relatives might know. Instead, while the rest of

America could not fly, and with all the chaos taking place, you still had time to sit and worry about what you could do to make sure the bin Ladens were OK and safe. Can you explain why this was such a priority? Why did the Saudis and the bin Ladens receive this extraordinary treatment?

5. At least fifteen of the nineteen hijackers were from Saudi Arabia. But you bombed Afghanistan. Did you miss? Or was it too difficult to go after the country that supplies 25 percent of our gasoline and contains so many of your daddy's business partners? I'm just trying to get a handle on the exact worth of 3,000 lives. How many tanks of gas do they equal?

6. As soon as your campaign to take control of Afghanistan was complete, you installed a former oil company consultant as the "interim leader." You then appointed a former Unocal consultant as our new ambassador to Afghanistan. Within a few months, a new deal was signed to build that pipeline across Afghanistan. Now that you've got what you want, can the troops come home?

These are all questions that must be asked of George W. Bush. But who will ask them? Who will demand the answers? The lazy, compliant press that is mostly owned by a few rich men who all contributed to the Bush campaign? Or the opposition party who spends more time trying to emulate the Republicans and is funded by the very same rich men who own the media? What hope is there for us if just the basic questions cannot be asked?

In order to keep the lid on all this, the Bush administration has gleefully used the attacks of September 11 as their excuse to start shredding our constitution and eliminating our civil liberties. There is no better time to do this. The public lives in a state of panic. No one knows when the next attack will come.

The people of Britain know something about living with this

kind of fear. A few bombings in London and suddenly the government is allowed all sorts of secret powers to do what it wants to combat "terrorism." No one has the time to ask about the terrorism instigated by the government or how that may be a factor in why there is so much death and destruction happening. How many Irish were falsely arrested and convicted? How many Irish were assassinated by operatives of the British government? We may never know. This is not what defines a free and open society.

And so now we have Bush's war on terrorism. What a perfect excuse to distract the people from the *real* problems which face the world right now. Tony Blair, an almost perfect clone of Bill Clinton, has now found his new best friend in George W. Bush. Perhaps he just likes how incredibly genius-like he looks whenever he stands next to Bush. Who could blame him? As Bush tries to speak the mother tongue and then segues into simply speaking in tongues, Blair just stands there and grins. Mr. Blair could do all the world a hell of a lot of good if he would wipe that smirk off his face and tell Bush that he will not back any more excursions to help daddy's oil buddies.

George Orwell had it pegged when he wrote *1984*. What most people remember from that book is "Big Brother." But even more relevant today is the part about how The Leader needed to have a "permanent war." He needed to keep the citizens in perpetual fear of the enemy so they would give him all the power he desired. The people wanted to live, so they gave up their freedoms and their liberties. Of course, the only way this could happen is if they were truly convinced that the enemy was everywhere, anywhere, and that they could die at any moment.

It worked in the book, and it is working today. The only thing that will stop it is if we completely and without equivocation reject the lies we're being told. Now is not the time to give up. We should never forget that there are more of us than there are of them. We have always held the power and we always will. It's just a matter of being fearless and deciding to use it.

NOTES AND SOURCES

Chapter 1—A Very American Coup

The information about Jeb Bush's wife and her run-in with US Customs is found in *The Hill*, "Gov. Jeb Bush: Florida Republican is Younger, Taller, and More Partisan than George W.," Marcia Gelbart, July 30, 2000.

The investigation into the purged voter lists was reported in *The Nation*, "Florida's 'Disappeared Voters': Disfranchised by the GOP," Gregory Palast, February 5, 2001; *The Nation*, "How the GOP Gamed the System in Florida," John Lantigua, April 30, 2001; *Los Angeles Times*, "Florida Net Too Wide in Purge of Voter Rolls," Lisa Getter, May 21, 2001; and Salon.com, "Eliminating Fraud—Or Democrats?," Anthony York, December 8, 2000.

Problems with blockades at some polling locations are discussed in the *New York Times*, "Contesting the Vote: Black Voters; Arriving at Florida Voting Places, Some Blacks Found Frustration," Mireya Navarro and Somini Sengupta, November 30, 2000; and also in the *Washington Post*, "Irregularities Cited in Fla. Voting; Blacks Say Faulty Machines, Poll Mistakes Cost Them Their Ballots," Robert E. Pierre, December 12, 2000.

The House of Representatives held hearings in February on the early calling of election results, as reported in the *Washington Post*,

"Election Coverage Burned to a Crisp; House Grills Networks' 'Beat the Clock' Approach," Howard Kurtz, February 15, 2001.

The Bush cousin connection is also documented in the Associated Press, "Fox Executive Spoke Five Times with Cousin Bush on Election Night," David Bauder, December 12, 2000; and the *Washington Post*, "Bush Cousin Made Florida Vote Call for Fox News," Howard Kurtz, November 14, 2000.

A series of articles in the *New York Times* chronicled the counting of the overseas absentee ballots: "How Bush Took Florida: Mining the Overseas Absentee Vote," David Barstow and Don Van Natta Jr., July 14–15, 2001; "How the Ballots Were Examined," July 15, 2001; "House Republicans Pressed Pentagon for E-Mail Addresses of Sailors," C. J. Chivers, July 15, 2001; "Timely but Tossed Votes Were Slow to Get to the Ballot Box," Michael Cooper, July 15, 2001; and "Lieberman Put Democrats in Retreat on Military Vote," Richard L. Berke, July 15, 2001. Following the release of these articles, Katherine Harris allowed inspection of her hard drives as reported in the Associated Press, "Computer Analysts Gain Access to Secretary of State Katherine Harris' Computers," David Royse, August 1, 2001; and the *New York Times*, "Florida Gives Computers in November Election to News Groups for Inspection," Dana Canedy, August 2, 2001.

The time of the Supreme Court decision can be found in *The Nation*, "The God That Failed; Florida Supreme Court's Rulings on the Presidential Elections," Herman Schwartz, January 1, 2001; CNN Saturday Morning News Transcripts 08:00, December 9, 2000; ABC News Special Report, 2:47 pm, December 9, 2000.

Justice O'Connor's comments regarding her retirement were reported in *Newsweek*, "The Truth Behind the Pillars," Evan Thomas and Michael Isikoff, December 25, 2000.

Information regarding the family connections between the Supreme Court and the Administration is from the *New York Times*, "Contesting the Vote: Challenging a Justice," Christopher Marquis, December 12, 2000; and the *Chicago Tribune*, "Justice Scalia's Son a Lawyer in Firm Representing Bush Before Top Court," Jill Zuckman, November 29, 2000.

Scalia's statement can be found in the text of the decision: Supreme Court of the United States, No. 00-949 (00A504) *George W. Bush et al. v. Albert Gore, Jr. et al.*, Scalia, J. concurring opinion. 531 US___(2000). December 9, 2000.

Theresa LePore's party switching is accounted for in the *Orlando Sun-Sentinel*, "Disappointed, Lepore leaves Democrats," Brad Hahn, May 9, 2001.

One of the best overall examinations on widespread illegalities and efforts to deny the right to vote to black citizens in Florida can be found in the report issued by the United States Commission of Civil Rights, "Voting Irregularities in Florida During the 2000 Presidential Election," June 8, 2001. It can be found at www.usccr.gov/vote2000/flmain.htm.

Cheney's history on abortion can be found in the *Boston Globe*, "Conservative Tilt in Congress Merged with a Moderate's Style," Michael Kranish, July 26, 2000; and the *Los Angeles Times*, "Would vote differently on ERA, Head Start, not Mandela," Michael Finnegan, July 31, 2000; CNN.com, "Dick Cheney voted conservative, played moderate," July 24, 2000. Cheney's defense department experience can be found in his official biography at www.defenselink.mil/specials/secdef_histories/bios/cheney.htm. Cheney's stock investments are detailed in Forbes.com, "Top of the News: O'Neill to Sell," Dan Ackman, March 26, 2001; www.Corpwatch.org, "Cheney's Oil Investments and the Future of Mexico's Democracy," Martin Espinoza, August 8, 2000; the *Sacramento Bee*, "A Go-Round on Foreign Policy Ride," Molly Ivins, March 11, 2001; *The Guardian*, "Eyes Wide Shut: Scruples Fade in Dealings with Burma," July 28, 2000. Further investigation into sales between Halliburton and Iraq is from the *Washington Post*, "Firm's Iraq Deals Greater Than Cheney Has Said; Affiliates Had $73 Million in Contracts," Colum Lynch, June 23, 2001.

Aschroft's record on abortion is discussed in "Controversy on Abortion, Civil Rights Liberties," at ABCNews.com, "An Ashcroft Justice Department," December 23, 2000. Ashcroft voted on the Employment Non-Discrimination Act S.2056, vote number 1996-281, September 10, 1996; and Aschroft's vote on the death penalty appeals bill can be found at Senate Bill #S.735, vote number 1996-66, April 17, 1996. Ashcroft's history with executions as governor and his stand on the war on drugs can be found at ABCNews.com, in the article "An Ashcroft Justice Department," December 23, 2000. Aschroft's vote on increasing penalties for drug offenses was a part of Bill S.625; vote number 1999-360 on November 10, 1999. Molly Ivins writes about Ashcroft's interests in Claritin in "Cabinet Diversity?; Check Out the Bush Team's Corporate Logos," February 12, 2001. His NO vote on including prescription drugs under Medicare is found on Bill HR.4690, vote number 2000-144, June 22, 2000.

Ann Veneman's background is discussed in Molly Ivins, "The Early Days of Bushdom are Not a Pretty Sight," Molly Ivins, January 29, 2001; and the *New York Times*, "Transition in Washington: Agriculture Department," Elizabeth Becker, January 19, 2001. Veneman's net worth is detailed in *The Guardian*, "History's Richest Cabinet Takes the Gilt off Bush's Tax Cut," Julian Borger, February 7, 2001.

Rumsfeld's background is described in *The Nation*, "Rumsfeld: Star Warrior Returns," Michael T. Klare, January 29, 2001; and *In These Times*, "The Rummy," Jason Vest, February 19, 2001.

Spencer Abraham's environmental record and history with the department of energy are from *The Nation*, "The Three Horsemen of the Environmental Apocalypse," David Helvarg, January 16, 2001; the Environmental News Network, "Energy Secretary Nominee Tried To Abolish The Energy Department," January 8, 2001; and www.alternet.org, "Who's Who in the Bush Cabinet," Geov Parrish, January 16, 2001.

Tommy Thompson's abortion record as governor can be found in www.alternet.org, "Who's Who in the Bush Cabinet," Geov Parrish, January 16, 2001; and his links to Philip Morris are described in another AlterNet article, "Bush's War on Children," Jonathan Rowe and Gary Ruskin, July 3, 2001.

Gale Norton's background is detailed in the *New York Times*, "Far, Far From the Center," Bob Herbert, January 8, 2001; and the *New York Times*, "Norton Record Often at Odds With Laws She Would Enforce," Douglas Jehl, January 13, 2001. C.R. Bard's court troubles are detailed in PR Newswire, "C.R. Bard, Inc. Executives Sentenced to Eighteen Month Federal Prison Terms," August 8, 1996.

Colin Powell's relationship with AOL/Time Warner is discussed in the Associated Press, "Stocks, Speeches Add to Powell Wealth," Greg Toppo, January 17, 2001; and *The Financial Times*, "The Americas: All the U.S. President's Very Rich Men," Peter Spiegel, March 8, 2001; Paul O'Neill's Stock Holdings Are Detailed, *The Nation*, "The Man from Alcoa," William Greider, July 16, 2001; and the *Houston Chronicle*, "Alcoa Strikes Curious Water Deal with San Antonio," Nate Blakeslee, September 3, 1999.

Karl Rove's industry connections are reported in the *New York Times*, "Bush Aide With Intel Stock Met with Executives Pushing Merger," June 14, 2001; and *Abilene Reporter-News*, "Mauro Raises Questions About Bush's Aides Link to Tobacco Industry," August 31, 1997.

The information about Kenneth Lay comes from the *New York Times*, "Power Trader Tied to Bush Finds Washington All Ears," Lowell Bergman and Jeff Gerth, May 25, 2001.

Additional information about the members of the coup comes from the Center for Responsible Politics and www.issues.org.

Chapter 2—Dear George

For information on the Bush Family fortune and its ties to Nazi Germany, check out the *Boston Globe*, "An American Dynasty" (Part 2), Michael Kranish, April 23, 2001; *Sarasota Herald-Tribune*, "Author Links Bush Family to Nazis," November 12, 2000; the *Jewish Advocate*, "The Bush Family–Third Reich Connection: Fact or Fiction?," Susie Davidson, April 19, 2001.

Information on the individual contributions to the GOP during election cycle 2000 can be found at the *New York Times*, "The Republicans: The Few, the Rich, the Rewarded Donate the Bulk of GOP Gifts," Don Van Natta Jr. and John M. Broder, August 2, 2000; and The Center for Responsive Politics, www.opensecrets.org.

You can keep track of what Bush did and does during his administration by reading Molly Ivins's column syndicated by Creators Syndicate (an archive can be found at www.sacbee.com/voices/national/ivins/) or by checking out the following Web sites: www.smirkingchimp.com and www.bushwatch.com.

The account about Bush's favorite book can be found in the *Arizona Republic*, "'Hungry Caterpillar' A Favorite with Bush," October 17, 1999. George Bush graduated from Yale in 1968. Eric Carle's "The Very Hungry Caterpillar" was published in 1969. The Associated Press ran a story, "Bush's Alleged Grades Published," by Brigitte Greenberg, November 9, 1999, that featured his transcripts. Information about Bush's reading habits comes from the *Washington Post*, "Shades of Gray Matter; The Question Dogs George W. Bush: Is He Smart Enough?," Kevin Merida, January 19, 2000; and the *New York Times*, "Bush Is Providing Corporate Model for White House," Richard L. Berke, March 11, 2001.

Bush's drinking and DUI past were found in the *Washington Post*, "1986: A Life-Changing Year: Epiphany Fueled Candidate's Climb," Lois Romano and George Lardner Jr., July 25, 1999; Associated Press, "Bush Pleaded Guilty to DUI," November 2, 2000; Dick Cheney's DUI charges are mentioned in www.Salon.com, "Bush Stays in the Clear—For Now," Jake Tapper, November 4, 2000. In addition to covering his DUI arrest, *Time*, "Fallout from a Midnight Ride," Adam Cohen, November 13, 2000, includes information on Bush's earlier encounters with the law.

The Laura Bush car accident details are discussed in *USA Today*, "Laura Welch Bush: Shy No More," John Hanchette, Gannett News Service, June 23, 2000; and the *Plain Dealer*, "Reserved Texas First Lady is Primed for National State," Julie Bonnin, July 31, 2000.

George Bush's response to the question of whether or not he used drugs is found in the *Washington Post*, "Bush Goes Further on Question of Drugs; He Says He Hasn't Used Any in the Past 25 Years," Dan Balz, August 20, 1999.

The *Boston Globe* traces Bush's experience in the National Guard in "1-Year Gap in Bush's Guard Duty: No Record of Airman at Drills in 1972-1973," Walter V. Robinson, May 23, 2000. James Baker's alleged comments were reported by conservative columnist William Safire in 1992, and fallout from the remarks is found in the Associated Press, "Report of Baker Remark Draws Ire in Israel," March 8, 1992; and the *Sunday Telegraph*, "Jewish Backlash Could Cost the President Dear," Xan Smiley, September 27, 1992.

Chapter 3—Dow Wow Wow

If you were as shocked as I was that your pilot may be on food stamps, here's where you can get the facts on that—and more: *Aviation Week & Space Technology*, "Old Values Clash in Comair Strike," James Ott, April 2, 2001; *Cincinnati Enquirer*, "Key Issues in the Strike," March 27, 2001; *New York Times*, "Small Jets' Big Stake in a Strike," David Leonhardt, June 16, 2001; *Star-Telegram*, "American Eagle Pilots Reject Contract," Dan Reed, August 17, 2000; Associated Press, "Express Pilots Vow to Strike as They Head Back to Bargaining Table," Pauline Arrillaga, June 28, 1998; Associated Press, "Continental Express Pilots Start Informational Picketing," M.R. Kropko, October 14, 1998; *Orlando Sentinel*, "High-Flying Job Doesn't Make Big Bucks," Roger Roy, March 16, 1997; *Philadelphia Daily News*, "US Airways Attendants Rehearse Strike Movements in Philadelphia," March 24, 2000; *Chicago Daily Herald*, "Airline Worried About Spring Travel as Flight Attendants Threaten Strike," Robert McCoppin, January 20, 2001; NPR/Morning Edition transcripts: "Holiday Airline Travelers May Experience Flight Problems Due to Full Flights and Labor Problems Between Workers and Airlines," November 21, 2000.

Statistics on personal and corporate wealth come from Associated Press, "Income of the Richest Up 157%," Alan Fram, May 31, 2001; and the Institute for Policy Studies Report: "Top 200: The Rise of Corporate Global Power," Sarah Anderson and John Cavanagh, December 2000.

Information regarding corporate taxes can be found in *The Cheating of America*, Charles Lewis and Bill Allison and the Center for Public Integrity (HarperCollins), 2001, pp. 11–13, 15, 79, 82–83.

Chapter 4—Kill Whitey

Many of the statistics about the economic and social state of African-Americans in this country can be found in a report by the Council of Economic Advisers for the President's Initiative on Race, "Changing America: Indicators of Social and Economic Well-Being by Race and Hispanic Origin," September 1998.

Information on the disparity in health care is found in the following articles: the *New York Times*, "Blacks Found on Short End of Heart Attack Procedure," Sheryl Gay Stolberg, May 10, 2001; the Associated Press, "Race Bias in Stroke Treatment Found," Melissa Williams, May 4, 2001; and the *Daily News*, "Black Maternal Deaths 4 Times the White Rate," Leslie Casimir, June 8, 2001.

The statistic about the use of guns in the home to shoot an intruder comes from The Brady Campaign to Prevent Gun Violence, "Guns in the Home" fact sheet.

Chapter 5—Idiot Nation

Literacy figures come from the Dept. of Education National Adult Literacy Survey; Literacy Volunteers of America.

Bush's gaffe is detailed in the *New York Times*, "Deep U.S.-Europe Split Casts Long Shadow on Bush Tour," Frank Bruni, June 15, 2001.

The contents of his commencement address at Yale are described in the Associated Press, "George W. Bush commencement address at Yale University," May 21, 2001.

Previous incidents of government officials' lack of knowledge came from the *St. Petersburg Times*, "Politics is Nothing New in Choosing Ambassadors." July 21, 1989; *The Economist*, "Ambassadors; What Price Monaco?," March 4, 1989; the Associated Press, "European Press Has Fun with Clark Performance," Jeff Bradley, February 4, 1981.

Accounts of Bush's lack of knowledge of the capitals of major countries were reported in Salon.com, "Briefs or No Briefs?," Jake Tapper, April 26, 2001.

The *Des Moines Register* reported on the basic history test that top college students failed in "America's Best & Brightest Are Clueless About Our History," Donald Kaul, July 7, 2000. It was also featured in *University Wire* (UVa), "Education without Knowledge," Bryan Maxwell, July 13, 2000.

Statistics about university class offerings came from the *Pittsburgh Post-Gazette*, "The Selling Out of Higher Education," Samuel Hazo,

September 3, 2000; and *New York Times*, "Much Ado—Yawn—About Great Books," Emily Eakin, April 8, 2001.

Negative quotes about teachers come from the *New York Times*, "Education Panel Sees Deep Flaws in Training of Nation's Teachers," Peter Applebome, September 13, 1996; the *New York Post*, "The Teacher-Pay Myth" (editorial), December 26, 2000; *Investor's Business Daily*, "Why Bad Teachers Can't Be Fired," Michael Chapman, September 21, 1998; Douglas Carmine, quoted in the *Montreal Gazette*, "Bring Back the Basics," Brandon Uditsky, January 6, 2001; *National Review*, "Firing Offenses," Peter Schweizer, August 17, 1998.

The story about hiring teachers from abroad: *New York Times*, "Facing a Teacher Shortage, American Schools Look Overseas," Kevin Sack, May 19, 2001. Teacher shortages in New York are from the *New York Times*, "Teacher Pact Still Far Off," Steven Greenhouse, June 5, 2001; *New York Times*, "Nation's Schools Struggling to Find Enough Principals," Jacques Steinberg, September 3, 2000; *New York Times*, "Survey Shows More Teachers Are Leaving for Jobs in Suburban Schools, Abby Goodnough, April 13, 2001. School facility information comes from the Department of Education, National Center for Education Statistics, Conditions of Public School Facilities. The *Washington Post*, "26 DC Schools Cleared," Debbi Wilgoren, September 12, 1997; and "Angry Judge Closes 4 More DC Schools," Valerie Strauss, October 25, 1997. The janitor shortage was reported in the *New York Times*, "Janitorial Rules Leave Teachers Holding a Mop," Shaila Dewan, May 28, 2001.

Information about Bush's library tax cut comes from the *Dallas Morning News*, "Libraries Want to Shelve Bush's Proposed Cuts," April 13, 2001. Jonathan Kozol's discussion of the state of school libraries, "An Unequal Education," was featured in the *School Library Journal*. Additional information on school libraries and Richard Nixon's connection to them can be found in the *Christian Science Monitor*, "Even in Information-Rich Age, School Libraries Struggle," Marjorie Coeyman, February 6, 2001; and *Education Week*, "Era of Neglect in Evidence at Libraries," by Kathleen Kennedy Manzo, December 1, 1999.

Sources for the answers to the pop quiz: Annual salary—Source: U.S.

Vital Statistics, Table #696—Bureau of Labor Statistics; 911 response—
Ladies Home Journal, "Before You Call 911: Is this emergency number
the lifesaver it should be?," Paula Lyons, May 1995; Extinction count—
Associated Press, "11,000 Species Said to Face Extinction with Pace
Quickening," September 29, 2000; Ozone hole size—the *Christian
Science Monitor*, "Ozone Woes Down Below," Colin Woodward, Decem-
ber 11, 1998; Detroit vs. Africa: Detroit = 19.4% (1991)—Annie E.
Casey Foundation, "Kids Count" Report, April 25, 2000; Libya = 19%,
Mauritius = 19%, and Seychelles = 13%—UNICEF; Newspaper Guild;
Justice Policy Institute, "School House Hype: School Shootings and
the Real Risks Kids Face in America," Elizabeth Donohue, Vincent
Schiraldi, and Jason Ziedenberg, 1999.

Much of the information about corporate presence in schools comes
from the Center for the Analysis of Commercialism in Education, Third
Annual Report on Trends in Schoolhouse Commercialism, September 14,
2000. Additional material comes from the Associated Press, "Marketing
to Free-Spending Teens Gets Savvier," by Dave Carpenter, November 20,
2000; "The Commercial Transformation of American Public Education," 1999 Phil Smith Lecture by Professor Alex Molnar, October 15,
1999; *Mother Jones*, "The New (And Improved!) School," Sept/Oct.
1998; *Mother Jones*, "Schoolhouse Rot," Ronnie Cohen, January 10,
2001; *New York Times*, "Five-Shift Lunches to End?," Richard Weir,
May 17, 1998; *Atlanta-Journal Constitution*, "Coca-Cola Learns a Lesson
in Schools," by Henry Unger and Peralte Paul, March 14, 2001; *The
Nation*, "Students For Sale: How Corporations Are Buying Their Way
into America's Classrooms," Steve Manning, September 27, 1999;
the *Washington Post*, "Pepsi Prank Fizzles on 'Coke Day,'" by Frank
Swoboda, the *Washington Post*, March 26, 1998.

The threatening kid profile came from "Risk Factors for School
Violence," Federal Bureau of Investigation Study of School Shootings,
September 2000.

Chapter 6: Nice Planet, Nobody Home

Pepsi recycling information comes from "Dumping Pepsi's Plastic," Ann Leonard, 1994 (article appears at www.essential.org) and telephone interview with the author; *Sword of Truth*, "India: Dumping Ground of the Millennium?" Keerthi Reddy, January 13, 2001.

The story about Congressional recycling was featured in the Associated Press, "Texas Congressman, Environmental Groups Target House Recycling," Suzanne Gamboa, September 20, 2000.

Air pollution rates were calculated with information from the Environmental News Network, "Air Pollution Kills, But Deaths Can Be Prevented," August 30, 1999; and the American Lung Association, "American Lung Association Fact Sheet: Outdoor Air Pollution," August 2000 update.

Information on gas mileage capabilities can be found in *Automotive News*, "Chrysler: CAFE Hike Possible," Arthur Flax, May 8, 1989; *Automotive News*, "More Horsepower!," Charles Child, June 24, 1995; and the *Washington Post*, "The Regulators; Battling to Raise the Bar on Fuel Standards," Cindy Skrycki, May 16, 2000. How much SUVs consume is from *Sacramento Bee*, "Scary Talk from Shrub and the Veeper," Molly Ivins, May 3, 2001. And the amount drilling in the ANWR would produce is quoted from the *New York Times*, "Cheney Promotes Increasing Supply As Energy Policy," Joseph Kahn, May 1, 2001.

Despite pressure from environmental groups to veto a transportation bill that protected the SUV loophole, Clinton signed it anyway, as reported in the *San Francisco Chronicle*, "Protecting Mother Earth and Gas Guzzlers," Debra J. Saunders, December 14, 1999.

The study on global warming was reported in the *New York Times*, "Panel Tells Bush Global Warming is Getting Worse," by Katharine Seelye and Andrew Revkin, June 7, 2001; and *USA Today*, "Climate Change Report Puts Bush on Spot," Tracy Watson and Judy Keen, June 20, 2001.

The *New York Times* articles referred to are: "Ages-Old Icecap at North Pole is Now Liquid, Scientists Find," John Noble Wilford, August 19, 2000, and a correction published on August 29; the asteroid article was "Asteroid is Expected to Make a Pass Close to Earth in 2028," Malcolm W. Browne, March 12, 1998, and "Debate and Recalculation on an Asteroid's Progress," Malcolm W. Browne, March 13, 1998.

Sacramento Bee, "America isn't Immune to Animal Diseases," Deborah S. Rogers, March 30, 2001—based on a 1989 study by the University of Pittsburgh that states that 5% of deceased Alzheimer's patients could have instead suffered from CJD.

Chapter 7—The End of Men

Where we stand with the women's movement: The only woman on the ballot of a major party was Geraldine Ferraro, who ran for Vice President with Walter Mondale in 1984. The five women governors are: Jane Dee Hull (AZ), Ruth Ann Minner (DE), Jane Swift (MA), Judy Martz (MT), and Jeanne Shaneen (NH) (National Governors Association). According to the Center for American Women and Politics, there are 13 women Senators and 60 female members of the House of Representatives (as of July 26, 2001). The four Fortune 500 companies which have women CEOs are Hewlett-Packard (Carly Fiorina), Avon Products (Andrea Jung), Golden West Financial Corporation (Marion O. Sandler) and Spherion Corporation (Cinda A. Hallman). The top 21 universities (according to *U.S. News & World Report* 2001 College Rankings) with women presidents are: Princeton University (Shirley Tilghman), University of Pennsylvania (Dr. Judith Rodin), Duke University (Nan Keohane), and Brown University (Ruth Simmons—who is also the first African-American president of an Ivy League institution).

Statistics on the poverty rate of divorced women come from the Society for Advancement of Education, "Count the Costs Before You Split," April 1998.

Equal Pay Day was 'celebrated' in 2001 on April 3, the same day the US Department of Labor released a report that measured the wage gap, the *Chicago Sun-Times*, "Women Still Earn Less Than Men," Francine Knowleds, April 3, 2001.

Men's and women's health comparisons come from *The Economist*, "Are Men Necessary? The Male Dodo," December 23, 1995; www.msnbc.com,

"Men May Be the Weaker Sex," Linda Carroll, January 16, 2001; and National Institute of Mental Health, "The Numbers Count: Mental Disorders in America"/Hoyert DL, Kochanek KD, Murphy SL; final data for 1997.

Chapter 8—We're Number One!

The World Health Organization of the United Nations estimates that there are 1 billion people in the world without access to clean drinking water. Using cost estimates of $50 per person (from the World Game Institute, www.worldgame.org), the total cost of providing clean water would be $50 billion. Since the Reagan administration, we have spent $60 billion on the insane Star Wars project. Over the next 15 years it is projected that we will spend another $50 to $60 billion, according to the Congressional Budget Office. We also give upwards of $100 billion a year in corporate welfare. In other words, the entire planet could have clean water tomorrow if our priorities were different. The Center for Defense Information has estimated that the total cost of the national missile defense system (including past expenditures and conservative estimates of future expenditures) will be approximately $200 billion. Center for Defense Information, "The Costs of Ballistic Missile Defense," Christopher Hellman.

Estimates for those without energy come from The World Bank in its report "Meeting the Challenge: Mural Energy and Development for Two Billion People Report," 2000. The number of people without phone service is from Internet pioneer Dr. Vinton Cerf in a speech at the Creating Digital Dividends conference in Seattle, October 17, 2000.

Information about the FY2001 Pentagon budget comes from the Council for a Livable World, "Fiscal Year 2001 Military Budget at a Glance," www.clw.org. College tuition figures are calculated from the US Vital Statistics—US Census Bureau Population Report Table #247 and the US National Center for Education Statistics, Digest of Education Statistics, #311.

Sources for "We're Number One!" lists: Children's Defense Fund,

"The State of America's Children Yearbook 2000"; UN Human Development Report 2000; U.S. Vital Statistics, Tables #1356, 1361, 1390, 1398; Energy Information Administration, "Official Energy Statistics from the US Government"; Amnesty International Facts and Figures on the Death Penalty, 6/1/01; Patrick Moynihan, "Family and Nation," 1986, p. 96.

Read more about Kim Jong Il's exploits in *Time Asia*, "Kim Jong Il: Asian of the Year," Anthony Spaeth, December 25, 2000; *Journal of International Affairs*, "The Kim is Dead! Long Live the Kim!," *U.S. News & World Report*, "A Not-So-Kooky Kind of Guy," Thomas Omestad and Warren P. Strobel, November 6, 2000; the *New Republic*, "North Korea Opens Up," by Peter Maass, June 12, 2000; Spring 2001; Associated Press, "North Korea's Monster Movie Flops in South Korean Theaters," July 28, 2000; Reuters, "South Korea Media Chiefs to Meet North's Kim Jong Il," August 6, 2000; www.CNN.com, "In-Depth Specials: Kim Jong Il: 'Dear Leader' or demon?"

Chapter 9—One Big Happy Prison

Reports of John Adams's death were covered in the *Tennessean* newspaper, October, 2000. Information about Koch Industries came from the *Corpus Christi Caller-Times*, "Federal Charges Against Koch Industries Cut to Nine," Michael Hines, January 12, 2001; Associated Press, "Government's Case Against Koch Industries Shrinks Again," March 18, 2001; Associated Press, "Texas Pipeline Company to Pay $20 million fine," Suzanne Gamboa, April 9, 2001; the *Washington Post*, "Oil company Agrees to Pay $20 Million in Fines; Koch Allegedly Hid Releases of Benzene," Dan Eggen, April 10, 2001; *Houston Chronicle*, "Koch Slapped with Big Penalty; Guilty of Pollution Violation," James Pinkerton, April 10, 2001; *Fort Worth Star-Telegram*, "Oil Company Settles Charges," Neil Strassman, April 10, 2001.

Information about Anthony Lemar Taylor's story comes from the following articles: the *Orange County Register*, "DMV Can't Catch Tiger by His ID," Kimberly Kindy, December 20, 2000; *Sacramento*

Bee, "Woods ID Thief Gets 200-to-Life," Ramon Coronado, April 28, 2001.

The Kerry Sanders case was documented in a *New York Times* article, "My Name is Not Robert," Benjamin Weiser, August 6, 2000.

The students at Medill School of Journalism at Northwestern University, led by Professor David Protess, continue to investigate death penalty cases and were featured in the June 21, 2001, episode of CBS's *48 Hours*.

The study of error rates in death penalty cases is "A Broken System: Error Rates in Capital Cases, 1973–1995," James S. Liebman, Jeffrey Fagan, and Valerie West, June 12, 2000; and was reported in the *New York Times*, "Death Sentences Being Overturned in 2 of 3 Appeals," Fox Butterfield, June 12, 2000.

The Death Penalty Information Center compiled statistics and information on the United States use of the death penalty on juveniles and the mentally retarded.

Polls measuring public support of the death penalty are published in the *Washington Post*, "Support for Death Penalty Eases; McVeigh's Execution Approved, While Principle Splits Public," Richard Morin, Claudia Deane, May 3, 2001; and the *Houston Chronicle:* "Harris County Is a Pipeline to Death Row," Allan Turner, February 4, "Complication; DNA, Retardation Problems for Death Penalty," by the *Chronicle* staff, February 6, "A Deadly Distinction," Mike Tolson, February 7, 2001

Chapter 10—Democrats, DOA

For more information about Clinton's history on faith-based charitable organizations: *New York Times*, "Filter Aid to Poor Through Churches, Bush Urges," Adam Clymer, July 23, 1999. On federal crimes and the death penalty: Bill Clinton, *Between Hope and History* (Random House), 1996, p. 80. On gay marriages: *Washington Post*, "Clinton Ad Touting Defense of Marriage is Pulled," Howard Kurtz, October 17, 1996; and *Washington Post*, "Ad on Christian Radio Touts Clinton's Stands," Howard Kurtz, October 15, 1996. On welfare: *New York Times*, "A War on Poverty Subtly Linked to Race," Jason DeParle and Steven A.

Holmes, December 26, 2000. On teen-age parents and welfare and adoption tax credit: *Minnesota Daily*, "Clinton's Waffling Reaches New Levels," May 7, 1996. On capital gains taxes: Republican National Committee news release, "Statement by RNC Chairman Jim Nicholson on the Tax Relief and Balanced Budget Agreement," July 31, 1997. On the death penalty: *New York Times*, "Charges of Bias Challenge U.S. Death Penalty," Raymond Bonner, June 24, 2000; and *New York Times*, "Clinton Is Urged to Declare a Moratorium on Federal Executions," Raymond Bonner, November 20, 2000. On new police and three strikes law: Clinton, *Between Hope and History*, p. 75–81. On rates of the uninsured: the *New York Times*, "A War on Poverty Subtly Linked to Race," Jason DeParle and Steven A. Holmes, December 26, 2000. On insurance to illegal immigrants: *Time*, "Clinton's Plan: DOA?," Michael Duffy, February 14, 1994; and the *Orlando Sentinel*, "Refusing a Helping Hand," Wendy Zimmerman and Michael Fix, September 20, 1998. Clinton on late-term abortions, *San Francisco Chronicle*, "Clinton Message on Christian Radio Back to Haunt Him," Marc Sandalow, October 19, 1996; and the *New York Times*, "Deal on UN Dues Breaks an Impasse and Draws Critics," Eric Schmitt, November 16, 1999. On the Land Mine Ban Treaty: *Boston Globe*, "US Should Sign Treaty Banning Land Mines," Susannah Sirkin and Gina Coplon-Newfield, August 11, 2000. On the Kyoto agreement: *New York Times*, "Treaty Talks Fail to Find Consensus in Global Warming," Andrew Revkin, November 26, 2000. On drilling on federal lands: *The Nation*, "Teapot Dome, Part II: The Rush for Alaskan Oil," Jeffery St. Clair and Alexander Cockburn, April 7, 1997; and *The Nation*, "Al Gore's Teapot Dome; Occidental Petroleum Acquires Large Portion of Elk Hills," Alexander Cockburn, July 17, 2000. On fuel efficiency standards: *New York Times*, "The Energy Plan: The Standards," Keith Bradsher, May 18, 2001. On activity on the Kyoto Agreement right before the election: the *Guardian*, "Sinking Feelings: Climate change is one of the greatest threats to life as we know it," Paul Brown, October 11, 2000.

Republican support for revising the arsenic standards was reported in the *New York Times*, "House Demanding Strict Guidelines on Arsenic Levels," Douglas Jehl, July 28, 2001. Information about the federal funding of faith-based organizations is from the *Christian Science Monitor*, "War On Poverty Enlists Churches," Gail Russell Chaddock, June 19, 2000.

Sources for policies on overseas funding for abortions are the *New York Times*, "Bush Acts to Halt Overseas Spending Tied to Abortion," Frank Bruni and Marc Lacey, January 23, 2001; and the *New York Times*, "Deal on UN Dues breaks an Impasse and Draws Critics," Eric Schmitt, November 16, 1999.

Statistics about the availability of abortion doctors come from Planned Parenthood/Family Planning Perspectives, "Factors Hindering Access to Abortion Services," Stanley K. Henshaw, 27(2), 54–59 & 87.

The tally for passage of the Bankruptcy Reform Bill in the Senate: Vote Summary, Vote Number 36, S.420, passed 3/15/01. YEAs: 83, NAYs: 15, Present: 1, Not Voting: 1 (Barbara Boxer, CA, did not vote).

Information about Clinton's last-minute executive orders and regulations comes from: *Washington Post*, "Racing the Clock With New Regulations," Dan Morgan and Amy Goldstein, January 20, 2001; *Washington Post*, "Clinton's Last Regulatory Rush," Dan Morgan, December 6, 2000; *USA Today*, "Arsenic Fouls Review of New Rules," Jonathan Weisman and Mimi Hall, April 20, 2001; *Washington Post*, "'Midnight Regulations' Swell Register," Cindy Skrycki, January 23, 2001; Environmental Protection Agency, "Further Revisions to the Clean Water Act Regulatory Definition of 'Discharge of Dredged Material,'" April 17, 2001.

Chapter 11—The People's Prayer

Anti-abortion politicians who are now in support of stem cell research are discussed in the *Washington Post*, "Conservative Pressure for Stem Cell Funds Builds; Key Anti-abortionists Join Push for Embryo Research," Ceci Connolly, July 2, 2001; *San Francisco Chronicle*, "Stem Cell Debate Creates Odd Alliances; Some Conservatives Break Ranks with the Religious Right," Marc Sandalow, July 22, 2001; *Associated Press*, "Thurmond Backs Stem Cell Research," June 30, 2001. Cheney's earlier history on gay legislation is chronicled in the *Badger Herald*, "Gay Republicans Left Out in the Cold," Chris McCall, November 2, 2000.

Chapter 12—Tallahassee Hi-Ho

Maria Cantwell received 1,199,437 of the votes while her opponent, Slade Gorton, received 1,197,208. Nader received a relatively strong 4% of the vote, or 103,002 votes. It can be safely assumed that many of those 100,000 Naderites also supported Cantwell as opposed to the Republican or Libertarian challenger (who received only 2.63% of the vote). Election results are from the Washington State General Election Final Report.

Molly Ivins' article, "Swing-State Progressives Ought to Think Back to '68," was published on November 1, 2000. The vote counts for all of the candidates are officially certified results from the Florida Department of State. Green Party standings come from the Green Party of California and Nader 2000/2004.

ACKNOWLEDGMENTS

I'D LIKE TO acknowledge, first and foremost, those of you who have read this book. I hope you had a few good laughs. I hope it has inspired you to go and raise a ruckus. You are the only ones who are going to change things. Promise me that you won't just put this book down and go back to playing solitaire on your computer or checking your E-mail for the tenth time today. I've checked mine two dozen times today already—and it's only noon. I'm not getting a damn thing done.

Next, I'd like to acknowledge those of you who bought *Downsize This* and made my first book a bestseller. That allowed this one to get published. I only get this platform if the beast gets fed. No one is publishing my book because they think it's a good idea to kill whitey or call the president the "president." If this book does well, you will hear from me again. If not, there's always something interesting to watch on Nick at Night.

I also want to thank those who stop me in the street and tell me their stories about living/struggling/surviving in America. All that you have told me or written to me has had a profound impact on my work and my being and I thank you for sharing your experiences with me.

Thanks to the good people at ReganBooks and HarperCollins for making this book happen, especially to Judith Regan, the publisher, for taking the risk and having the patience. Also, thanks to my editor, Cal Morgan, for teaching me words I have never heard of (words of which I have never heard?). And thanks to everyone else there who goes unheralded but who has made it possible for me to have my say and see it end up in real bookstores: Jennifer Suitor, Lisa Bullaro, Shelby Meizlik, Cassie Jones, Kim Lewis, Lorie Young, Kurt Andrews, Andrea Molitor, Carl Raymond, Paul Olsewski, Jamilet Ortiz, Tom Wengelewski, Lucy Albanese, Kris Tobiassen, Brenda Woodward, Adrian James, and Westchester Book Composition. Thanks to Paul Brown for the book jacket design. Thanks also to Susan Weinberg at HarperPerennial for first bringing me to HarperCollins.

I also want to thank all of you who work in the bookstores selling these books and to the librarians out there who help steer kids to some good reading. Your efforts are truly appreciated. And thanks to Don Epstein and all the people at GTN who organized the "Stupid White Men Tour Across America" that will accompany this book. Without you there never would have been "The Big One."

Thanks to those who helped me research and pull this book together and keep it as timely as possible. The publisher had to literally pry the manuscript from us and drive it to the printer at the last possible moment as we were still waiting for one more forest or artery for Cheney to destroy. First and foremost, Kathleen Glynn, who helped me get started and stayed with it to make this the book that it is. My co-conspirators include Ann Cohen (whose greatest contribution, among many, to this book was explaining to me how a toilet seat and a bar of soap works), Amy McCampbell (who came here for a few days to work on my movie and ended up staying five months to help me with this book), David Schankula (a Sarah Lawrence College student who toiled into all hours of the night on this book and got my head screwed back on straight in the final chapter), Rehya Young (no amount of words could express my gratitude toward this wonderful individual who has been in the trenches with me for the past two years, and who thanks me for her first whiff of tear gas in Seattle), and my unofficial editorial board of friends and family who perform the all-important "butthead check"—making sure I don't totally embarrass myself by acting like a jerk, checking that I have sufficiently covered up my lack of education and manners, and generally offering their constructive and supportive comments, in addition to some great research. They are, for this book, Anne Moore and John Hardesty (whose writing—and whose lives—were both the inspiration for and the engine behind the criminal justice chapter), Jeff Gibbs (who gave me lots of help and ideas on the environmental stuff and whose prognosis for the planet has scared the PBBs outta me), Joanne Doroshow (our good friend since our days together at Nader Central), and Al Hirvela, Ben Hamper, Harold Ford, Veronica Moore, Natalie Rose, and K. G. (who all read various chapters and made it feel like we were back sitting on the floor at the *Flint Voice* trying to put the paper together before the sun came up or we ran out of border tape!). And special thanks to my agents, Mort Janklow and Anne Sibbald, at Janklow & Nesbit.

Twenty years ago this year, life got good. My deepest thanks to those responsible.

ABOUT THE AUTHOR

MICHAEL MOORE is a writer, filmmaker, and voter. His films include *Roger & Me*, *The Big One*, and the surprise hit of the Cannes Film Festival, *Canadian Bacon*. His next film is *Bowling for Columbine*. He is the author of the bestseller *Downsize This: Random Threats from an Unarmed American*, and coauthor with Kathleen Glynn of *Adventures in a TV Nation*. All four seasons of his and Kathleen's shows, *TV Nation* and *The Awful Truth*, have been nominated for Emmy Awards (with *TV Nation* winning the Emmy in 1994, the only year they had the money to buy the votes). Mike is an active outdoorsman who likes to swim, bike, hike, rock climb, fish, hunt, paint, build boats and gliders, go whitewater rafting, bungee jumping, mountain cycling, scuba diving, and skydiving, and he's a three-time champion of the Mesick Triathlon and the Burton Toughman Contest. His hobbies are cooking and crafts, and he likes to spend his time riding dirt bikes with Tony and reading Proust to his nieces Rosalyn, Madison, and Molly. He is an Eagle Scout, and once accidentally burned down the community center in his hometown while cleaning up after a bingo game. He divides his time between Flint and Paris. He often checks his E-mail at mmflint@aol.com and occasionally visits his Web site at www.michaelmoore.com. Barring success, this will be his last book.

ABOUT THE TYPEFACE

The typeface used in this book is Bermuda Demi-Bold. It is a serif style face with a touch of postmodern, postfeminist graphic movement. The Bermuda family of type was invented by Walt Higgins, who is also the creator of the Bermuda shorts. Though Walt had never been to Bermuda, he lived his life in that carefree style common to the islands of the Caribbean (although Bermuda is not technically in the Caribbean). Always one to shun pants, Higgins was fond of carrying around a tailor's pencil and a pair of scissors and would randomly go up to strangers, draw a circle below the knee, and hack off the lower portion of their slacks. It was while performing this procedure one day in Muncie, Indiana, that Walt Higgins discovered that the pencil he used could also be used to write notes on the discarded fabric. Soon, the Bermuda typefaces were born—but Walt found himself serving out his final years in the Kokomo Correctional Facility for a "slip" he made with his pinking shears on an elderly gentleman (the man's pants were riding up fairly high that day). Walt's defense that he had done the man "a favor" by performing a "rabbinical procedure"—did not sit well with the jury. Though Walt Higgins passed away in 1934, his legacy lives on through his typefaces and his summer outerwear—and we are proud to display both within this book.